Norberto A. J. Laguy

*f*P

STRATEGY AND PLACE

MANAGING CORPORATE REAL ESTATE
AND FACILITIES FOR
COMPETITIVE ADVANTAGE

Martha A. O'Mara

THE FREE PRESS

THE FREE PRESS
A Division of Simon & Schuster Inc.
1230 Avenue of the Americas
New York, NY 10020

Designed by MM Design 2000 Inc.

Manufactured in the United States of America

10   9   8   7   6   5   4   3   2   1

Library of Congress Cataloging-in-Publication Data

O'Mara, Martha A.
    Strategy and place: managing corporate real estate and facilities
for competitive advantage/Martha A. O'Mara.
        p.   cm.
    Includes bibliographical references and index.
        1. Real estate management. 2. Corporations—Real estate
investments. 3. Facility management. 4. Strategic planning.
5. Real estate management—United States. 6. Corporations—Real
estate investments—United States. 7. Facility management—United
States. 8. Strategic planning—United States. I. Title.
II. Title: Managing corporate real estate and facilities for
competitive advantage.
    HD1394.044   1999
    658.2—dc21   99-22122
                                                                      CIP

ISBN 0-684-83489-8

The author gratefully acknowledges the sources of material reprinted in this
volume as listed below.

Page 105: Schematic map of Fidelity's downtown Boston locations appears
courtesy of Fidelity Corporate Real Estate, Inc.

Page 170: Photos of Sun Microsystems' Menlo Park Campus appear courtesy of Backen, Arrigoni & Ross Architects. Other illustrations regarding
Sun (chapters 4 and 7) have been used with permission.

Page 194: Illustration reprinted with the permission of The Free Press, a
Division of Simon & Schuster Inc., from *Competitive Strategy: Techniques
for Analyzing Industries and Competitors.* Copyright © 1980 by The Free
Press.

Pages 196 and 252: Illustrations reprinted with the permission of The Free
Press, a Division of Simon & Schuster Inc., from *Competitive Advantage:
Creating and Sustaining Superior Performance* by Michael E. Porter. Copy-
right © 1985 by Michael E. Porter.

To Robert for his patience,
to Sierra, Aidan, and Jonah for their promise,
and to Jack and Connie for their parenting.

My love and appreciation.

CONTENTS

PREFACE AND ACKNOWLEDGMENTS

This book stands as a milestone in a personal journey.

The compass for this book was first set during my freshman year in college at the precast concrete marvel that is the University of California Irvine. Disillusioned with my chosen field of study, I enrolled in a course in Environmental Psychology taught by a young professor named Dan Stokols. This new field of study, in its infancy at the time, examines how the physical environment affects behavior. I was hooked. Nearly twenty-five years and a few detours later, I have reached what became over time my destination—recognition of the important role *Place* plays in the behavior of organizations. There are more journeys to follow, but at this point I am delighted to stop along the path.

After my undergraduate studies I sought employment as an architectural programmer. According to this new specialty, the social sciences would be the savior of architecture. However, hardly anyone had even heard of it. Fortunately I gained employment with Theodore Barry at his eponymous management consulting firm. Ted, the quintessential visionary, did what most resembled programming in his firm and had recently branched into the practice of building architecture and engineering. I stayed with TB&A for four years during which we extended the firm's services into office interior design, especially to accommodate these new objects called personal computers, and this new product idea called systems furniture, into the workplace. I then joined another firm which specialized in interior design and helped develop services in office automation consulting and the nascent profession of facility management. By this time I knew I needed an MBA if I was ever going to understand what my clients were really trying to accomplish. I entered Harvard Business School in the early 1980's when the MBA had just become the hot degree and we all thought we were at the center of the known universe. I soon noticed that the cases we were studying about behavior in organizations and effective management all but ignored any physical dimension. *Where* were these people I wondered—in the office? On the phone? In a plane? On another planet? Why was the physical setting of organization action totally ignored, while six years of consulting had shown me what an intense, controversial, and semiotic place the office was to most organizations. I had the temerity to question this omission, to which my professors typically replied: "Hmm, interesting question, but hardly anyone has ever studied that in organizations." I picked up the gauntlet and while my classmates went off to gainful employment I signed up for four years of graduate study in organizational behavior, my dissertation topic already well in mind.

That milestone reached, I joined the faculty of the Graduate School of Design at Harvard, where I taught real estate development to pay for my position, and where I tested a range of disciplines and ideas to find my voice.

Although the work began with my dissertation, serious effort on the book began in 1994, two years after giving birth to my first child, Sierra. Interruptions invariably followed as I attempted to not only have work that I loved but a family to love as well. This effort accounts for the long recitation of thank yous to follow.

Through my research and this book I have attempted to integrate the concerns and real life practical decisions faced by the many corporate real estate and facility managers I worked with over the years, with the broader management frameworks of strategy and organization which have endured the tests of time. In particular my work is indebted to the influence and warm encouragement of Professors Paul Lawrence, Philip Stone, and Rosabeth Moss Kanter. My MBA studies first helped me to see the interrelationships between strategy, behavior, and systems. I am especially grateful to Michael Porter in strategy and competition, to Michael Beer in organizational behavior, and to the management control systems faculty. I was fortunate to be admitted to the second cohort of Harvard's innovative Ph.D. in Organizational Behavior and learned much from the Sociology Faculty in Arts and Sciences. That was a time of few boundaries, great curiosity, and wonderful compatriots. During that time, I also joined forces with the Center for Executive Development and learned from its founders Richard Hamermesh, Doug Anderson and John Cady to translate management theory into an inspirational and practical educational experience for managers.

While I am truly indebted to my teachers, however, I bear the responsibility for the applications of their concepts to corporate real estate. However flawed, I hope the ideas presented are useful to corporate real estate and facility professionals and to general managers alike.

Over the years, the research was supported by a variety of grants from the International Development Research Council (IDRC), the Real Estate Research Institute, and through the professional support of the Institute for Corporate Real Estate, the International Association of Corporate Real Estate Executives (NACORE), the International Facility Management Association (IFMA), and the Milton Fund of Harvard University. My professional clients also underwrote some significant studies, whose particulars remain confidential. Special thanks to Robert Patterson, Ron Duff, Stephen Bell, Sally Mertens, Klaus Kramer, David Streeter, and Bill Agnello among the many strategic thinkers in corporate real estate who were generous with their time and insight.

On a personal note, it took me longer to complete this book than I ever fathomed but what I learned through the process is that life happens. The birth and nurturing of children, the sustenance of a marriage, the support deserved by aging parents and friends in crisis, even simply making a living, are the companions of adulthood as we strive to meet our most precious self-centered goals. I am thankful for what I didn't give up. There are so many people who deserve recognition for the support they gave me and this is my one best chance to do so. I beg the reader's tolerance.

My husband Robert sacrificed a lot to see me reach my goal. I am grateful. My family encouraged me even when they sometimes didn't understand my obsessiveness. Love and thanks to Maureen and Anthony Stevens, John O'Mara, and Herm and Esther Schwartz. I sorely miss Connie O'Mara, my mother, who did not live to see this book in print.

I am blessed with wonderful and encouraging friends whom I collectively thank here. Joyce O. Thompson has been my inspiration throughout this project. Her courage through adversity and the loving support of her husband Jim Thompson, family, and friends, has constantly reminded me to keep my priorities straight and to appreciate the pure and simple gifts of life. Denise Dupré, Mark Nunnelly, Kelan Barry Thomas, Pam Germain, Tanya Pole Giovacchini, Mike Friedman, Elise Blaxill, Donna Horton Novitsky, Susan Lehmann, Sally Chicotel, and the rest of our Book Club are among many cherished friends who cheered me on when I felt discouraged.

Superwoman and I have never met. The only way I ever completed this work while keeping my children happy and healthy and my home in livable condition was through the help of many dear people over the years who deserve recognition: Laureen Evans, Jim Chen, Sheela Manandhar, Kevin O'Brien, Sally Long, Mercy Krua, and Gina Reitano.

Research assistants who helped get the book material ready for production include Heather Culp, John Lee, Sharon Tepper, Hilary Lewis, Jack Glagola, Mauricio Silva, and Donald Gibson. The Harvard Graduate School of Design provided valuable resources: particular thanks to Peter Rowe, Francois Vigier, John Seiler, and Jerold Kayden. At The Free Press, my editor Robert Wallace deserves special recognition for his prescience, his patience, and for not giving up on me completely when I called to say that the book would be further delayed because I was expectant with twins! To the rest of The Free Press team my thanks as well.

Finally I want to acknowledge the dedication, energy, and professionalism of the many corporate real estate and facility management professionals whom I have worked with while writing this book and through my work with the Institute for Corporate Real Estate. I hope I have helped to bring greater recognition to the important role they play in enabling competitive advantage for their organizations, and to the vital contribution they make to their companies every day.

Martha A. O'Mara

Cambridge, Massachusetts

March 1999

INTRODUCTION

For the past ten years, I have examined how corporations make real estate and facility management decisions about their offices. Mostly I've looked at companies for whom information is the raw material, and intellectual capital—the creation and application of knowledge—is the essential component of their product. One observation holds true for all the companies I have studied:

Organizations hate making decisions about real estate and facilities.

Why is this so? Decisions about facilities are highly visible and take a long time to implement; and once made, the building lasts for decades, reminding everyone whether the firm made a good long-term decision or not. Today, the planning and management of corporate real estate is further complicated by advances in information and telecommunications technology. These technologies have literally opened up a whole new world—the virtual world—where information can be created, accessed, and transformed into knowledge and action across spatial and temporal boundaries. People do not have to go to a specific place to access and manipulate that information, all they need is a computer, a phone line, software, and a modem.[1]

Most of us still assume that office buildings are always a necessity. Until recently, the tools we information workers need could only be found there: the telephones, the mainframes, our computers, and of course, our co-workers. Inside, offices look pretty much the same from one company to another. Most everyone has a desk, surrounded by either fabric panels or walls. You can identify the most important people by the amount and quality of their office space. Places to work together, such as conference rooms, are often in scarce supply and tucked away out of view. Everyone comes at

1

the same time for a set number of hours per day. The job of corporate real estate is to supply the space for these offices while facility management oversees daily operations. In this scenario, the phrase *corporate real estate strategy* sounds suspiciously like an oxymoron. How can something be strategic if people have no choice as to whether they use it or not?

The ability to work in the virtual world now allows us to choose how we work in space and time. As a result, many of our assumptions about how we organize work and where it takes place are changing. Since we are no longer tied to a specific place by the physical tools of our work, we can choose how often, where, and in what ways we come together. Whole new ways of doing business are evolving, with both confusion and unprecedented opportunity at hand.

We often hear predictions these days that corporate offices are going to disappear in the future—that all information work will be conducted in cyberspace. Some futurists claim we all will work from home—our electronic cottages will be tied together through the Internet and private corporate networks.

Those of us who have spent our lives either working in or studying large, formal economic organizations suspect otherwise. Corporate facilities are not going away, but they need to absolutely change, inside and out. Virtuality alters many of the traditional functions of the office. While it may lessen the importance of some functions, virtuality highlights the importance of other things the workplace provides.

Rather than making real estate disappear, virtuality makes corporate real estate decisions even more complex and difficult. We must decide not only *what* to build, but *whether* to build and *where* to build it.[2] For most companies, corporate real estate and facility costs are second only to people costs, or third after people and technology. Since we no longer can assume automatically that a central place of work—an office—is absolutely necessary, companies must look harder at what sort of investments should be made.

Our approach in this book is to consider *corporate real estate* as encompassing all aspects of the physical settings of organizations. These myriad functions include determining the location of new offices and factories, choosing the design and construction of corporate headquarters and other facilities, determining whether to lease or purchase property, deciding on the disposal of excess property, designing office interiors and workstations, and purchasing furnishings and equipment. The definition also includes those tasks relating to the operation of these properties—

facilities management. It is not limited by departmental boundaries: Many real estate and facility issues have more to do with information technology or human resources. And it is not something that either senior management or line managers can afford to ignore in the business environment of the future. A lot of money is at stake. United States corporate real estate assets are estimated to exceed $3 trillion, with real estate representing about 25% of a typical corporation's assets, according to the International Association of Corporate Real Estate Executives. But even these numbers are dwarfed by the enormity of supporting the people who do the work.

Choices about where and how to house our knowledge workers are now strategic. We must decide who should come to the office, when, and what they should do when they get there. *Place* is where people and technology come together to interpret, process, and act upon information. Place unites the organization in space and time. Now that we can chose whether to work in the same place or not, the true benefits of Place in an organization can be understood. In the future, organizations will make different choices about Place based upon their competitive strategy. The way they make these choices and how they use the unique features of Place will help them produce products better, faster, and more cheaply than their competitors. The challenge is to make the link between *Strategy* and *Place* that will enable your company to build and maintain competitive advantage.

Although the formal planning and management of Place usually falls under the staff functions of corporate real estate and facilities management, decisions about Place are now an important concern for general managers who seek to maximize the value of their employees and to utilize technology intelligently and cost effectively. Corporate real estate professionals and general managers must work together in making those choices about Place *which enable their companies to build and maintain competitive advantage.*

WHERE DOES *STRATEGY* BELONG IN *PLACE*?

Strategy has gone from being the hot management buzzword of the 1980's and 90's to the very core of how organizations think as the twentieth century closes. Today, everything is supposed to be strategic. Strategic information, strategic cost cutting, strategic this and strategic that—even strategic waste management! The essential message is: If it doesn't support the core purpose of the business, it shouldn't be part of the business. Yet, despite the current rhetoric about the need for corporate real estate decisions to be grounded in the strategic needs of the business, very little guidance exists for how this is actually done.

This book provides the link between strategy and corporate real estate, between Strategy and Place. It presents a framework for making corporate real estate decisions which support the business strategy of your company.

The most important step to put real estate in a strategic context is to accept that real estate is of no value to the corporation, regardless of its economic value in an external real estate market, if the real estate does not support the objectives of the organization. *The decisions you made about Place and its daily management must emphasize maximizing its value in helping your organization to compete and thrive.*

Classic measures of real asset performance such as return on equity or internal rate of return, or even measures of asset utilization such as return on capital employed, only measure real estate's effectiveness in past terms. Those methods use metrics relating only to already established lines of business—how the world *used* to work. It is much harder to quantify the value of real estate which puts you at an advantage for tomorrow's competitive environment. A future orientation requires both vision and a belief that Place does matter.

Real estate and facilities fulfill two critical roles supporting the work of the organization and the realization of its competitive strategy. The first role is to physically support the production process. Real estate provides a central place for people to gather and work to be done. Depending upon how they are designed and managed, facilities can either support or impede communication between people and the actual flow of work. The second role is the symbolic representation of the organization to the world. The physical setting of the organization is seen by its employees, customers, and suppliers as the embodiment of the company's values and goals. A sound corporate real estate strategy harnesses both the logistical and symbolic power of place and puts it to work to complement the competitive strategy. This book addresses both of these dynamics.

This book's approach to corporate real estate strategy formulation and implementation is based upon recognizing, understanding, and managing uncertainty. A strategic perspective on corporate real estate recognizes that the volatility and predictability of a company's competitive environment greatly impacts the appropriate time horizon for planning and the ability to make major commitments of capital and resources. To assess how real estate and facilities can be managed best in the face of this uncertainty, the company's strength within its industry must be understood. Then the impact of real estate decisions on customers, suppliers, labor, competitors, and the community must be diagnosed. Only then can the correct real estate strategy be formulated and implemented. Further, different parts of the business may require different strategies, depending upon the competitive forces within their own marketplace and their effect on uncertainty. Buffering the organization's operations from the effects of uncertainty is a key task of the corporate real estate manager.

While it is true that no real estate or facility strategy, no matter how well-delivered, can ever compensate for a lousy product or poor customer service, real estate and facilities play an important role as *enablers* of strategic actions. Enablers are those things which help get the product out the door better, faster, or with less cost. They support the people who do the work and provide an environment where innovation flourishes and common goals are well understood.

Does your company compete through low cost or through differentiation? What work processes are used and what physical setting is needed to best support those processes? Who works at your company—what are their preferences? Can the workplace provide them an important source of support in their daily living needs? What influence does you company's history have on the way it does business today? Can your facilities help nurture your corporate culture by supporting certain behaviors and sending the right signals? How does this all fit in with the preferences and goals of the company's leadership? By asking these and other probing questions, you begin to develop a vision of the workplace that best fits you company's needs and provides your workers with the support required to perform at high levels of productivity and quality. This workplace you envision will help orient the company toward its future goals. While the organization, its competitive environment, and the real estate market are in a constant state of change, the real estate manager must provide a sound, secure, and stable physical home for the business, balancing short-term needs with long-term investments.

There is no one set of rules a company can follow for developing the optimum physical configuration and work environment; instead, it is a constantly evolving effort to find the best fit which meets current and future demands. A unified workplace solution solves more than just spatial needs. Corporate real estate or place integrates the three critical corporate resources—people, technology and strategy—so that they are mutually supportive. Although the best fit between these elements can be felt by the occupants and sometimes outsiders as well, fit is hard to quantify and can even be difficult to articulate clearly. Figure I–1 below illustrates fit.

THE AUDIENCE FOR *STRATEGY AND PLACE*

This book provides a bridge between general managers who set and implement the business's strategy and the corporate real estate and facility manager who must support that strategy. It translates between corporate strategy and myriad physical and behavioral considerations the workplace must accommodate.

Most companies make a major real estate or facility decision every three to five years. Managers responsible for making new facility decisions for an organization or business unit will find *Strategy and Place* an efficient way to get up to speed on the many types of decisions they will face. These include a wide range of strategic issues such as personnel and resource allocations, geographic relocation, contracting and purchasing, and physical plant design decisions. In particular, the methodology for linking corporate real estate strategies to the external strategic demand and internal characteristics of the company will be highly useful. The book relates changes in office interior design and the allocation of space to many of the

Figure I–1
Corporate Real Estate Integrates Strategy, People, and Technology with Place.

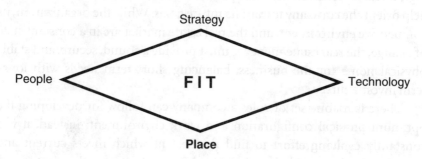

structural changes organizations are experiencing today. These changes include the greater use of project and high-performance teams, networked links with customers and suppliers, increased telecommuting and virtual methods of working, and many other trends which challenge conventional thinking about the location, design, and management of the office. It will help line managers translate their strategic and operational requirements into spatial and physical responses, and then communicate them to senior management and boards of directors.

Those in businesses related to real estate will be eager to better understand the decision maker's perspective which *Strategy and Place* provides. Several of the cases presented in this book profile the decision-making process for purchasing land, buildings, design services, and furnishings. The book provides insight into the behavior of corporations when they make facility decisions, and therefore will be of great interest to those professionals who sell goods and services such as real estate developers, architects and interior designers, and office furnishing and equipment manufacturers. The trend toward greater outsourcing of facility management and corporate real estate activities has resulted in a service sector eager for new insights and improved methods for serving their clients. *Strategy and Place* introduces these professionals to the strategic language their clients speak and helps them to translate their ideas into the client's lexicon.

This book is above all, for the manager in action; however, academics and educators also will find it of value. It is a useful addition to any syllabus relating to corporate real estate or facility management. The book also makes a contribution to the management literature on decision-making processes within organizations, since to date there has been very little research documenting real estate and facility decisions.

Whether you are a line manager responsible for getting the product into the customer's hands, or a real estate manager within the company or a service provider working from the outside, the concepts presented here will help you to better align real estate and facilities with your company's needs. Not all of the benefits of the strategic real estate perspective are quantifiable, in fact, many of the most powerful ones are very difficult to quantify on a direct cost-benefit basis. They do however, follow distinctive and understandable patterns which help us to diagnose a company's needs and develop an approach to decision making that maximizes the usefulness of that real estate in meeting the company's strategic goals. We highlight many winning examples of how real estate can enhance a company's competitive strategy throughout the book.

ORGANIZATION OF THE BOOK

The book is organized in three parts. Examples of corporate real estate strategies in action are given throughout and cover more than forty different companies of various sizes, industries, and histories. *

Part One sets the context for why Place is now strategic. Chapter One examines the changing relationship between the virtual world and the office, and explains why it is not new technology but long-standing issues of strategic uncertainty that make corporate real estate decisions so difficult. The impact virtuality already has had on the ways we use the office are assessed. Although virtuality give us so many more choices, Place remains a key organizational resource. It provides context to information, uses the power of symbols to influence behavior, and still provides the most suitable location for many types of information work. Yet we must completely reconceptualize how we approach making real estate and facility decisions. The focus will not be on the real estate market or minimizing facility costs; it will be on supporting the organization's strategy and the people who make the strategy happen.

Chapter Two discusses why the profession is undergoing such dramatic changes and the ways the profession is responding to these challenges. This chapter puts the past career experiences of corporate real estate managers into perspective and identifies what skills are most needed to meet the changes underway in the profession.

We examine the evolution of the corporate real estate and facility management functions from an externally focused market mindset and from a cost-minimization mindset to today's strategic perspective in Chapter Three. For general managers who are less acquainted with the issues of corporate real estate and facility management, these two chapters provide a helpful introduction.

In Part Two (Chapters Four though Seven) we identify three basic approaches to real estate and facility management decision making. Each strategy relates to the degree of uncertainty found in a company's strategic environment at the time the decision is made. A company will use one of these approaches more than the others depending upon the predictability of its requirements and the need for longer-term commitments. Each of these strategies possess advantages and disadvantages: The key is to apply them in the correct context supporting your competitive strategy.

In brief, the three approaches to corporate real estate decisions are

Incrementalism: *Only short-term commitments to space are made and capital expenditures are minimized. Decisions and purchases are made on an as-needed basis. Very little long-range planning is done.* This strategy is most frequently used by start-ups, but it is also useful for companies which have frequently shifting marketplaces or high rates of technological change. While incrementalism seems like a good way to avoid making long-term decisions, over time, incremental decision making can lead to poorly configured and supported facilities and higher real estate costs.

Standardization: *Control over both design and management procedures are strictly maintained with centralized decision making. These standards are largely based on the need for efficiency, economy, and control.* Standardization is especially appealing to large companies with multiple locations. While standards can lead to substantial economies in purchasing and can make relocating employee offices easier, they are often too inflexible and easily become out-of-date. They can produce excessive bureaucratic procedures which impede the company's ability to change.

Value Based: *Symbols and values of the organization are considered when design decisions are made. Procedures are flexible to meet the needs of individual parts of the organization.* A value-based approach is frequently used by companies with some competitive stability, and by those with large populations of highly educated and trained employees. Value-based decision making can lead to well-designed, highly serviceable facilities, but the decision-making process and the implementation of decisions can consume more time. If the process is not well managed, higher fixed or operating costs may result. Higher project development also can result if the process is not well managed.

Chapters Four, Five, and Six take an in-depth look at the process of real estate decision making at companies operating in each of these three modes. In practice, these strategies are dynamic and their use changes over time as a company's strategic uncertainty shifts in response to its competitive environment. The most appropriate strategy changes over time as competitive conditions change, and different parts of the business may require different strategic approaches. Chapter Seven illustrates this dynamic process and offers suggestions for integrating the strategies to meet your company's unique requirements.

Once the relationship between corporate real estate and uncertainty is understood, and options to approaching decisions are identified, the task still remains to find the best fit between Strategy and Place for your own organization. You can begin by having a systematic approach for gathering information about business requirements.

Part Three (Chapters Eight through Eleven) presents a method for diagnosing your own company's strategic environment and internal organizational demands and relating them to the corporate real estate and facility management requirements you must meet.

Chapters Eight and Nine highlight the external factors influencing real estate decisions and provide a framework for better understanding your company's competitive strategy and the relationship of real estate and facilities in enabling competitive advantage.

Chapters Ten and Eleven focus on the internal characteristics of your organization which make it unique from other companies, even those in the same industry.

In Chapter Twelve, we look ahead to the future of Place in organizations. We see that every company must develop its own unique approach to Place—to allocating those scarce resources of face-to-face personalization

Figure I–2
Diagnostic Framework for Corporate Real Estate Decision Making

and immediacy in ways which best support the strategic and operational requirements of the business.

THE RESEARCH BASIS FOR *STRATEGY AND PLACE*

This book encompasses both my research and professional practice activities in corporate real estate strategy for the past decade. Watching leading-edge companies—such as Sun Microsystems, Fidelity Investments, and many others—use their work environments as a source of competitive advantage encouraged me to investigate the relationship between real estate and facilities and the ways in which companies build and maintain competitive advantage.

The research for this book was initiated in the late 1980's as part of my doctoral dissertation at the Harvard Business School. The initial study was of real estate and facility management decision making at eight high-technology companies including Digital Equipment Corporation (now part of Compaq), Sun Microsystems, Pacific Bell and Pacific Bell Directory (now parts of Southwestern Bell), New England Telephone (now part of Bell Atlantic), Millipore, G-Tech and Molecular Devices, a small start-up. Since 1989, periodic updates of each company's real estate activities have been made, providing not only a rich and detailed description of how these high-profile companies made their real estate decisions but also the opportunity to study the results of each decision's outcome later in time. This research resulted in the typology of decision-making approaches outlined in Part Two of the book.

During my nine years on the faculty of Harvard University's Graduate School of Design, a number of research efforts further advanced the thinking contained in this book. Along with my own continuing work on corporate real estate decision making, and my development and testing of the diagnostic frameworks contained in Part Three, I supervised graduate student research on topics ranging from outsourcing, supervision of remote workers, alternative officing, telework centers, and the location preferences of new media companies. I also directed a two-year study of location decision making by information-age companies, and a study of economic development practices in high-performing office markets. For the past several years, I have served as a core faculty member of the Institute for Corporate Real Estate, sponsored by the International Association of Corporate Real

Estate Executives (NACORE) for whom I conduct seminars on competitive facilities strategies for corporate real estate managers. I have also taught management courses through the International Association of Facility Management (IFMA) and the International Development Research Council (IDRC). Along with my work with these professional associations, I have provided management development seminars for the corporate real estate staffs of several major companies including Fidelity Investments, Merrill Lynch, NationsBank, and Thompson Financial Services. Most recently I have participated in the Corporate Real Estate Portfolio Alliance, a research consortium consisting of corporations, service providers, and academics. I have been joined in this effort by fellow academics Joseph Gyrouko of the Wharton Business School and John McMahan of the Haas Business School of the University of California at Berkeley; and corporations including Boeing, Microsoft, Sun Microsystems, Fidelity Investments, Bell South, Pacific Gas and Electric, U.S. West, CB/Richard Ellis, Johnson Controls, Florida Power and Light, State Farm Insurance, TriNet, and the U.S. General Services Administration. Our research aims to develop portfolio analysis tools for managing corporate real estate holdings and improving strategic planning; it is coordinated by the McMahan Group of San Francisco. The results will be complete soon after this book is published.

In all, the corporate real estate strategies of more than forty companies have been examined in detail for this book, in addition to a review of the best practices across the spectrum of the corporate real estate and facility management profession.

PLACE—THE NEW OPPORTUNITY
FOR COMPETITIVE ADVANTAGE

The title of this book, *Strategy and Place,* alludes to the seminal book *Strategy and Structure,* authored by noted business historian Alfred Chandler in 1962.[3] Chandler was one of the first observers of managerial behavior to make the connection between the choices firms made in how they structured their supervisory and reporting relationships, and the advantages they were able to establish in the marketplace. He recognized that there is no single best way to structure a complex organization. Instead, the organizational structure of an enterprise should be based upon its competitive strategy.

Today, a new range of opportunities presented to organizations enables competitive advantage. *Strategy and Place* argues that there is no one best way to physically house a company and its workforce. Instead, the greater range of choices we have in how we organize our businesses in space and time, makes *Place* an element of competitive strategy, rather than merely a tactical or functional consideration. Each company must find its own unique set of solutions which best support the way the company competes and succeeds in its markets. However, decisions about Place must still be made within the physical parameters of land, buildings, and technology and within the behavioral parameters of people and organizations. This book defines the processes organizations use to make decisions about place, and links place to the strategic and organizational demands which must guide the implementation of those decisions.

Let us take advantage of opportunity... presented to improve our situation.

...to gain a personal competitive advantage... therefore we must...

...range of choices we have... how we organize our influences...

...we must... and... considerations... company must...

...set of solutions... the... the competitive context...

...within the physical environment of this building...

...and within the biological... of... organization...

...before... time the processes and situations... that shape...

...final analysis in... light... of their decisions.

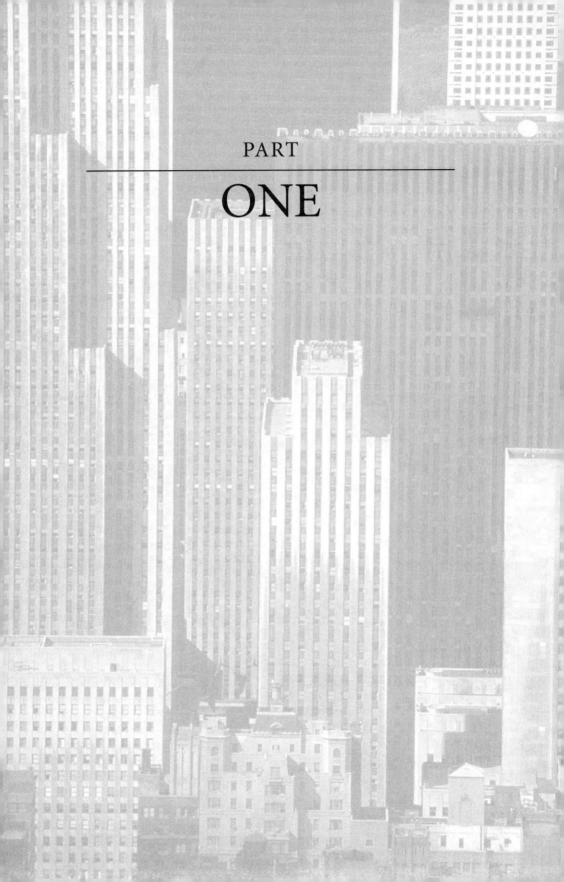

PART

ONE

INTRODUCTION TO PART ONE

Enabling Competitive Advantage Through Place— The Corporate Real Estate Imperative

The changing role of Place, from a banal but necessary component of business to a dynamic catalyst leveraging the workforce in space and time, is already affecting the corporate real estate profession. In Part One, we examine the context for this change, and what such change portends for corporate real estate decision making.

Chapter One examines why Place is even more important in the virtual world. It sets the groundwork for the basic premise of this book: Decisions about Place—rather than being supplanted by technology—are even more critical to organizational success today.

To the practicing corporate real estate professional, much of what is contained in Chapter Two will be old news. Yet, it is important to understand how we got where we are today and why we are seeing such dramatic changes in the entire commercial real estate industry. This chapter is also a helpful overview for general managers who in the past have dealt only casually with corporate real estate issues.

Chapter Three calls for a new way of viewing corporate real estate and facility management. It challenges the old assumptions about what drives decisions regarding the location, construction, use, and management of Place. Rather than viewing real estate and facilities as generators of highly undesirable costs, or as uncontrollable external components of supply subject to the whims of the commercial real estate market, this chapter advocates viewing Place as a strategic asset. This new perspective may be difficult for some managers to embrace if they are used to approaching real estate decisions from mindsets grounded in the past. The strategic perspective I advocate makes full use of not only the logistical functions of Place—bringing people together in space and time to solve difficult problems—but fully realizes its influence on individual and organizational behavior. Place then indeed becomes a valuable tool for enabling competitive advantage.

CHAPTER ONE

THE ROLE OF PLACE IN A VIRTUAL WORLD

The ability to work in the virtual world greatly impacts the planning, design, and management of corporate real estate. This chapter provides the context for understanding the role of Place in the virtual world. We examine the changing relationship between the virtual world and the office, and we explain why it is not new technology but very old issues of strategic uncertainty that make corporate real estate decisions so difficult. We then assess the dramatic impact virtuality has on the ways we work together and how companies are responding to virtuality in the design and management of their corporate real estate. Many of the points brought up in this chapter are expounded upon in later chapters of this book. Those references are noted throughout the discussion.

Most organizations are still in the early stages of adapting to virtual capabilities. Innovation has lagged because the true integration of technology with Place requires a total commitment to changing our approach to the planning, design, development, and occupancy of corporate real estate. Virtuality has changed many of the traditional functions of corporate real estate and facilities, lessening the importance of some but highlighting the strategic importance of others. The emphasis of corporate real estate in the future will not be on responding to the real estate market or minimizing facility costs; it will be on supporting the organization's strategy and the people who make the strategy happen. To do so, we must understand how Place helps the organization function.

THE RADICAL NOTION OF VIRTUAL WORK

The idea that we can now work from anyplace—that the tools knowledge workers need can be carried around on personal computers or accessed through a network, and that we can speak to anyone anywhere and be contacted anywhere at any time—is quite radical. It challenges the entire concept of work which developed in the twentieth century. We no longer need to be at the factory, in the workshop, or tethered to a mainframe computer to process information, communicate, produce a product, or conduct commerce. There is no historical precedent for how to think about organizing and housing virtual work. Our traditional concept of the office, one place for every worker, with the space designed to reflect that person's place in the pecking order, is based on very old assumptions about how people work together.

As communications and information technologies advance, the hierarchical, highly controlled organizational structures which evolved during the industrial age are falling apart. New ways of working together are constantly being innovated. The hierarchy is being replaced with different ways to coordinate economic activity both within the organization and beyond its boundaries; they include project teams, networks, and alliances.[1] In later chapters we examine these changes in relation to corporate real estate and facilities and look at some innovative approaches to better fitting structure and work process to Place.

While so much else in the world of corporate real estate is changing, driven by dramatic social, technological, and organizational changes, one major obstacle to effective corporate real estate management hasn't changed at all. *Places are still very expensive to build and to maintain; they are costly to alter.* The stakes are even higher when unpredictable, rapid change makes future requirements uncertain. This uncertainty is the essential dilemma that corporate real estate must deal with. It is nothing new, but technology has raised the stakes higher than ever. Let's begin by examining the challenge uncertainty always has presented to organizations.

STRATEGIC UNCERTAINTY, NOT TECHNOLOGY, IS THE REAL VILLAIN

Remember that long before the tools of virtual work were developed, companies still hated making real estate and facility management decisions. Commitment to these long-lived assets embody the most fundamental challenge organizations face: *forecasting the future.*

It typically takes at least a year, and often several years, for a company to identify a need for more or different office space, agree upon the need within the company, plan for its requirements, find the site or building, build it out and, finally, occupy the space. This commitment to space is typically for a minimum of five years, often longer.[2] In the meantime, the company's business requirements may change a great deal, perhaps also changing the reasons why the space is needed. This uncertainty over future needs, as we detail in Part Two, is at the core of the corporate real estate strategy dilemma.

My research has found that companies use different sorts of criteria for making real estate and facility decisions depending upon the strategic uncertainty in their competitive environments at the time the decisions are being made. This is why companies with highly turbulent, rapidly changing competitive environments are the least likely to make long-term facility commitments. Faced with the uncertainties of fast growth, rapidly changing technology, deregulation, or globalizing markets, these companies only act incrementally. They wait until the last minute to make major real estate decisions, and then take only the amount of space that is critically required, and avoid building costly facility improvements. In contrast, well-established companies with more predictable strategic environments can plan their real estate commitments with a view to the long term and can more easily standardize their facility policies and practices. Of course, broad changes in global markets and technology mean that there are fewer predictable industries these days.

Most companies fall somewhere in the middle range of uncertainty. They have the size and scope to benefit from larger-scale commitments, such as a customized corporate headquarters or new regional office locations, but they don't really have a clear picture of what their company will need in the future—their technology, their markets, or their competitors may be changing too quickly to permit confident long-term forecasts. To help them make decisions about the future, these companies try to articulate their corporate values and strategic goals. Such companies then try to symbolize these values and goals in the way they design, allocate, and occupy their business facilities. Efforts are made to deliberately reinforce the company's message, and to influence their employees' behavior through the design and management of their workplace. By establishing the reasoning behind their real estate and facility decisions, they can be more consistent in their actions over time which then helps to shape the company's future direction.

Part Two examines these strategies and the business conditions that underlie them, in great detail. But it is important to underscore here that real estate and facilities are not just simple logistical tools, although that remains a critical role. They also greatly affect behavior and attitudes both within and outside the organization's boundaries. This book argues that both the functional and the symbolic roles of the work setting take on even greater importance in the context of virtual work.

Some observers herald the proliferation of virtual work tools as an easy solution to the difficult and expensive problem of housing our workforce. Instead of making all these perilous expenditures on long-lived assets in times of uncertainty, they ask, "Why don't we just go totally virtual and work in cyberspace? We can then avoid all those annoying corporate real estate and facility management decisions and costs." They foresee the demise of the office building and imply we'll all move to the hinterlands and work in virtual space.[3] *That won't happen.* Here's why.

PLACE IS STILL NEEDED
IN THE VIRTUAL WORLD

Organizations need a place to help transform information into knowledge and action, to harness the power of symbols for the organization, and to support the physical needs of workers.

INTERPERSONAL CONTACT AND CONTEXT

A long and distinguished line of research in the social sciences has shown in many ways that people require the presence of others to interpret complex information and to get others to act on that information. The earliest work in the field of organizational behavior, the Hawthorne studies, found that the physical setting of work—where, how, and when workers communicated with each other—affected the formation and maintenance of the informal organization. It is those networks of personal ties which hold an organization together.[4]

Through a process behavior theorists term the *social construction of reality,* we establish a common understanding of what we believe to be reality through our interactions with others.[5] This understanding of the world channels our behavior, focuses our attention, and sets our priorities. The messages forming our attitudes rely on clues which are physical and interpersonal. They provide rich context. The physical setting plays an important role in our social interactions because it frames every piece of the information we receive.

Information is ubiquitous today. Companies can no longer sustain a competitive advantage merely through exclusive access to information, or thorough accomplishing higher speeds of processing information. The transformation of that information into knowledge and action is where critical competitive advantages are found.

People need to be in the same place at the same time (termed *colocation*) to aid the speed and quality of this information transformation. Matching the appropriate mode in which a transaction takes place is discussed further in Chapter Ten. Interpersonal contact helps us to capture the moment and build a sense of urgency, especially when there are many competing demands for attention. According to a 1997 study, the average office worker gets 178 messages every day, about one every three minutes.[6] Context is needed to help set priorities.

Think about the myriad interpersonal tasks the average manager performs in a typical day. Among these she observes the performance and learning needs of subordinates and colleagues, may realize that family pressures are affecting an employee's performance, notes the gung ho attitude of a new employee, hammers out a final budget that requires negotiation and compromise, chooses a vendor for a major piece of outsourcing, solving both short-term crises and making longer-term plans. During this time she must separate truth from fiction, urgency from panic, priorities from politics.

How much of that work could truly be done through virtual technologies alone? Could many of these tasks be accomplished as well without this manager meeting face-to-face with the players involved? Although tremendous things can be done rapidly in virtual space and over networks, two or more people in a room often are required to reach final understanding and agreement. Smiley faces in E-mail aren't enough for the tough stuff. Virtuality is a great tool that can be used in many ways to make organizations smarter, faster, and more cost effective, but the true essence of organizing is collective action, and that takes people working together both physically and interpersonally. Face-to-face is still the preferred method of communicating important information and solving difficult problems.

If interpersonal context is important for interpreting and prioritizing information, then it follows that the greater uncertainty there is about the meaning and importance of information, the greater the need for context. People in complex organizations need lots of ways to help them deal with uncertainty if they are to make decisions and take action. Not all communications media translates well into cyberspace. We all know that to truly understand something, we often have to go and see it, to kick the tires. We are communal creatures. We need each other, and we need places to be together.

CREATURE COMFORTS AND SYMBOLIC MEANING

Place matters. Anyone who has ever designed or managed offices for programmers or engineers will know exactly what I mean. Knowledge workers are extremely sensitive to their surroundings. First of all there is the obvious matter of ergonomics, and these can be directly tied to the health and welfare of the worker. Virtual tools, especially computers are tough on the body. For example, repetitive stress disorders, such as carpal tunnel syndrome, are now the leading cause of workplace disability claims.[7] Second, there are the symbolic, aesthetic and, social elements of the workplace that influence behavior and satisfaction; they either facilitate or impede individual and team effectiveness.

Place allows us to harness the powerful effect which symbols in our environment have on our behavior. Cues from our surroundings influence our actions. We behave differently in different places: a church does not invoke the same conduct as a sports stadium. We see, and react to, symbolic messages in all of our surroundings. The clever company uses clearly articulated symbols to reinforce its culture and values and to encourage people to behave in ways that most contribute to sustaining competitive advantages. As a strong, appropriate culture becomes increasingly recognized as an essential element of implementing strategy—especially in knowledge work businesses—an office environment which supports the culture becomes even more necessary.

Many of these symbols are fairly obvious, even to outsiders. A company with all open offices with same-size cubicles assigned to everyone from low-level managers all the way to the CEO is trying to send a message about egalitarianism and openness. A firm providing luxurious private offices for its partners is probably trying to tell its associates, "Strive and someday you'll have these perks, too." Of course, the symbols need to be a realistic depiction of the actual culture, or the direction in which the organization would like the culture to evolve.

In my research, I found that companies coping with moderate levels of uncertainty in their strategic environments made the greatest use of symbols in the design of their offices. They had a lot of discussion about the corporate culture and the values of the company whenever a major facility commitment was made. These companies put special emphasis on the symbols which proclaim who they are and where they are going. A clear articulation of values provides a basis for going forward to make capital commitments even when uncertainty over specific future operational needs persisted. This value-based strategy is further described in Chapter Six.

BODIES IN SPACE ARE STILL BODIES

A very practical reason why offices will not disappear is that we all have to work somewhere. As a knowledge worker with a wonderful home office, a full-time nanny, and a part-time secretary, I can tell you that working from home can be convenient, but it is not the perfect solution all the time. Expecting workers to do all of their work at home, unless it directly supports the worker's lifestyle, merely shifts the real estate burden from the company to the worker. Few middle-level managers and line workers have the home space for a dedicated office, so the company encroaches upon family space in the living or dining rooms, or the bedroom, or they require a larger home, and the salary increase to pay for it. Working at home is not a comfortable full-time option for most people, and forcing home-based work on employees limits the pool of talent available for hiring. Increasingly it is more difficult to shift this burden to employees when qualified labor is in shorter supply.[8]

Although Starbucks may have emerged as the corporate headquarters of the independent consultant, no other places have come forward as viable, full-time alternatives to the office. For example, not long ago telework centers were much ballyhooed. These offices set up close to residential areas and occupied either by employees from a single company or by individual workers from many different employers. They have had only limited success so far.[9]

The physical place of work is still so important that its quality is frequently used as a recruiting tool at even the most technologically sophisticated companies such as Sun Microsystems, Cisco Systems, Adobe, and Microsoft.

Virtual technologies certainly add value under the appropriate conditions. They are especially useful tools for people who already worked outside the office in the old days of paper, ink, and the post office. The regional managers, salespeople, or independent professionals whose work requires them to be out in the field can now do so more easily and productively. Independent contractors, people whose work can be clearly separated from others, also find virtual work opportunities convenient and attractive. For those who primarily work in offices, virtual technology can loosen our tethers to the workplace by helping reduce some onerous commutes and increasing our productivity while on the road. And nearly everyone can benefit from some time away from the office to quietly work elsewhere, escaping that very same social interaction that makes the workplace more than just a space to work in.

Virtual tools also can make us less tied to place within the boundaries of the entire corporate facility. People can use them to move more easily from place to place, using different parts of the office for different tasks. In fact, freeing up office workers from the tyranny of hard wiring makes it even easier for them to work in communal spaces. Rather than remaining in separate boxes tied to a computer and phone, now employees equipped with laptops and cordless telephones can easily roam freely throughout the workspace and beyond. Although this still might seem like a radical idea, the concept of *your office is where you are* was under discussion as early as 1985.[10]

As our choices of where and how we can work increase, and the social component of the office grows in importance, we now make more conscious decisions about how we work at the office. The critical resource to be managed is not just the cost of the physical asset, it is what the Place enables the organization to accomplish, that matters.

PLACE AS A CRITICAL STRATEGIC RESOURCE

Face-to-face contact in knowledge work today has become, in a sense, optional because technology has freed us from places, and yet context is even more critical in helping us to interpret and act upon information. Therefore, face-to face contact becomes an important resource to allocate. It costs a lot to put people together in a facility, or to have them travel to be together, and those costs are rising.[11] One result is that an office won't just be automatically assigned to everyone in the company. Instead Place will be allocated as needed according to the requirements of the work to be done, and it will change as those requirements change.

Rather than assuming we are always together in the same place when we work, even though we might have spent all of our time there working in solitude with a monitor or a telephone, we must now identify when and how face time should occur. We will need to examine what context the information requires. What do we hope to gain from a face-to-face interaction? Have we used other, cheaper forms of communication in advance so that we can take the most advantage of our personal time together? Is this a "flesh pressing" matter where the personal contact is more symbolic than substantial? Assessing the degree of interpersonal contact most useful for a particular task is an essential part of analyzing work processes within the organization. A framework for evaluating the degree of personalization and immediacy a particular exchange of information requires is presented in Chapter Ten, Figure 10–3.

The office is here to stay. Place provides the context to organizational action, fulfills a symbolic role as the physical embodiment of the organization, and not insignificantly, still provides a physical space for many kinds of tasks. Yet it is radically and rapidly changing from the traditional one person-one place approach with space assigned according to the management hierarchy, to a more complex and dynamic setting. Given virtual technology, how is the workplace changing and what changes might we anticipate in the future?

FIRST-WAVE RESPONSES
TO VIRTUAL TECHNOLOGY

Organizations are responding already to the challenges of virtuality, but much remains to be done. Companies are using virtual technologies to help eliminate underutilized space. The boundary between home and work, once so clearly delineated by office walls, is increasingly blurred. Improvements in virtual tools, especially software, have made virtuality more real, and thus more responsive to organizational context. Let's look at what is happening on these three fronts.

ELIMINATING UNUSED SPACE

The first wave of adopting virtual technologies, especially laptop computing and modems combined with enterprise software applications, gave essential office tools to those who already spend much of their work time out of the office. Sales and service professionals used to maintain a space back at the office so they could use the phone, computer, or fax to file their orders and reports or to have their presentation materials updated. All of that can now be done electronically, not only from home but from a hotel, a car, or even an airplane. Some of these mobile workers have completely given up having a company supplied office, although most set up some sort of home office arrangement or shared workspace arrangement back at the office. The space savings at many companies have been dramatic. Ernst & Young moved its auditing staff to "hotelling"—providing office space on an as needed basis with little individually assigned space—and saved at least 15%–18% of its space requirements, and estimated a 25% increase in productivity. When Dun & Bradstreet converted to a virtual system supported by hotelling, occupancy costs dropped between 32% and 48% and sales productivity rose nearly 30%. By using a variety of alternative officing techniques and better support of remote workers, Anderson Consulting has reduced by half the amount of space per person in a number of its offices.[12] Facing severe business pressures in the early 1990's, IBM cut its real estate holdings from 44 million SF in 1993 to 21 million SF by the end of 1995 through some layoffs but mostly through more effective use of space.[13] IBM converted much of its sales staff to remote work systems and used productivity centers instead of traditional offices and reduced sales office space by over 60%.[14]

Remote work isn't new. Senior management has always done a lot of their work away from the office using that old buggy whip of a tool, the briefcase. The difference today is that remote work is done by people much lower in the organizational hierarchy. It is most successful when the job performance has a measurable output, and collaboration and communication between co-workers is not important. New types of software are allowing previously office-based work to be performed from remote locations, but implementation of many of these programs is difficult. For example, although software is now enabling customer service to be done from any location, including an employee's home, the need for training and supervision, as well as a place to work, remains unchanged.

Telecommuting (working from home using virtual technology) has dramatically increased, driven not only by better technology and the desire for worker convenience and real estate cost savings but also by legislative mandates for cleaner air.[15] Telecommuting does not save a lot of office space when most employees just telecommute a few days per week and still maintain assigned places of work at the office. Telecommuting only saves on real estate when alternative officing supports telecommuting. This ability to easily work away from the office has, however, dramatically changed the old dividing line between home and the office, for better and for worse.

BLURRING THE BOUNDARY BETWEEN OFFICE AND HOME

Using virtual technologies, many of us now are doing more of our work from home. Working from home is not such a new idea, after all. The office as a central place employing people away from their homes is less than seventy-five years old. Large-scale office employment is a post–World War II phenomena. For most of history, people worked at or near their homes. A ground-floor room might be set aside for commercial activities, and the rhythms of life between work and home were fairly seamless. In contrast, the modern office clearly defined the place where paid work was done, and it was far away from the home.

Today many of us spend part of our time working from home and we often manage some of our home obligations from the office (like all those personal phone calls we make). Many companies are recognizing the crossover between our home life and our working life. Our offices are becoming more homey as companies provide home support services in the workplace: big things like child care or elder care, or small conveniences like dry cleaning service, a sundry store on site, extensive food services, and health clubs. Some are even providing concierges to run errands. To better support home-based work, companies also may supply office furniture and technical support to home offices.

Although the home office can rarely provide a complete substitute for a corporate supplied facility, it can help to lessen the burden on the corporate infrastructure and be a benefit to the employee. However, it is important to distinguish between supplementing our work from home, and having home be our primary place of work.

The challenge now becomes balancing our time between work and home, and not letting work take over at the expense of our home life. Too often, we escape from the chaos of our homes into the orderliness of the workplace.[16] The question remains whether we are going to use this blurring of boundaries between the home and the workplace to help us be better parents, partners, and neighbors, or whether it will only serve to make us work more at the expense of our personal lives. How the new vision of the workplace is realized holds the answer to that question.

MAKING VIRTUAL MORE REAL
(THE ENTERPRISE SOLUTION)

A host of new software applications, enabled by the migration from mainframes to client/server architectures, are providing much more timely and easily managed information. Enterprise Resources Planning (ERP) software from companies such as SAP, Oracle, PeopleSoft, and Baan can link widely dispersed organizations by creating a common view of dynamic financial, manufacturing, inventory, distribution, and human resources information. It is easier today to get needed information to the front-line worker without a lot of middle-management manipulation. More important, increasingly that information can be obtained away from the workplace. The newest generation of packaged enterprise software promised to take advantage of the Internet to bring customers, suppliers, and other vendors into the information network. Using ordinary commercially available browsers, customers can track the status of orders, vendors can enter bids for jobs, and employees can update their human resource records, all from any location.

Groupware, such as Lotus Notes or GroupWise is deployed by project teams whose members may be working in many different places. Coordination tasks that used to require secretarial support—messaging, mail, scheduling, and setting up appointments and meetings—are now easily coordinated in virtual space. Each person working on a document can use his own personal font, size, and color when editing shared documents. Project files, as well as corporate databases can be accessed anytime, anywhere, using the Internet as the backbone for global communications.

These projects have been employed to speed up project delivery, improve quality, and lower costs.

These advances in sharing and communicating information and taking action are certainly changing the way people in organizations are managed and how they work together in space and time. But they have not eliminated the need for a place to work. Indeed, even optimistic projections of reduced space needs by corporations are relatively modest—in the neighborhood of 4% to 12% per employee from 1995 to 2000.[17]

DECISIONS ABOUT PLACE—THE NEXT WAVE

Although the first wave of adapting our organizations and offices to virtual technology is underway, it is not enough. What we learned during this first wave is that while underutilized space can be easily eliminated, that which remains may change its use, but still will remain. There is still a need for a Place to work. The many more choices we face today in organizing our workforce in space and time require a new approach for making those difficult decisions. We must better understand how Place allows our organizations to respond to fast-breaking competitive challenges, and how Place reinforces our internal work processes and cultural development.

CHAPTER TWO

FORCES DRIVING CHANGE IN THE MANAGEMENT OF CORPORATE REAL ESTATE AND FACILITIES

The professions of corporate real estate and facility management have greatly evolved over the past twenty-five years. This chapter explores the forces of change that are driving the more strategic role played by corporate real estate and the people who specialize in its management.

The history of their professional associations shows just how young this profession is. The International Development Research Council (IDRC) was founded in the early 1960's primarily as a vehicle to aid companies in the industrial site selection process.[1] The other major association is NACORE (which changed its name from the National Association to the International Association of Corporate Real Estate Executives). NACORE was incorporated in 1974, with a majority of members concerned with retail site selection. It wasn't until 1980 that a professional association of facility managers was started, the International Facility Management Association (IFMA).

By 1999 the collective membership of these associations included more than 21,000 senior managers and executives.[2] IFMA members in the United States and Canada alone account for over $24 billion in annual purchasing power.[3] While these professional associations maintain separate identities, the topics of their sponsored research, conference topics, and educational programs all exhibit a great deal of crossover between the tasks of corporate real estate and those of facility management. In their role of supporting the Place of the organization, the functions of corporate real estate and facility management are far more alike than different, which is why they are considered a single domain in this discussion.

Along with the development of the profession in the past decade, corporate real estate and facility management functions in the United States have undergone a dramatic metamorphosis. Ten years ago most corporate real estate managers would tell you that their primary job was to interact with the external real estate market. Today the profession recognizes the need to more closely link its focus and activities to corporate strategy and to the internal operating requirements of individual companies. But change is not easy, especially for longtime corporate real estate managers, because it requires that they change their entire professional orientation.

Six major sources of change are driving the transformation of the corporate real estate profession: the globalization of customers and competitors, radical advances in computers and communication, lifestyle and demographic changes, changes in the corporate form, changes in the external real estate environment, and overall, increasingly rapid rates of change in society at large. These trends are all interrelated, as shown in Figure 2–1. While these trends have been analyzed by many people in many ways, let's look at how these social and economic changes specifically affect the corporate real estate function.

GLOBALIZATION OF CUSTOMERS, COMPETITORS, AND EMPLOYEES

A major driver of change is the transformation to a global economy and with it, global competition. Improved standards of living across many

Figure 2–1
Sources of Change Are Interrelated.

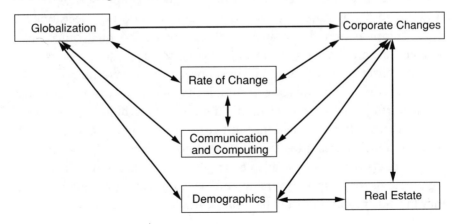

parts of the world are leading to more demand for goods and services. Although this global product demand is increasing the demand for U.S. goods worldwide, it also is spawning localized producers who are becoming formidable global competitors in their own right. In their home markets, low-cost labor, high quality, and rapidly growing domestic markets have enabled international competitors to succeed where American and European competitors once dominated. Further, companies which have largely operated in the mature markets of America and Europe need international markets to sustain growth. Today, customers—and competitors— are everywhere. The numbers on direct foreign investment bear this out; it increased from an average of $100 billion per year during the 1980's to $350 billion in 1996. Foreign direct investment worldwide was expected to reach $400 billion annually by 1999.[4]

In addition to manufacturing, improvements in communications technology and international logistics now allow knowledge work to be dispersed globally. Countries as disparate as Ireland and India can provide high-quality information-processing labor at much lower comparable wage rates than the United States. Indeed, the national boundaries between ownership, markets, and production have disappeared completely for many companies. A company may access the capital markets in the United States by being listed on the New York Stock Exchange, have its manufacturing done in Southeast Asia, its software developed in India, its advertising designed in Great Britain, and its corporate executives housed in a comfortable office building located near their suburban homes.

The global disaggregation of business activities has led companies to seek cost and quality advantages worldwide and to rethink their parochial boundaries. The work process can be more easily geographically separated, resulting in many more locations to choose from. Location decisions are more complex, and the strategic importance of the final outcome is greater. Corporate real estate must now be managed on a global basis.

Globalization requires several responses from corporate real estate. The first is the obvious increase in complexity that comes from managing a global portfolio of properties with different real estate, building, and workplace cost dynamics, regulations, and customs. Second, design standards may not translate well into other cultures, and the same building and interior products may not be available globally. Third, different political and legal systems may affect ownership and development rights which in turn may increase risk and shorten planning horizons.

New types of facility requirements arise when a company operates on a twenty-four-hour basis across the globe. Telecommunications systems interact with complex logistics as daily operations as well as special projects move electronically from place to place. These global networks are made possible by radical advances in computers and communication.

RADICAL ADVANCES IN COMPUTERS AND COMMUNICATION

In the previous chapter, we looked at the impact virtual technology has had not only on how the place of work is planned and managed but also on the actual way organizational activities are carried out. This technology may have been developed specifically for management tasks, such as office automation hardware and software. The Internet, although not originally designed for use in managing organizations, may be the source of the most radical changes in the future.

The use of office automation technology has first-order and second-order effects on the planning, design, and management of corporate real estate. The impacts of using computer and communications technology equipment on the physical design and management of the workplace are first-order effects. Second-order effects on real estate come from accommodating the organizational changes made possible by technology, particularly software.

Corporate real estate and facility managers must now become conversant in matters of computer and telecommunications hardware. Extensive use of computers in an office setting can greatly tax the building infrastructure. Both the initial design as well as the ongoing management of the space are greatly affected. Computers require large amounts of power, the heat they generate requires more air-conditioning, and their use presents many ergonomic challenges. The need to provide a healthful environment for workers who spend most of their time working on keyboards and gazing at screens, determines the selection of lighting, furnishing, and sound control systems. Even moving individual work areas within the building envelope can be more complicated if cables or wiring must be moved as well. Portable technologies such as notebook computers and cellular phones only provide a partial solution as ergonomic and security issues are still unresolved.

A new generation of building and computer hardware products has been designed to better cope with demands on infrastructure and the need to rapidly change workers' locations and interior layouts. These new products further complicate the purchasing decision, and concerns over unused depreciation on existing equipment may be an impediment to their rapid implementation.

The Internet is changing how companies manage and transmit information, both internally and when communicating with their customers. Businesses directly producing an end product or service for customers are finding new ways to conduct or supplement that relationship over the Internet. In the not too distant future, the many ways retailing is conducted will change.[5] Unseen to the customer, the changes fueled by the Internet may be even more dramatic. For example, customers may order many goods directly from the factory rather than through a retail middleman; this eliminates or reduces inventories and therefore distribution facilities.

LIFESTYLE AND DEMOGRAPHIC CHANGES

The face of the American office workforce has been changing over the past fifteen years. Most notably, more women are returning to the paid workforce after having children. A corollary, of course, is that there are more men with working wives, more two-career families. Balancing work life with the responsibilities of parenting is a greater issue than ever before. This issue is magnified for the growing number of single parents in the workforce. There is also more racial and ethnic diversity in the knowledge workplace, resulting from high levels of immigration and from higher educational achievements by minorities.[6]

Employee attitudes are changing as well. The massive middle-management layoffs by blue-chip employers during the early 1990's weakened the bond between employers and employees. In the information age, "the brand is you."[7] People are encouraged to invest in their own careers and personal networks. They are less likely now to stay with the same company through their entire work life, and they are more likely to switch careers and interests several times during their lives. Downsizing had another, more onerous impact. The number of hours people spend at work is actually increasing as companies try to do more business with fewer resources.[8] An actual shortage of workers, particularly information workers, is predicted as the demographics of the "baby bust" generation and the expanding U.S. economy collide.[9]

Greater family pressures, more diversity, and a change of attitude toward their employers have all increased people's expectations of their work environment. These in-demand workers are more critical and vocal about their needs. They expect a greater voice in selecting their workplace location as well as in its design and daily management. Spending more hours at work means that better working conditions and more conveniences and amenities are expected. Workers also desire greater flexibility to help them balance between work and home. These demands have broadened the scope of corporate real estate and facility management services. On-site support services such as child care, convenient food service, and provision of personal services such as dry cleaning, ATMs, and sundry shops now are regularly on the corporate real estate agenda.

Some of the need to provide flexible work hours and alternative work arrangements such as telecommuting come more from workers' demands than the demands of the work. Companies must extend building operating hours to accommodate flextime schedules and late-night work sessions. Diversity is accompanied by a multitude of new facility requirements. Some changes, such as providing access for disabled workers, are legally mandated. Other changes are made to show sensitivity to personal needs. For example, some companies now provide space for their Muslim employees to perform their brief, but frequent daily prayers. Providing a workplace responsive to the personal as well as professional needs of the workforce is extensively explored in Chapters Ten and Eleven.

CHANGES IN THE CORPORATE FORM

The form of the corporation is undergoing change. We are innovating many more ways of organizing economic activity, blurring the boundary between customer and supplier, employer and employee. The traditional corporation was based upon a purely hierarchical approach characterized by long-term formal employment relationships, broadly defined job descriptions, and a distinct chain of command that designates authority and responsibility. In contrast, simple market relationships are based upon a single, clearly defined exchange of goods or services for a predetermined price. Today, most companies conduct activities through hybrid organizational structures which have the characteristics of both hierarchical and market relationships. People may report to more than one boss, and move from project to project, rather than directly up the corporate ladder. Networks of relationships are more important to the company's success than the formal organizational structure. A picture of these relationships would resemble a spiderweb rather than the inverted tree which depicts a hierarchical structure. These eclectic ways of organizing make extensive use of joint ventures with customers, suppliers, and sometimes with competitors; use contract employees on a project basis; and may outsource not only corporate support services but also even core functions such as customer service or manufacturing.

These hybrid organizational forms make the job of forecasting, managing, and cost accounting for real estate and facilities even more complex. The official company head count may not accurately describe all of the people who need a place to work on site. Suppliers may require space, or a firm may have its own employees housed on a customer's premises. These blurred boundaries between suppliers and customers require more creative facility solutions in terms of both the way space is provided and how the cost is charged back appropriately. When most of the company is being managed on a short-term project basis with teams comprised of employees and alliance members, there is little predictability of demand for amounts and types of space. Fewer line managers are willing to take responsibility for the long-term space commitments still mandated by the real estate industry. As a result, the corporate real estate function takes on the responsibility of providing flexible assets for the business units and for maximizing asset utilization over time.

The redefinition of corporate boundaries also has affected how corporate real estate and facility management services are provided within the company. More companies today believe that any functions retained within the formal boundaries of the company must relate to the core business objectives or directly contribute to the core competencies of the company.[10] Anything that can be as easily accomplished by an outside service provider at a comparable or lower cost is a target for outsourcing. In fact, many corporate real estate and facility management tasks have been targeted for outsourcing at most large companies today.

Ownership of public companies is more broadly held than ever before due to the abundance of mutual funds and other easy ways for small investors to participate in the stock market. As a result, there is greater public scrutiny of corporate decisions. Highly visible commitments of capital, such as real estate, often attract the critical eye of stock market industry analysts. In making corporate decisions about expenditures managers often ask, "What will the analysts think?"

More attention also is paid to managing asset performance at the business unit level. Improved management information systems allow closer tracking and more detailed analysis of real estate and facility management costs. It is easier for these costs to get more attention from general managers than ever before. Line managers' interest in corporate real estate increases even more when companies begin to evaluate and reward executive performance based upon asset utilization measures. The visibility and the pressure upon corporate real estate managers increases accordingly.

CHANGES IN THE EXTERNAL REAL ESTATE ENVIRONMENT

The crash of commercial real estate values during the late 1980's to early 1990's transformed the real estate development industry. Although the industry always rode the crests and trenches of the general economic cycle, some fundamentals—how projects are developed, financed, operated, and managed—were altered irrevocably. This change has given greater power to the corporate real estate function while limiting flexibility at the time it is most needed.

Most notably, the bust in commercial real estate greatly limited the production of speculative office space; that is, construction of space prior to commitment by tenants. Financial institutions which were once badly burned by their reckless real estate lending practices are loath to lend money for development unless the risk is perceived to be low. This greater caution has increased the power of corporations in the office leasing transaction since a commitment from a corporate tenant is usually needed before any significant financing can be obtained. On the other hand, a lack of speculative development in many markets has decreased the amount of space available for lease at short notice, putting even greater pressure on corporations to make development commitments farther into the future. By 1998, purely speculative developments were starting to be funded in locations with low vacancy rates, but industry analysts doubted that another cycle of overbuilding would occur.[11]

One approach to ameliorating the lack of readily leasable office space is a hybrid between speculative and custom-designed facilities. This build-to-suit approach uses a developer to acquire the site and oversee construction. The corporate tenant has some input on the design of the facility, but care also is taken so that the building could serve other tenants easily at a later date. Build-to-suit projects often take advantage of off-balance sheet financing methods which improve asset performance ratios while retaining the tax advantages of ownership.

In the late 1990's stability in the commercial real estate industry came in large part from the securitization of ownership. Large funds composed of individual investors purchased great numbers of properties and pooled the assets to offset individual fluctuations in performance. Because these securities can be traded in the same way as stocks, they are far more liquid than traditional real estate investments. Some developers, such as the giant Hines Corporation raised its own pool of equity capital in 1997 to fund the development and financing of corporate build-to-suit projects.[12] A few corporations, especially those rich in real estate assets, have converted their real estate holdings into securitized assets even though the corporation remains the major tenant.[13]

A final result of the changes in the commercial real estate industry is that a lot of experienced real estate development professionals are looking to put their expertise to use in other ways. Many developers have become service providers working for fee income rather than equity participation. Large, globally operated real estate service firms offer one-stop shopping for a range of services—project development, brokerage, property management, and portfolio management. Corporations now have many more resources to choose from when developing and managing their facilities. However, this also has produced greater competition for internal corporate real estate managers who must now prove their worth to their employers.

OVERALL, INCREASINGLY RAPID RATES OF CHANGE

Change itself is a phenomena to be reckoned with. As management theorist Charles Handy points out, continuous, predictable change is not threatening because the past can be used as a guide to the future. Today, in what he calls the age of unreason, change is discontinuous without pattern or precedent. Handy believes that the greatest source of change for how we will live our lives in the future is the change in how our work is organized.[14]

As a result of changes in product development, especially in high technology fields, industries have higher rates of new product development and shorter product life cycles than ever before.[15] Instantaneous global communication means new ideas are shared rapidly. Competitive advantages are harder to sustain over time.

For many industries, the increase in the velocity and depth of change means that time more than cost, becomes the basis for competition.[16] As overall quality levels improve, supporting time-based factors—innovating new products faster and getting those products to market ahead of the competition—are critical.

The conundrum for corporate real estate is that while the rate of discontinuous change has increased, the time-consuming process of building facilities is not much shorter. The real estate capital markets also are based upon long time commitments at odds with corporate realities.

CHANGES IN PLACE MEAN A GREATER STRATEGIC ROLE FOR CORPORATE REAL ESTATE AND FACILITIES

Change in society's use of space and time—as demonstrated by the increasing ways economic activities are being conducted and the speed at which they take place—is accelerating. The changes just outlined all point to the need for a more strategic perspective on corporate real estate and facilities. However, this strategic perspective is unfamiliar territory for many corporate real estate and facility managers who have developed their careers operating under a very different set of priorities. In the next chapter, we explore how the perspectives of corporate real estate are changing, and why a strategic point of view is required to meet the challenges of change.

CHAPTER THREE

CHAMPIONING THE STRATEGIC PERSPECTIVE:

Making Place a Competitive Advantage

Tremendous changes are impacting the planning, use, and significance of corporate real estate (CRE) and facilities. How should CRE professionals respond? To best craft a response, it is helpful to understand how the focus of the profession also is changing from tactical deal making to strategic integration with business objectives.

SHIFTING THE CORPORATE REAL ESTATE MINDSET—DOMINANT MODELS

Like all career specialists, corporate real estate professionals have an image of their profession which they carry internally. It frames the way they view the world. These mindsets, or cognitive biases, are like a lens through which potential decisions and actions are viewed. Mindsets usually are formed by critical experiences during the early years of career development, and once formed, can be difficult to change. These mindsets to change bias the decision-makers point of view when a decision is required.[1]

Three perspectives on the roles and responsibilities of the corporate real estate manager are found today. Each perspective influences how problems are identified and the types of solutions sought. Figure 3–1, Milestones in the Development of Corporate Real Estate Mindsets, traces the historical events accompanying the development of these three perspectives since the 1970's.

First, the *market mindset* relates corporate real estate holdings to their external commercial market value. This mindset was formed in the late 1970's as a response to the undersupply and increase in value of corporate

Figure 3–1
Milestones in the Development of Corporate Real Estate Mindsets

DOMINANT CORPORATE REAL ESTATE MINDSET:

	MARKET	MINIMIZE-COST	STRATEGIC
Technological Change	Hand Held Calculators 1970 • Personal Computers 1978 • Electronic Spreadsheets 1982 • Computer Aided Design 1984	Cellular Telephones 1987 • Notebook Computers 1992 • First Graphical Web Browser 1993 • Video Conferencing 1994	Palm Pilot Debuts 1996
New Management Ideas	The Organization and the Environment 1969 • Discounted Cash Flow 1970 • Scenario Planning 1973 • Competitive Strategy 1980 • In Search of Excellence 1982 • The Changemasters 1982 • Competitive Advantage 1985	Benchmarking 1989 • Core Competence 1990 • Outsourcing 1992 • Reengineering 1993	The Virtual Organization 1996
Financial Markets	REIT Boom 1970–72 • REIT Bust 1973–75 • Rents Skyrocket 1979–81 • Tax Act 1981 • Recession 1981–82 • S&L Deregulation 1982–89	Tax Reform Act 1986 • Stock Market Crash 1987 • Credit Crunch 1990 • Sale Leaseback Agreements 1991	REIT Boom 1996–98
CRE/FM Milestones	NACORE Incorporated 1974 • IFMA Founded 1980 • NACORE establishes MCR/MCRS Designation 1980	Journal of Real Estate Research First CRE Issue 1989 • CRE 2000 Published 1992	IDRC Certification 1998 • Journal of Corporate Real Estate 1998
Historical Events	Oil Embargo 1973 • Carter Elected 1976 • Oil Embargo 1979 • Reagan Elected 1980	Bush Elected 1988 • Berlin Wall Falls 1989 • Desert Storm 1990 • Clinton Elected 1992	European Union 1999

| 1970 | 1975 | 1980 | 1985 | 1990 | 1995 | 2000 |

real estate and then to the ensuing speculative development furor of the mid-1980's. It may be that professionals who began their careers by selecting sites and acquiring and developing property are more likely to possess this mindset.

Second, the *minimize-cost mindset* intensely focuses on reducing direct occupancy costs. The progenitor of this mindset was the reengineering movement, and subsequent downsizing of the late 80's and early 90's. It may be possible that CRE professionals with a facilities management background are more prone to have this attitude.

Third, the *strategic mindset* acknowledges that real estate and facility decisions can be made only in the context of what the organization must do to compete and succeed in the marketplace.

These responses to corporate real estate exemplify each mindset:

Figure 3–2
Dominant Mindset Response to Real Estate

Dominant Mindset	Unchanging Truth	CRE Response
Market	Real estate is expensive.	Get a deal on it!
Minimize-cost	Real estate is expensive.	Get rid of it!
Strategic	Real estate is expensive.	Allocate it!

Let's look more closely at each of these three mindsets and what they imply for CRE decision making. What are the historical reasons each mindset evolved? What are the advantages and pitfalls of each point of view? Can you recognize yours?

Sidebar 3–1
CRE 2000

In 1992 the International Development Research Council (IDRC) began to examine the ways the corporate real estate profession was changing through a series of studies called Corporate Real Estate 2000 or CRE2000.[2] This extensive research project was funded by a number of leading corporations. One early effort identified five basic approaches to corporate real estate management. These evolving stages require different skills and competencies with a shift toward a more strategic focus at the higher stages. Of the first three approaches, *taskmasters* are primarily concerned with the technical aspects of supplying buildings, *controllers* are analytic and focus on minimizing building costs, and *deal makers* try to solve specific organizational problems through real estate solutions. A fourth stage, the *intrapreneur,* provides services to the lines of business at market costs, matches CRE strategy to those of competitors, and acts as a profit center. It is not until stage five—*business strategist*—that real estate executives become primarily concerned with influencing competitive advantage, productivity, and shareholder value. IDRC's 1993 report observed that CRE professionals were just beginning to explore the possibilities of this stage.

The IDRC scheme does not go nearly far enough in calling for a radical refocusing of the profession. It still gives great validity to the earlier stages. The first three sets of tasks often can be performed by outside service providers with greater quality and lower cost. In the quest for real estate profits, the *intrapreneur* often loses focus on meeting the business's needs. Only the *business strategist* role integrates with the strategic needs and internal demands of the organization. The approaches to decision making and organizational analysis advocated here will help develop *business strategists* the profession now requires.

THE MARKET MINDSET

The market mindset views corporate real estate as a portfolio of assets whose cost and performance can be compared to outside standards. This mindset has its origins in the era of rapidly escalating real estate values which began in the late 1970's, and the commercial building spanning the 1981 tax act and the 1986 tax reform act.[3] Three aspects of corporate real estate decision making were affected by the real estate development frenzy during this era: location of facilities, the balance between ownership and leasing of property, and the organization and emphasis of the corporate real estate function.

ORIGINS OF THE MARKET MINDSET

As speculative real estate markets heated up in the early to mid-1980's, so did the profile of corporate real estate. Space was scarce: nationwide downtown vacancy rates were in the range of 5% between 1979 and 1981. Vacancy rates in New York, San Francisco, and Los Angeles were less than 3%. Office space lease costs in New York City rose from less than $19 per square foot in 1980 to over $27 at their peak in 1985. Similarly, San Francisco rents rose from under $12 per square foot in 1979 to over $22 by 1984. Boston skyrocketed from about $10 per square foot in 1980 to over $17 in the mid 1980's. Corporations that needed additional space or had leases come up for renewal experienced major sticker shock. Facility costs also rose from the more intensive use of office automation.[4]

Due to the high cost of downtown real estate, along with advances in computing and telecommunications, corporations were encouraged to relocate their support operations from expensive city centers to lower-cost suburban locations. In the suburbs, land was cheap and plentiful. Custom facilities could be developed at a price competitive with the leasing of standard speculative high-rise space in the city. The suburbs were most attractive to middle managers who would relocate: housing was more affordable, the streets appeared safer, the schools seemed better, and the welfare burden lighter than in the cities.

Many large companies added to their real estate incrementally in the 1970's and early 1980's. This often left them with less than optimum adjacencies between departments. For example, New England Telephone (NET) found itself spread out into 2,000 sites and 12,000 buildings throughout New England. At the time, NET was also the largest user of office space in downtown Boston, occupying eight major buildings, along with many smaller pieces of space. In Northern California, Pacific Telesis held 57 leases in the San Francisco area alone.[5] Many of the older buildings occupied by these companies could not support the more sophisticated wiring and technological infrastructure required by intensified computer use. It was often less costly to build new space than to upgrade to support the additional power and HVAC requirements of computer intensive work environments.

Not all corporations were on the losing side of the run-up in values of real estate. Corporations that either purchased land before the market rise or held long-term leases began to realize the hidden value that these properties held. Some companies took advantage of their low cost basis in real estate and sold off some holdings to the highest bidder, directly contributing income to the bottom line. Some executives started viewing their real estate holdings as potential sources of cash.

As the cumulative cost of leasing over time began to exceed the cost of developing and owning the property, it became easier to justify owning core facilities. Since many companies maintained the general notion that space they built should not cost more than leased space, as the cost of leased space went up, the benchmark for owned facilities rose accordingly. Customized buildings have other attractions as well: They can be designed to more closely suit the company's needs and might better accommodate a large number of employees in a location less accessible to outsiders.

The specter of continually rising real estate costs also encouraged companies to lock in the current cost of facilities by owning. The real estate manager of a major computer manufacturing firm explained his push towards ownership of real estate assets: "We can fix our real estate costs today and benefit from lower relative costs tomorrow." In an age of continually increasing property and construction costs, managers believed they could gain competitive advantage over new entrants in their industry whose cost of real estate and facilities would be higher at a later time.

The market mindset led real estate managers to further differentiate their jobs from those of facility managers. Real estate managers were the deal makers and the real estate developers while facility managers were the day-to-day maintenance people. Real estate managers became more focused on the art of the deal and took a project-by-project focus. Real estate typically reported to the finance function; in many organizations this gave it higher status than facilities management which reported to administrative support or local operations. Real estate managers had less at stake in the longer-term impact of their decisions on the organization; their primary mandate was to get a good deal in the context of the current market. Some major corporations even began to run their real estate operations as separate real estate development profit centers.

CONSEQUENCES OF THE MARKET MINDSET

There were several positive outcomes from this era. The market mindset encouraged companies to take a more sophisticated view of their real estate holdings. Real estate began to be viewed as a portfolio of properties whose relative cost and performance could be compared to outside standards, rather than merely an accumulation of properties acquired over time as short-term business needs dictated. It encouraged better information systems about real estate holdings. The market mindset led to greater recognition of corporate real estate's ability to uncover hidden wealth.

Over time however, many disadvantages to approaching corporate real estate with a market mindset become evident. With the external real estate market setting the standard for what real estate should cost—a result of commercial space being in short supply—many companies accepted higher expenditures for real estate and facilities. The prevailing logic became if our competitors are paying that much for their space, anything less we pay gives us a cost advantage. Managers should have asked, "What is the true value of this space to our company and how much should we spend on it?" Flush with highly leveraged debt, developers competed for corporate tenants with increasingly lavish tenant improvement packages, so that corporate offices looked more like granite and walnut lined palaces than serious profit-making places.

Some decisions to acquire or sell property were based more upon the financial attractiveness of the deal than the physical needs of the company, resulting in bad operational logistics. For example, a major consumer products company headquartered in New York sold off half of its midtown Manhattan property in 1985 and relocated its occupants to less costly space in New Jersey. A handsome profit enhanced corporate earnings that quarter. However, major coordination problems arose because some of the operations in New Jersey needed to be closer to the company's New York headquarters. Coordination problems became even more acute when the company began to organize many of its functions, including new product development, into high-performance teams. Can the cost of this move, which physically separated key product development functions be quantified in terms of lost opportunities to forge new market segments and attain market leadership? Of course not. However, we do know that in the past ten years this company has been beat to market consistently by a competitor which houses all of its key employees in one location specifically designed to enhance teamwork.

Of course, some businesses always have managed their real estate from a proactive profit-making perspective, but these are generally businesses for whom real estate holdings are a by-product of core business activities. Successful examples include companies who own a great deal of long-underutilized land such as forest products companies, utilities, or railroads.

Operating under the market mindset, corporate real estate managers closely identify with peers in the external real estate community, such as brokers, developers, and financiers. This external focus can distract CRE managers away from building closer ties with the line managers of their own company and undermine their ability to more fully understand their company's real estate and facility needs. They come to be seen by others within the corporation as outsiders with expertise rather than as valuable partners in the business's growth. Not surprisingly, when the impulse to outsource strikes, these highly compensated real estate managers are early targets for replacement by outside service providers.

Finally, real estate markets go down as well as up. A market mindset can provide short-term cash when prices are rising, but exposes a company to unnecessary financial risk when markets fall. Part of the payback analysis for New England Telephone's move to a new headquarters was based upon the potential appreciation of the company's share of the equity in the project. However, by the time the building opened, the downtown Boston market was in a slump and some of the debt on the building defaulted. NET's profits from the equity never materialized.

THE MINIMIZE-COST MINDSET

The next wave of corporate real estate thinking—one many companies still operate under—is the minimize-cost mindset. This perspective views real estate and facilities as consumers of investment capital and generators of operating costs which should be minimized as much as possible.

ORIGINS OF THE MINIMIZE-COST MINDSET

This mindset's intense focus on reducing real estate and facility costs has the same midwife as the massive reengineering, downsizing, and operational streamlining many large corporations pursued in the late 1980's and early 1990's. Many companies did find significant real estate and facility savings when they reexamined their work processes, especially in light of new ways of doing business made possible by office automation, improved delivery logistics, and advanced telecommunications capabilities. The market mindset of the previous decade caused companies to put on excess real estate poundage because corporate real estate costs had been compared to the inflated values in the external real estate market. The minimize-cost mindset was initiated at companies either as part of an overall corporate cost-cutting initiative, or by corporate real estate and facility managers in an effort to show the added value of their functions to senior management.

CONSEQUENCES OF THE MINIMIZE-COST MINDSET

There are many important benefits to the minimize-cost mindset. It helps to ferret out waste, it argues against pretentious and expensive design elements, and above all, it makes line managers more aware of the effect of real estate and facility costs on the profitability of their business.

The minimize-cost mindset helps cut facility fat. At its simplest, it looks for opportunities to eliminate unused space. For example, improvements in delivery service logistics have allowed many companies to sell off unneeded or underutilized distribution facilities, sometimes even at a profit over the book value of the property. Another common minimize-cost tactic is to reduce overall occupancy costs by shrinking office space per employee. Workstations and private offices are made smaller, while alternative officing arrangements reduce the need for traditional office space. Companies often justify shrinking space standards by comparing their space utilization to other companies in their own or similar industries. These comparative benchmarking studies became very popular in the early 1990's, providing cross and within industry comparisons of space utilization and costs.

Since there is often substantial investment in interior construction and furnishings based on the old space standards, companies tend to act on space reduction incrementally. New facilities or the remodeling of older ones offer the opportunity to reduce square feet per person. For example, over five years, financial giant Merrill Lynch was able to reduce its average space per employee by 20% as it remodeled or vacated spaces in downtown New York and built new space in other locations. We'll examine Merrill Lynch's strategy in further detail in Chapter Seven.

Lower facility operating costs also are sought through outsourcing building services to contractors who pay less or offer fewer benefits to their employees.

The minimize-cost mindset also lessens the corporate emphasis on glitz. It not only argues against gold plating and rare wood paneling but also encourages occupancy of lower-cost locations. High-profile companies such as AT&T and IBM largely abandoned their downtown trophy buildings for lower-cost suburban locations during the late 1980's and early 1990's. While this blue-chip exodus depressed downtown lease rates in some locations, it encouraged other companies to remain in downtown locations at lower renegotiated rates.

A minimize-cost mindset toward corporate real estate is also held by some line managers. This attitude is most likely when individual facility costs are allocated directly to the specific lines of business which occupy them instead of being blended into a companywide square-foot rate that ignores the real cost of the actual space occupied. Further cost-cutting efforts occur when companies begin to measure their managers' performances based upon the return on capital employed.[6]

Although many of the benefits of the minimize-cost mindset do provide quick quantifiable results, it can lead to a preoccupation with facility cost reduction at the expense of the company's longer-term competitiveness. Muscle is cut along with fat. Short-term cost reductions many impede longer-term flexibility. By reducing the issues of corporate real estate and facility management decisions to only cost considerations, it inhibits a value-based perspective on real estate and facilities.

Direct costing and measurement of asset performance can help raise line management's awareness of facility costs, encouraging them to identify opportunities to save money, but these measures also can lead to a preoccupation with cost reduction which detracts from efforts to increase the effectiveness of those assets.

Short-term cost minimization can actually lead to higher indirect costs, or worse, impede longer-term competitive advantages. Obvious examples include choosing a cheaper location for an office, even if it means longer commutes for employees, or providing inadequate on-site services so that employees need to leave the facility for meals, meeting space, and client contacts. Locking in a lower lease rate in exchange for a longer-term lease commitment may lessen the company's future flexibility and the company may end up paying for space it doesn't need.

Examples of short-changing interior facilities at the expense of organizational effectiveness are plentiful. Space standards may become so tight that the noise and distraction levels reduce employees' ability to get their work done and increase their stress. How well the workplace supports the business can be overlooked in the quest for cost reduction. Employees who try to flee to conference rooms because their workspaces have poor acoustics may find that the company has converted conference rooms to offices, so there is nowhere to have a meeting or work without interruption. The popular cartoon "Dilbert" often chronicles the unintended results of facilities cost cutting gone wild.

Facility cost reduction efforts can increase costs in other areas by shifting, not solving the problem. Costs from lost productivity are one obvious result. Information technology and support staff costs often increase when office space is eliminated.

In order to reduce the impact of facilities costs on their performance reviews, line managers may play all sorts of games to reduce costs. Some ask to be moved to cheaper space, even though they occupy space designed for them. Property may be sold off to lower asset utilization ratios.

No corporation intentionally sets out to waste money. Much cost reduction is straightforward. Eliminating waste and redundancy are unassailable. The question remains, *How do you decide what you really need?* The choices managers face about where and how to spend money on real estate and facilities are difficult and complex. Without a clear understanding of your organization's strategy and the role real estate and facilities can play in enabling competitive advantage to be developed and maintained, those choices cannot be made. When cost is the sole arbiter of a critical resource decision, opportunities for finding new sources of competitive advantage, for being better and faster, for discovering creative sources of differentiation will be lost.

THE STRATEGIC MINDSET

The coming wave of thinking is strategic corporate real estate. This perspective acknowledges that real estate and facility decisions can be made only in the context of what the organization must do to compete and succeed in its marketplace.

While a careful eye must always remain on the activities of the external real estate market, and while costs must be carefully monitored, the strategic mindset emphasizes that decisions about real estate markets and costs must be viewed from the perspective of the company strategy. To paraphrase a mission statement at one of the companies I studied:

> Corporate real estate enables competitive advantage by supplying the right resources in the right place at the right time at the right cost.

ORIGINS OF THE STRATEGIC MINDSET

The need to place corporate real estate decision making in the context of competitive strategy, while certainly never a novel idea, gained currency in the 1990's. This focus on strategy was fueled by several new perspectives on organizations which focused on improving internal organizational processes and support. One of the major influences on strategic thinking to emerge in the early 1990's was the notion of core competencies.[7] Core competence refers to the intelligence within the organization, its ability to learn and coordinate a wide range of production skills and technologies. Most valuable are those competencies which competitors have a hard time imitating. This common sense concept urged companies to give attention and resources to those things they do best which contribute most directly to economic success. Activities better done by outside providers and not directly related to the firm's core activities should be outsourced. Better information systems and the ability of customers and suppliers to work more closely together also permits close coordination of upstream and downstream activities without requiring ownership of those activities. All activities which remain within the company should make a direct contribution to building and maintaining competitive advantage. With its emphasis on capturing the knowledge within the company and increasing the quality of organizational learning, the core competency approach also highlights the importance of workplace quality.

CONSEQUENCES OF THE STRATEGIC MINDSET

The strategic mindset enables competitive advantage by providing the right facility solutions for the company's unique needs. It optimizes the logistical requirements of the work to be done and utilizes the symbolic dimensions of space to enhance the culture of the organization. The strategic mindset improves communication between corporate real estate and the line businesses. It encourages more realistic and accurate cost analysis by factoring in the uses and costs of people and technology. However, it is not easy to implement the strategic mindset because it requires a fundamental change in attitude about corporate real estate management. New skills may need to be developed.

Real estate and facilities clearly play a critical role in operational logistics. As discussed in the previous chapter, technology has changed the dimensions and the complexity of the choices we must make. Facilities designed with a clear understanding of the work process and its effect on all dimensions of a company's operations maximize the value of the workplace and either directly or indirectly the productivity of the employees. We address work process issues further in Chapter 8.

Place is fraught with meaning. Although plant, property, and equipment are lumped together in the financial report, real estate cannot just be treated like some piece of capital equipment. Limiting it to the same sort of analytic and decision-making process is similar to forcing a machine or computer to waste a great deal of its power to convey symbolic information and to influence attitudes and behavior. The importance which facilities take on in organizations was well-described by the founding CEO of G-Tech, Guy Snowden, one of the companies profiled in Part Two:

> There are tremendous hassles, debates, and struggles between physical space and budgets. Senior management is not at all well equipped to handle the process. You need professional assistance and a lot of people involvement. It is almost always divisive—top management plays Solomon. You can't finesse it or smooth things out. It is the most visible, most political resource to manage and the most status significant.

Space—how much, where, and how it is designed and decorated—conveys prestige. Although some designs may try to minimize status symbols in the workplace, they will never be eliminated. People seek and respond to ways that help them differentiate themselves. Any corporate real estate strategy which ignores the powerful role facilities play in the emotional context of the organization is doomed to failure. The savvy approach uses its symbolic nature to advance organization's goals by reinforcing assumptions, attitudes, and behaviors complimenting the strategic goals of the company. As we will see in Chapter Six, incorporating values and symbols into the corporate real estate decision-making process helps an organization make sense of its longer-term plans even when there is uncertainty over specific future requirements.

The strategic mindset requires a clear understanding of the business strategy and organizational demands of the company. It encourages improved communication between corporate real estate managers and line managers. Many of the line managers interviewed complained, "The real estate department doesn't understand my needs." Meanwhile, corporate real estate professionals inquire, "Where do I start?" and "What should I ask?"

OBSTACLES TO THE STRATEGIC MINDSET

The strategic mindset sounds like a no-brainer: *Do what the business needs.* Then why do so many companies find it hard to view their corporate real estate and facilities from this perspective? One stumbling block is that the benefits of strategic solutions may be difficult to quantify in the short term. Also, the strategic mindset can be difficult to maintain *if there is no clear corporate strategy.*

Productivity measurement has always been the holy grail of workplace design. And just like the holy grail, it is ever elusive. But productivity measurement, especially when applied to knowledge work, is as flawed as any performance measurement and compensation system. Some performance can be measured directly using sales, task completion, and cycle time. Ergonomic design efforts can be assessed against injury claims. But a lot of things information workers do and the quality with which they do them are not easily measured and certainly cannot be neatly attributed to cause and effect.

What can often matter is that people *think* the quality of their physical work environment affects their productivity. The investment made in their physical well-being and comfort tells them they are important to the company. Satisfaction surveys can provide insight, and even subjective estimates of productivity increases can be useful.

The strategic mindset assumes, of course, that there is a clear strategic direction within the company. A clear strategy may not exist at your company due to high environmental uncertainty or a lack of leadership and vision at the senior level. Mergers or acquisitions may abruptly shift strategy. Sometimes, major real estate decisions trigger strategic soul-searching. A large capital commitment, such as a new corporate headquarters or major plant, may be the catalyst for a larger examination of strategy before the commitment is made.

Effective corporate real estate professionals do not merely wait to be told what the plan is, they actively seek out strategic insight. Maintaining an active dialogue with line management and voraciously reading industry publications can help. Most strategy setting is an incremental, iterative process. Don't assume that senior management has a grand plan hidden away somewhere. It is not so much that secrets are being kept from the real estate function as it is that a great deal of uncertainty exists over future competitive conditions. Strategic plans are constantly revised as the competitive drama unfolds and new information becomes available. Expect to provide flexibility.

CHAMPIONING THE STRATEGIC MINDSET TOWARD CORPORATE REAL ESTATE AND FACILITIES

The strategic perspective challenges some long-time corporate real estate managers because it requires that they expand their expertise beyond their traditional knowledge base of deal structuring and development. The strategic real estate manager also must have a sophisticated comprehension of the company's overall competitive strategy—the distinct requirements of its industry and the ways that the company attracts, serves, and retains customers. Of course, different parts of the company may compete in different industries and markets and thus have different requirements, further complicating the real estate professional's duties.

Once the strategic mindset is adopted by corporate real estate, awareness of the strategic role of real estate and facilities must be increased throughout the company. If you have sold facility innovations within your company on the basis of their costs savings alone, you may need to work to change senior and line management attitudes toward corporate real estate.

Making corporate real estate strategic and communicating its contribution to the rest of the organization requires a new breed of corporate real estate and facility professional. However, there are only a few formal educational programs focused on corporate real estate skills. Companies must grow their own talent. Opportunities for corporate real estate management development to meet the challenge of the strategic perspective are discussed in the final chapter, "The Future of Place."

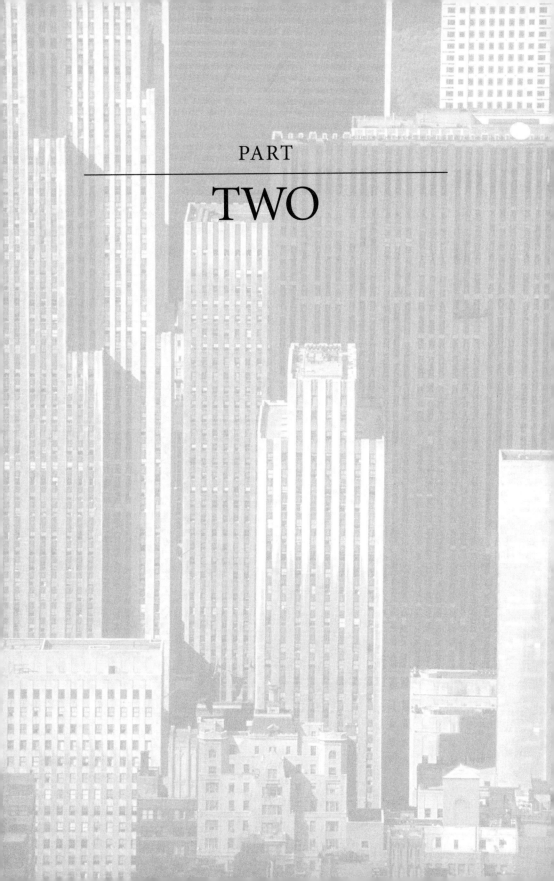

PART

TWO

INTRODUCTION TO PART TWO

Decision-Making Strategies

My initial research on corporate real estate strategy examined how companies make real estate and facility management decisions. I found that all organizations do not approach corporate real estate decision making in the same way and identified essentially three distinct approaches.

The following four chapters illustrate these strategies in action at a variety of companies. After looking at each approach individually, we see how they interact in more complex situations, and how they change over time. By seeing how other companies have approached making real estate decisions over the years, we can develop an appreciation for how corporate real estate and facilities can enhance the strategic goals of the organization.

The highly turbulent competitive environments many companies must operate in today are at odds with their need to make real estate commitments which often require physical and financial obligations far into the future. The level of confidence the company has in forecasting its future business situation—its competitive environment and the strategies needed to thrive in that world—best explains how companies approach making real estate decisions. The degree of strategic uncertainty in the company's competitive environment at the time the real estate decision is being made sets the context for how we understand those decisions.[1]

Understanding how strategic uncertainty influences corporate real estate decisions and the advantages and disadvantages of the three different strategic approaches can help decision makers craft strategies that best help their companies cope with uncertainty, while still making possible the sorts of long-term commitments real estate decisions require.

In my initial research on corporate real estate decision making, I examined fourteen different corporate real estate or facility management decisions at eight high-technology companies of various sizes and ages. A summary of how that research was designed and conducted is contained in the endnotes to this introduction.[2] Since that earlier project, I have worked with hundreds of corporate real estate and facility managers from many other companies in a variety of industries. I have found that this simple observation holds true: *strategic uncertainty drives corporate real estate decision making.*

THEORETICAL PERSPECTIVES ON ORGANIZATIONAL ACTION

Apart from a practical desire to help companies make better corporate real estate decisions, I also wanted to explore what these decision processes suggested about behavior in organizations. As we discussed in Chapter One, the physical setting of a company plays functional and symbolic roles. Real estate and facilities are both logistical tools that support the tasks of the organization and visual and symbolic representations of the organization and its values.[3] These two roles also represent two different ways of interpreting behavior in organizations. Without getting into a detailed and largely theoretical discussion of these theories, let's examine the basic premises behind the functional and the symbolic perspectives. References to management theory literature are explained more fully in the endnotes to this introduction.

TWO VIEWS ON ACTION IN ORGANIZATIONS

There are essentially two opposing, but not necessarily exclusive, ways of viewing what drives action in organizations.[4] Some theories claim that organizational behavior is primarily driven by an economically rational response to production requirements or environmental constraints. This *rational-instrumental* perspective implies that decisions about facilities are made in an economically rational way, taking into account available external resources, the technological requirements of production, and embedded resource allocation systems. By economically rational we mean that the highest value output is sought at the lowest investment cost. Such approaches view the physical setting of the organization as an influence on social interaction and the formation of networks as a mechanism for controlling behavior by structuring work flows, interactions, and visual supervision, and particularly as a scarce resource which conveys power to those who control space. Facilities are designed to house an organizational structure which best serves the production technologies, available resources, and the demands of its external environment.[5]

Another group of theories, which I collectively refer to as *valuational-symbolic* theories, presume that behavior in organizations is based upon social and emotional criteria. Decisions are made in the organizations based upon individual preferences or driven by random events. The reasons for the decisions are then retrospectively attributed to functional goals. How values are symbolized plays a large role in the decisions. Theorists with this point of view conduct research which views organizational phenomena as socially constructed.[6] Their research focuses on how myths and symbols are used in the organization. Through the organization's interpretation of these myths and symbols, distinct cultures develop which bind employees together with a common historical perspective and with norms of acceptable behavior. According to the valuational-symbolic perspective, the basis for real estate and facility decisions is how well they reflect the management style, the hierarchy, and the status and power of the organization's members. These value-driven criteria are more important than the rational-instrumental requirements. The facility serves as a symbol of the organization's culture.[7]

This dual role, the functional and the symbolic, is reflected in the different decision-making criteria used in the three structuring strategies. Simply put, companies which operate in a highly rational-instrumental manner either make real estate decisions incrementally, taking only what they need when they absolutely need it, or else they standardize both the design and the management of their facilities. Companies whose behavior resembles more of what the valuational-symbolic perspective describes, make real estate decisions which reflect their corporate values. These approaches will each be discussed in much greater detail in the following four chapters.

STRATEGIC UNCERTAINTY

I originally identified uncertainty as a major influence on real estate decision making based upon what I heard during my interviews at the companies I studied. These managers frequently complained that uncertainty about future needs, based upon a lack of clear vision of the company's future business opportunities, inhibited their efforts to make long-term plans. These quotes illustrate their dilemma. They may sound very familiar to you:

> This is a tough environment to plan in because your vision is only good for six months—no one would even believe a three-year forecast . . . and you can't build any faster.
>
> Real Estate Manager
> East coast computer manufacturer

> Last year we projected sales to be $350 million but they were $530 million instead, which meant we had a 300,000-square-foot difference in space needs. This year our budget forecast was right but we were still 200,000 square feet short.
>
> Planning Manager
> High-growth hardware and software company

> During the planning, the building changed from a rabbit warren to a corporate headquarters, because we were planning for divestiture at the same time.
>
> Project Architect
> Regional telecommunications provider

Comments such as these suggested that uncertainty from outside forces such as competitors' actions, customers' responses, or government regulation had a great effect on real estate decisions. The challenge then was to compare the uncertainty experienced by the companies in the study with each other, and at different periods of time for the same company.

Previous research had attempted to measure uncertainty in an objective manner using quantitative measures, or by surveying managers within the company about their perceptions of uncertainty. I devised a way to systematically compare levels of external uncertainty across the organizations and time periods under study. I identified those factors which most contribute to uncertainty by using the industrial economic model of industry structure and competitive forces identified by Michael Porter in his highly influential work on competitive strategy. Also included were factors such as financial uncertainty, technology,[8] and the political and regulatory environment.[9] To distinguish this particular type of environmental uncertainty from many other different interpretations found in organizational theory, I refer to this collection of external factors as *strategic uncertainty*.[10] In Chapter Seven, you will be able to rate your own company's level of strategic uncertainty using a method adapted from my research. Later, this set of factors forms the basis for the diagnostic framework described in Chapters Eight and Nine.

When I compared the level of strategic uncertainty a company faced at the time a real estate or facility management decision was being made, an interesting pattern emerged. Each level of uncertainty—whether highly uncertain, moderately uncertain, or fairly certain—corresponded with a different approach to real estate decision making. Figure One depicts these relationships.

While we examine each of the structuring strategies separately, and although one approach will predominate at a particular time, all strategies are used to some extent every time a corporate real estate decision must be

Figure II–1
Decision-Making Strategies Vary According to Strategic Uncertainty

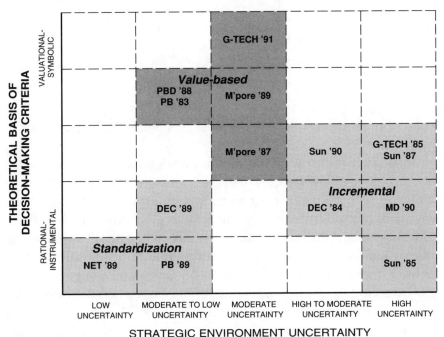

Figure II–2
Basic Model of the Structuring Process

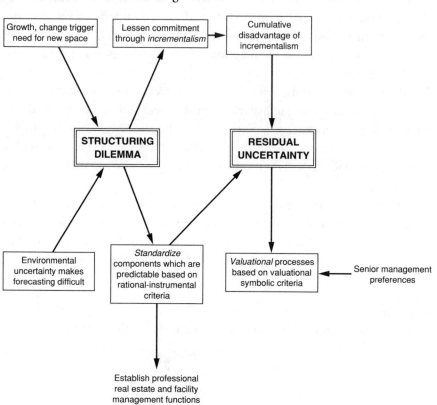

made. The model shown in Figure II–2 represents the overall decision-making process.

First, a need for new or different space is triggered. This can be from an internal cause, such as the growth of the business or a new product line, or it can be caused by external factors, such as the expiration of a lease. Since environmental uncertainty makes the forecasting of future needs difficult, the *structuring dilemma*—the need to make a long-term commitment under conditions of uncertainty—results. Second, because real estate decisions are time consuming and costly, the initial impulse is to minimize the commitment through incrementalism or for those parts of the operation which can be predicted, to use standardized solutions based upon previous decisions and established procedures. However, incrementalism is not a perfect solution—there are cumulative disadvantages. And some future needs cannot be precisely predicted. The *residual uncertainty* is a third point in the model. Here, in order to make long-term commitments which are consistent with the strategic direction of the company, valuational-symbolic processes are used. Senior management preferences are also evident in value-based decision making.

The three strategies are each examined in detail in Chapters Four through Six. A variation of the decision-making model, according to the level of strategic uncertainty at that time, is presented for each.

CHAPTER FOUR: *INCREMENTALISM*

Some organizations use rational-instrumental criteria in a highly incremental manner. They commit their resources very cautiously, obtaining only as much space as they need in the short term, and invest in amenities and large capital items only when production or technology requires it. An incremental strategy corresponds with a highly uncertain strategic environment. It is a very commonly used approach, especially in the start-up and fast-growth stages of a company. In this chapter we look at how four different companies use incrementalism to cope with high strategic uncertainty, fast growth, or financial conservatism. We especially focus on the experience of Sun Microsystems as it grew from a start-up to a billion dollar contender.

CHAPTER FIVE: *STANDARDIZATION*

The other rational-instrumental approach is characterized by standardization of both decision processes and design outcomes. Many aspects of the facilities, such as building design, office size, furniture, and surface materials, are written down and enforced by management. Established bureaucratic procedures exist for long-range planning, property acquisition, selection of vendors or consultants, and for other tasks. Standardized strategies are found in relatively certain and stable strategic environments.

CHAPTER SIX: *VALUE-BASED STRATEGY*

Real estate decisions in some organizations fit more closely with valuational-symbolic theories of organizational action. Members described certain projects using symbolic, rather than economic justifications. Their companies spent time and expense on aesthetics. This value-based approach is often a hallmark of companies dealing with moderately uncertain strategic environments. Although these companies have built up enough of an installed base or market position to make longer-range plans, other requirements were still speculative. Without some basis for decision making, these companies could not commit the resources necessary to continue moving their organizations forward. Suitable facilities would not be in place when new employees or functions were added; branch offices would not be located to take advantage of new business opportunities. Discussions about values, symbols, and meaning were used to establish decision-making criteria when there were insufficiently clear rational-instrumental demands to use as a basis for planning. Instead, these managers relied on their judgment and innovation, and left room to make changes in the future. Along with observing Sun Microsystems make the transition from incremental to more value-based decision making, we look at the ways several other companies express their corporate values and vision through their real estate and facilities.

In the last chapter of Part Two, we look at how these basic strategies interact.

CHAPTER SEVEN:
REAL ESTATE STRATEGIES ARE DYNAMIC

Most organizations in the study did not use one strategy exclusively, but shifted strategies over time as their level of strategic uncertainty changed. They also may have used one strategy for one particular line of business, and another for a different business, depending upon the particular strategic requirements of those businesses. Although the typical progression is toward greater standardization as the organization grows and its environment stabilizes, an increase in strategic uncertainty can lead to a new value-based emphasis and a move away from established facility standards. We return to two of the companies we first observed using incremental strategies and see how their use of strategies changed over time as their strategic and organizational demands evolve. We also observe how financial service giant Merrill Lynch uses very different strategic approaches in its diverse lines of business.

While you read Part Two, compare the real estate and facility management decision-making processes at your own company with those profiled. What strategies tend to predominate? Are you overcoming the disadvantages of that strategy? Have you changed your approach over time? Do different parts of your company use different approaches? What can you learn from the experiences of these companies over time that might help your company make better quality real estate decisions which are more supportive of your company's competitive strategy?

CHAPTER FOUR

INCREMENTALISM

The more uncertain managers are about their company's future, the more they want to delay major commitments until either better information or a clearer vision is available. Long-term commitments to facilities or capital improvements are avoided as much as possible. A company coping with high uncertainty will only acquire more space when the shortage of space is critical. Even at that point, often it will commit to only space that can be clearly allocated to a current urgent need. Is this bad management? A failure to take action? Not necessarily. That level of commitment may be all the company is capable of at that moment in time. Such an *incremental* strategy, acquiring real estate only when the need is acute, is very common. Companies using this strategy are unable, or unwilling, to confidently forecast their future needs. We can identify an incremental strategy through several characteristics: a preference for short-term commitments, a lack of long-range planning, and a reluctance to invest in either facilities or furnishings. Incrementalism is a sensible reaction to a highly uncertain strategic environment. Under these conditions, the primary concern of the company is to meet the physical requirements of the work to be done— that which is immediately identifiable and tangible. Investments in property, plant, or equipment are not made unless they can be directly linked to an immediate business requirement. Companies pursuing an incremental strategy rarely put much emphasis on employee amenities or visual aesthetics. Designer frills are not tolerated.

An incremental strategy is apparent when space is acquired in bits and pieces over time:

> Previous to 1988, we didn't think about getting any more space until we would run out.
>
> COO, medical products company

71

Acquiring space here is like cooking porridge in a pot—it starts to spill over one pot so you scoop it up and put it into another pot and then that pot boils over and you get another pot, and so on.

Facility Planner, high-technology company

Conveniently, as our need for space grew, the other tenant's need for space declined. We gradually took over this space with a series of short-term subleases and then started to expand in pieces in the next building.

CFO, biotechnology start-up

When applied to corporate real estate decision making, an incremental strategy includes taking short-term leases on space, not committing to space until current working conditions become unbearable, substituting lower cost materials for typical office furnishings, and making use of alternatives for office space such as working at home or renting temporary quarters.

With an incremental strategy, companies try to avoid long-term commitments in the hope of retaining future flexibility. Not surprisingly, most start-up companies begin with an incremental strategy. High-growth companies also use incremental strategies to keep up with new, unanticipated demands. Some of these companies continue to approach real estate decision making incrementally long after they have reached the size, scale, and financial means to take longer-range commitments. Incrementalism persists after the start-up or high-growth phases for several reasons: continuing high uncertainty from particular parts of the strategic environment, the desire of senior management to perpetuate a sense of urgency among the employees, or a reluctance to make resource commitments that are visible to outsiders.

The incremental version of our decision-making model in Figure 4–1 shows the relative weight of the considerations made by firms pursuing incremental strategies. Incrementalism is the primary path. Value-based processes are used only in critical areas, especially those relating to the organization's culture. Design and policy standards are based upon the preferences of senior management who often relate these standards to their experience at previous companies. Dedicated corporate real estate and facility management functions and the staff assigned to them within the company are minimal.

Figure 4–1
Incremental Decision-Making Model Under Conditions of High Strategic Uncertainty

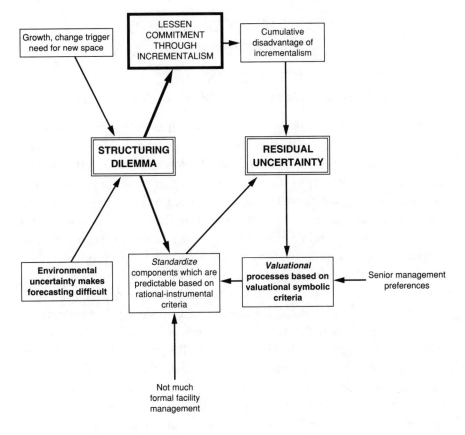

There are three major reasons why companies pursue incremental real estate and facility strategies. Uncertain competitive conditions are the drivers of two reasons: first, an inability to forecast space requirements based on *uncertain product demand in the future;* and second, *a lack of management time to plan and make decisions* during periods of high growth and rapid change. A third set of reasons for making decisions incrementally are based upon *financial considerations:* a desire to conserve capital for future commitments, or to take advantage of late-breaking opportunities in the real estate market. Next, we examine how each of these reasons influence corporate real estate decision making, and look at examples of companies operating under these conditions.

INCREMENTALISM AND
HIGH STRATEGIC UNCERTAINTY
THE START-UP: INABILITY TO
FORECAST DEMAND FOR NEW PRODUCTS

A common reason for taking an incremental approach is the difficulty in forecasting future real estate needs when the potential success of the company's new products cannot be predicted. Uncertainty about future success can come from a variety of sources, many of which are outside of the direct control of the organization. For example, the company cannot predict the *actions of its competitors.* This may be because the product is new and the company does not know when or how strongly other firms will enter its market. When Sun Microsystems pioneered the concept of open systems computer workstations, this new product concept was offered only by other start-ups. In hindsight, Sun benefited greatly by the reluctance of market giants IBM, Hewlett-Packard, and DEC to jeopardize their existing product lines with a high-performance stand-alone machine that could be built from commonly available components. By the time these major competitors awakened to this emerging opportunity, the market for workstations had expanded so broadly that there was room for both Sun's success and for the other companies to offer workstation products as well. In this example, such rapid product acceptance even caught Sun by surprise.

New products also face *uncertainty over customer acceptance.* How fast will the product sell in the marketplace? How price sensitive are potential customers—will they pay a price for the product that is high enough to allow enough profits to grow the business? When a customer tries a new product, often it is still easy for that customer to switch back to using the older, previous product—otherwise the switch to the new competitor would not have happened in the first place. It is not until it becomes more difficult for a new customer to leave—when the cost of switching back to a competing or previously used product is unattractive to the customer— that the company with the new product will feel secure enough to make longer-range commitments. We will see in later chapters why those companies with a great deal of confidence in the future loyalty of their customers are more likely to standardize their approach to real estate and facilities decisions.

Uncertainty over operating technology is particularly vexing for an organization which prefers to approach its real estate and facilities incrementally. The use of new technology, such as a new management information system, usually implies investment in something prior to it being highly tested in the marketplace; that is, it is still uncertain. Since incremental firms don't want to make the expensive leap of faith required by the adoption of new technology unless they can strictly justify it according to business requirements, they tend to hang on to existing technology longer compared to companies with more insight into their future.

Financial constraints over the acquisition of facilities are particularly severe for companies lacking an income stream from their products and largely dependent upon venture capital funds. Start-ups requiring costly laboratory space to support their operations are even more cash constrained. Not surprisingly, start-ups are hampered not only by competitive uncertainty but also by a lack of investment capital. They may know the kind of space they would like to have, but do not have the wherewithal to fund the additional space. All available money must be directed toward the goal of getting the product into the hands of customers, before the competition beats them to it.

To look at some examples of incrementalism in action, let's begin with a classic start-up situation—a venture capital-funded high-technology product idea which began in the research laboratory of a major university. Many of its experiences are typical of companies in the start-up phase—cutting-edge technology, high levels of competition, uncertain customer acceptance, and potential regulatory constraints—combined with limited capital and a pressing need for facilities to support getting the product out the door ahead of the competition.

CASE STUDY OF A START-UP: MOLECULAR DEVICES
THE EARLY YEARS

Molecular Devices (MD) was founded in 1983 by a Stanford University scientist and three of his post-doctoral students. They were exploring biosensors—ways in which biological materials could be used to transmit electrical impulses. Biosensors were being studied at other universities and by some companies, and related research had been going on for over a decade. They believed that biosensor technology would ultimately replace many of the slower and more labor-intensive laboratory analyses of chemical and medical samples conducted today. Able to provide both speed of assay and a portable, self-contained medium, biosensors had great future potential as an important medical and research tool. Based upon the commercial potential of biosensors, a group of venture capitalists provided funding for the enterprise, although most of their work in early 1984 was purely scientific research. Later that year, the investors brought in a president to manage and grow the business. He had previously been with Genentech, and earlier with McKinsey & Company, the management consulting firm he joined after receiving his MBA from Stanford. Additional administrative and marketing staff were gradually brought in over the next two years.

Several venture-backed companies, as well as researchers in larger medical product companies, also were attempting to develop biosensor products. The MD scientists had made progress on a simple version of the biosensor which they developed into a micro kinetic plate reader. By early 1986 they had introduced the V-Max plate reader. The V-Max was an effective and improved substitute for more expensive machines currently in use. They hoped it would provide an entry into the biomedical equipment marketplace and be a catalyst for ramping-up their manufacturing and distribution. It would provide a source of sales income, while the biosensor devices were still under development.

At its beginning, the company was in an ideal situation for incremental facility growth. MD scientists began working in a laboratory borrowed from the Linus Pauling Institute at the Stanford Industrial Park, which was adjacent to the Stanford campus. Conveniently, MD was able to grow incrementally room by room at this site because the Pauling Institute's space needs were declining at the same time MD's were expanding. MD gradually took over that space with a series of short-term subleases. Since the wet labs already had been built and amortized, MD avoided making this costly investment up front. Additional space for manufacturing and offices was needed in early 1986 as the V-Max was developed. Fortunately, across the courtyard from the Pauling laboratories was another small, single-story building with 5,000 SF of vacant space. In July of 1986, the manager's offices were moved over there and some panel systems furniture, poster art, and additional office furniture were procured. Labs stayed in the original building and engineering and manufacturing (primarily component assembly) moved across the way. The tree-shaded courtyard between the buildings often was used as a meeting area, as well as for lunches and parties. The company leased another 5,000 SF in January of 1987 and then leased the rest of building (another 10,000 SF) in phases. By mid-1988, MD occupied both courtyard buildings. By the end of that year, the company employed about 40 people but was still dependent upon venture capital to support operations.

Like many other start-ups, real estate and facilities issues were the responsibility of the chief financial officer. The CFO, who joined MD in February 1986, had previously been with another high-technology company in the area and held a Stanford MBA. Human resources was handled by the president with the help of a part-time outside consultant. The CFO also reviewed most facility decisions, but the small size of the company made it possible for all interested persons to participate in decision making. The company had a three-year planning horizon for space needs, but as the CEO admitted during an interview, "Our real estate needs in the first year's projection are clear, but the next two years are crystal ball." The plan showed the company running out of space by the third or fourth quarter of 1988. Since they knew the space in their present location would soon be filled up, by the summer of 1987 they had started to think about relocating to a larger space.

A START-UP LOOKS FOR A NEW SITE

During their search for a new location, the MD executives had to find a balance between the preferences of its powerful research scientists and the financial pressures imposed by its venture capitalists.

The first priority for a new location was that it be within a fifteen minute drive of Stanford University because the founding scientist came into the labs every day but still taught full-time at Stanford. The executives also believed it was very important to remain physically close to Stanford for the symbolic value, since they were trying to build credibility within the scientific research community. They realized that they might have to pay a price premium for such space in the immediate Stanford area, which was in great demand.

The first candidate for relocation was a vacant 33,000 SF building next door to their present location, but the building was full of hazardous waste from the previous tenant. MD spent several months negotiating a lease for that property, but couldn't get a lender to finance the building improvements because of uncertainty over the cost of waste removal at the site, estimated in the range of $2 million. They also considered staying within the Stanford Industrial Park, but the limited amount of space available had become very expensive as office space users, who could afford higher rents, displaced research and development tenants.

Flexibility to accommodate future growth was also a high priority because they anticipated MD would soon need 60–70,000 SF of space. However, the time line for the expansion was uncertain because it greatly depended upon when products would be ready for the market. Ideally MD wanted to initially lease 40,000 SF, but then be able to expand to a total of 60–70,000 SF within the same building.

The location of key employees' homes helped MD focus on other options within the vicinity of Stanford. To determine whether to move north or south of campus, the locations of existing employees' homes were plotted on a map. Although equal numbers lived in either direction, moving north of the present location was favored because traffic in the south, toward Mountain View, was more congested. Incidentally, but conveniently, the CEO also lived to the north of Stanford in San Mateo.

Financial feasibility was the most critical factor once potential sites were narrowed down. Along with low rental rates and an ability to expand incrementally, MD needed a developer who could finance the tenant improvements and amortize the cost into the rent.

Like most start-ups, one senior manager led the search process with consultants used as needed. The real estate broker was selected haphazardly because people in the lab had contacted him prior to the CFO's selection of a broker, so he already was on record as having MD as his client. Once a number of site options had been identified, the president, CFO, and some other managers rented a van and toured each site at 7:30 in the morning to assess local traffic congestion during rush hour. The search engendered a lot of discussion within the company—everyone had an opinion.

In October of 1987, the executives selected a location from a group of seven buildings under development in nearby Menlo Park. The buildings at Menlo Oaks Corporate Center were not yet constructed but the footprint and the exterior shell was designed. The building's excellent location but higher than desired cost forced MD to make an important strategic decision: proximity to Stanford or lower cost. The building was on the west side of the Highway 101 freeway, rather than the less expensive east side, and it was a steel frame building rather than of "tilt up" construction. Although the rate was lower than what MD would have paid to stay in the Stanford Industrial Park, where space was $1.71 SF/month and went as high as $2.00–2.10 per SF/month, it was higher than space farther away from Stanford. For example, good-quality tilt-up space across the Bay in Milpitas was about $0.75 SF/month. But this more expensive site had other advantages: good freeway access to Highway 101 and high visibility from this major artery. There was expansion space available within walking distance or a short drive in case the company needed to expand faster than they foresaw.

The developer was eager to have a potentially high-growth company located on his site so he offered an attractive lease allowing MD to absorb higher rental rates as it occupied more space. Of the total 63,000 SF, MD initially committed to lease 50,000 SF with the right of first refusal on the remaining 13,000 SF in the building. Initially MD had to occupy and pay rent on only 35,000 SF, while they still were able to immediately build improvements to a total of 45,000 SF. The monthly rent negotiated was $1.37/SF on a triple net lease for six years with a $30 per square foot tenant improvement allowance to pay for interior fit-out, including the labs which required extensive plumbing and ventilation. The final cost of the tenant improvements was over $1.25 million. As part of the deal Molecular Devices received sign rights, and an illuminated blue and black sign with the company logo was installed on the building's exterior, in clear view of passing cars in both directions.

INTERIOR PLANNING

Employees at start-ups expect to have a lot of say in the daily workings of the company. At the beginning, there was a lot of participation at MD in the planning of the interior space, but the process soon got out of control as the cost estimates began to outpace the strict budget. The president and CFO then became more autocratic about decisions. The CFO selected a space planner with whom he had worked before at another start-up but no formal written design program was produced. Because the project began to take up too much of the CFO's time, he hired a consultant to coordinate the project with the developer and the city of Menlo Park's building department and to handle myriad details such as phone installation and coordination of the move. Although the consultant was more experienced in the design of manufacturing operations and laboratories than offices, he also interviewed the department heads to determine office design requirements and drew up the interior space plan.

Although layout of space is rarely an issue for start-up companies since they are usually small enough for easy face-to-face interaction, the process of developing the space plan for MD's new location produced some conflict. The R&D staff felt that additional lab and office space for R&D should be maximized at the expense of space for administrative functions. Others thought that R&D should be integrated into the same space with engineering. After much discussion and controversy, sometimes extending to the evening hours, the original plan to place the two departments in separate areas of the second floor remained unchanged, although more lab benches were built.

A Spartan attitude toward interior decoration often accompanies an incremental strategy. Companies in their early years usually give little thought to the aesthetics of their surroundings. The overwhelming concern is to house a growing number of employees and simply to survive until product launch. Any expenditures made must directly support the product. At Molecular Devices, the great majority of the capital investment went to provide top-quality laboratory space. To save money, MD did not hire an interior designer. The building architect drew the construction documents the way the consultant laid them out, only checking for code compliance. The two-story building had long rectangular shaped floors with an open stairway in the center of the longer side. Fire code regulations in the city mandated that long fire-proofed hallways be placed down the length of each floor. These closed halls made open circulation more difficult. The long rectangular shape of the building did allow lots of access to windows. The laboratories were located along the prime window area. This gave the labs extensive outdoor views, a pleasant innovation not found in most conventionally designed labs. The employees selected the color of the carpet from choices presented by the developer. A blue color scheme, first established in the Palo Alto offices, was continued and inexpensive poster art brightened the walls.

The size of the workstations was extensively discussed during planning. The director of engineering insisted that the engineers' open offices be 10' by 10' although that dimension fit awkwardly into the building's interior layout. He based this assessment on the layout of the existing equipment each engineer needed in the workspace. The allocation of closed offices was also controversial. In the Stanford Research Park location, many people had private offices because they had been built by previous tenants. In the new building, the R&D staff were adamant they be given closed offices instead of open cubicles. In the end, the president raised the management level at which one qualified for a closed office, although some of the more vocal R&D staff were also given closed offices. The majority of MD employees were placed in open-office cubicles with 60" high movable fabric partitions. MD reused partitions it had purchased previously and added new ones. Freestanding furniture from a variety of sources was used inside most of the workspaces.

Start-ups also are uncomfortable with a lot of formal hierarchy. The president of MD didn't want to have a closed office that was larger than that of the department heads and other executives, but he did need more space for meetings in his office. The solution was to give him a private office the same size as other managers, with an adjoining conference room. When he was out of the office, the door between his office and the conference room could be shut and the room could then be used by others who entered from another door.

Moving into their new space at year's end was a major event for the company, and they celebrated by holding an open house party for both business associates and friends of the company to view the new space. After the move, the head of manufacturing took over the day-to-day facility management functions.

Many start-ups are plagued by a chronic shortage of space. While this can increase interaction and collaboration, it can also fuel rivalry and conflict. As it turned out, MD suffered from the opposite problem. Employees were not added to the company as quickly as MD had planned: a major joint venture partner had delayed its agreement and sales of the V-Max were moving more slowly than projected. Although they began to pay rent on the space, the managers at MD did not want to occupy the excess space they had for two reasons. "We didn't want those from the venture capital community who come visit our operations to think we are being extravagant," explained one manager. They also had learned from their first location that once people started to use a space, they were much more reluctant to give it up when conditions became more crowded. Therefore they started with the small office size that they planned to use when the facility was filled, and partitioned off the unused space from view.

As it turned out, this conservatism toward excess space was justified. The biosensor faced uncertain technologies, fragmented competition, and unexplored product applications. While staying afloat, the company did not grow at nearly the rate that the founder and investors had hoped. The president left in 1991 for another start-up, and MD continued to sublease the excess space in Menlo Park. As soon as the first lease renewal came up in 1994, the company relocated to the southern Silicon Valley and took 60,000 square feet of office and R&D space in Sunnyvale—a lower-cost location overall. MD did go public in 1995 and remains a respected niche player producing innovative analytical technologies which help scientists create better ways to analyze cells and biomolecules.

HIGH GROWTH MANDATES
INCREMENTALISM FOR SURVIVAL

The high-growth company also pursues an incremental strategy, but this time the inability to forecast future requirements is compounded by the lack of time that management can devote to long-range planning. High growth also can be accompanied by high product margins. These high margins may cause the company to be less disciplined about cost containment, even though generating enough cash to fund continuing growth is still critical. In practice, this means that although high growth can later cover up a lot of real estate and facility mistakes, managers in these companies are still reluctant to make any major long-term investments in facilities.

What happens when a start-up begins to grow beyond even the most optimistic dreams of its founders? While such growth is enviable, it also engenders high visibility. Over the past fifteen years, high-growth companies (other than retailers or franchisers) have been found most often in new product-market areas such as specialized computer hardware and software, telecommunications, and financial services.

The explosive growth of Sun Microsystems from 1982 to 1989 illustrates many of the opportunities and pitfalls of high growth and the pressures such growth brings to bear upon corporate real estate and facilities.

CASE STUDY OF HIGH GROWTH: SUN MICROSYSTEMS
THE RISE OF SUN

In 1982, Sun Microsystems pioneered a revolutionary product concept that was to transform the computer industry. Its three founders shared ties to Stanford University; the name *Sun* comes from the acronym for the Stanford University Network. The founders were Andreas Bechtolshem, a Stanford University engineer, and Vinod Khosla and Scott McNealy, two Stanford Business School classmates. They were young and they had a vision. The first Sun computer was assembled from available off-the-shelf components. Shortly after shipping the first Sun product, the founders were joined by Bill Joy, a computer sciences graduate student at the University of California, Berkeley, who even then was a leading authority on the Unix operating system which the Sun hardware employed. Sun's first product was a new kind of computer known as a technical workstation. It could outperform personal computers in speed, capacity, and the ability to display graphics. The Sun workstation featured an oversized high-resolution screen which could display information from several programs at once and it could perform more than one task simultaneously. Since this workstation was much less costly than a mainframe or minicomputer, it could be assigned to an individual user rather than shared. Further, a series of workstations could be networked together to produce as much computing power as a mainframe at significantly lower cost.

Sun's founders turned their off-the-shelf design into a unique marketing idea. They based the design of their products on an open systems philosophy; Sun hardware could be linked to systems provided by many other vendors and its software was based upon the popular Unix operating system. Until this time, the accepted wisdom in the computer industry was that you needed to lock your customers into a proprietary design to keep them loyal to your product. Computer companies had traditionally sought to capture their customers by providing their hardware and software which would work with only their own products. This enabled them to sell these products at a premium price. Corporate buyers of computer systems were reluctant to experiment with computer systems because of the complexity and the cost. Sun changed the rules of the game. Its computers put the power of the machine on the desk of the user; in this case, the engineer or technician who was hungry for the latest and greatest technology. However, no one could predict how fast this product concept would be accepted in the marketplace, or what technological innovations would soon increase performance or lower price.

AN EARLY LOCATION CHOICE BECOMES EMBEDDED

As with many start-ups, the location of the firm's founding determined its ultimate headquarters location. Sun originally located its operations in Mountain View, adjacent to Highway 101, so that it was within a short drive to the Stanford campus. In the area, there were many other start-ups constantly developing out of the various research labs at Stanford, or spinning off from larger high-technology companies in the area. Although Mountain View had been primarily agricultural, developers were rapidly putting up relatively small (40–50,000 SF) two-story buildings which accommodated small start-up companies. These low-rise buildings easily housed the extensive electrical and mechanical equipment needed to support heavily computerized operations. They could accommodate from one to four companies.

Sun's rapid growth caught Sun's founders, as well as the computer industry, by surprise. An early, half-hearted attempt to move the company out of its expensive location near Stanford was met with so much resistance from Sun's employees, many of whom were working upwards of 75 hours per week, that the idea was quickly dropped. Sun began to lease a series of buildings in Mountain View as fast as they could be built.

From 1982 to 1985 Sun had little in the way of formal facility management. The finance department managed real estate and facilities decisions until early 1985 when a vice president of corporate resources was hired, and human resources, MIS, and facilities were placed under his charge. HR and facilities were brought together because as he explained, "HR is an entry point for engineers and they are very touchy about space." The sensitivity of engineers to their workplace surroundings would continue to shape Sun's approach to real estate and facilities. Two months after the VP of corporate resources arrived, Sun hired its first experienced senior manager of facilities. He had previously worked at Intel and another local start-up. At the time, Sun occupied about five buildings in Mountain View and 226,000 square feet in total. During the chaotic next two years, the senior manager of facilities' primary mandate was to manage the physical demands of Sun's phenomenal growth. As one Sun manager later observed: "During the first five years there was a lack of any real estate asset management strategy here—the basic concern was getting space and ramping-up the company."

RAPID GROWTH ACCOMMODATED THROUGH INCREMENTALISM

The computer workstation market and its related peripherals and software changed rapidly in the period from 1983 to 1988. Products had an average shelf life of eighteen months. As workstations became more powerful (in terms of processing speed and capacity) and their price lowered, they began to seriously erode the demand for higher-end machines. Distinctions between products blurred. The open systems approach quickly won Sun a large following of users, especially among engineers who were most concerned with getting the greatest speed and performance at the lowest cost. The market exploded: by 1987 it was $2 billion; by 1988, $2.8 billion; and it was projected to grow to $6.3 billion by 1991. By 1986, Sun was the hottest workstation company in the business with the greatest market share. In 1987 Sun developed its own microprocessor chip, the SPARC, based upon reduced instruction design. It also developed and sold software to accompany its workstations, along with networking hardware and software for linking Sun computers to each other and to other manufacturers' products.

CEO Scott McNealy boasted in an interview, "What's important is that customers love having a standard and being able to buy from different vendors . . . I think we are going to turn the whole computer industry upside down."[1] Such assertions awakened the large established computer makers, particularly IBM, DEC, and Hewlett Packard. By 1988 other major vendors were offering open systems products and Sun Executive Vice President Bernie Lacroute observed, "To compete, we have to be faster out the door and better than everyone else." To protect against such increased rivalry, Sun concentrated on developing new products, spending over 13% of its revenue on R&D versus the computer industry average of 8.2% during this time.

Sun's meteoric growth from 1985 to 1989 can be illustrated by several metrics. Sales grew 114% annually, which translated into nearly doubling the company every year: from $115 million in 1985 to nearly five times that amount in 1987 ($538 million) to nearly double the next year to $1.7 billion in 1989. Reflecting this growth, the number of employees at Sun nearly doubled from 2,907 to 5,233 from 1987 to 1988.

Sun managers keenly analyzed their competitors' offerings and the experiences of other computer start-up companies. "We've studied every crash and burn in the industry, and we don't want to repeat any mistakes," exclaimed McNealy to *Fortune* magazine.[2] Yet much of Sun's rapid growth in capabilities and products was unprecedented in history.

1988—THE YEAR OF GROWING DANGEROUSLY

With such phenomenal growth, it was difficult to take care of even basic physical needs, let alone make future predictions about demand. As one real estate planner related: "It's been difficult to forecast space requirements; for example, in 1987 we thought sales would be $350 million but they were $530 million and so we had a 300,000-square-foot difference in the amount of space we needed. In 1988 we we were right about sales but we were still 200,000 square feet short." In 1988, a senior facility manager reported that "So far we have an office space and a telephone for 90% of our new employees ready for them when they arrive." This was considered an accomplishment.

To accommodate the 200 new employees per month that were being added to the company during this high-growth period, Sun needed about 50,000 additional square feet of workspace. This was the equivalent of one building per month by Mountain View real estate standards. In this time of rapid growth, obtaining contiguous space was a greater priority than obtaining space at the lowest

Need another 50,000 SF? No problem: The simple, two-story office buildings which housed Sun in its early years sprung up from former agricultural fields in Mountain View.

cost. Sun continued to concentrate on leasing space in Mountain View because managers wanted to avoid having people spread out geographically as they were at competitors HP and DEC. According to a facility manager: "Sun became entrenched in Mountain View early and didn't anticipate the company's phenomenal growth." This unpredictable growth gave the local developers the upper hand in lease negotiations. Every new building Sun attempted to lease cost more than the last. The senior facility manager complained, "It was often difficult to bargain for the best rates because the developers would already know that Sun needed the space because the engineers would call them." Sun was able to build some sort of campus identity in Mountain View by occupying several buildings in clusters sited by developers. Signs and graphics were added to Sun buildings to help unify the look of the scattered sites, but most of the buildings were so far apart that people drove rather than walked to meetings away from their building. Early leases in Mountain View were for seven to ten years but shorter subleases were later obtained in the local area for flexibility in the event of a business downturn. As Sun continued to grow, more bean fields adjacent to their Mountain View location were plowed under and another cluster of 50,000 SF buildings with surface parking appeared. Soon however, most of the land adjacent to Sun's existing Mountain View buildings was fully developed. Figure 4–2 is a site plan of Sun's Mountain View facilities in 1989.

The short life cycle of Sun's products heightened competitive uncertainty. The company introduced a new workstation product line every twelve months on average, and each new Sun line offered at least twice the power of the previous line at about the same price. Since product lines were expanding at uneven and unpredictable rates, departments continually reorganized and employees' offices were moved frequently. The churn rate (percent of office occupants moved in one year) exceeded 100%. A 200-person building would be stretched to hold 225 or 250 employees, then a replanning would take place. The process was vividly described by one space planner: "Acquiring space here is like cooking porridge in a pot—it starts to spill over one pot so you scoop it up and put it in another pot and then that pot boils over so you get another pot!"

Figure 4–2
Sun Mountain View Campus 1989

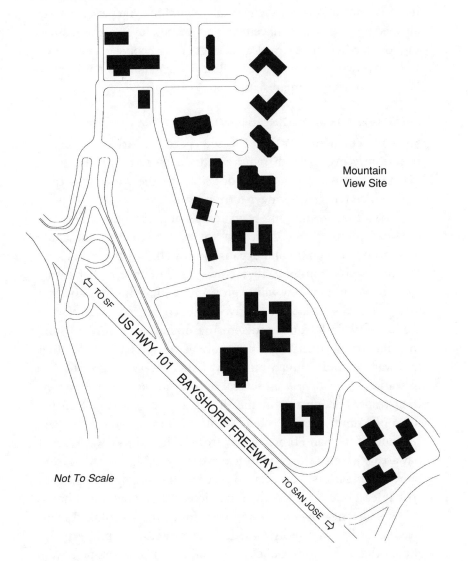

Mountain
View Site

TO SF

US HWY 101 BAYSHORE FREEWAY

TO SAN JOSE

Not To Scale

The extreme space shortage experienced by Sun during its high-growth phase was compounded by senior management's reluctance to add space more aggressively. The space problem was aggravated by frequent reorganizations at Sun. A space planner with years of experience at other high-technology firms explained the dilemma: "Although you try to keep moves to a minimum, business reorganizations can change that—you think you have the space all lined up, and then management reorganizes. If you are reorganizing you need a lot of extra 'flex space' to move people in and out of. But in a downturn, this space is often given up and then it is much harder to quickly reorganize to regain competitiveness."

STRATEGIES FOR MANAGING GROWTH

Sun's incremental addition of leased space was driven largely by uncertainty over growth requirements. However, Sun did make two basic strategic real estate decisions in the company's early years which reflected a longer-term perspective.

Sun's first major long-term real estate commitment was to establish another site dedicated to manufacturing that could accommodate incremental expansion as well. Just two years after the company's founding, there was already concern that future space in Mountain View would grow increasingly limited, and that local real estate costs were relatively high compared with adjacent areas, particularly for manufacturing operations. Most of Sun's manufacturing consisted of assembly of components from other hardware manufacturers, but it was still a very space-intensive operation. After reviewing several options in the Bay Area, a new industrial development on the site of an old golf course in the town of Milpitas was selected. Milpitas is located across the narrow end of the San Francisco Bay from Mountain View. This east bay area is about a thirty-minute drive away (without traffic) from Sun's headquarters. Commercial space in this rapidly growing area cost at least one-third less than in Silicon Valley. Lower-cost housing was also nearby—more appropriate for the semiskilled labor needed for light assembly. One developer owned the property but three others also were building on the site. The developers were willing to accommodate Sun's need to acquire space incrementally and Sun contracted for one building at a time. Sometimes the company would lease buildings under construction on a speculative basis by one of the developers. The site manager explained: "It has been hard to plan in advance for our needs beyond 30 to 60 days. They change quickly even during shell construction; one building had to have 14" added to its wall height after the tilt up had been done." The short time horizon is illustrated by the comment of a planner at a project review meeting held at the end of May 1988: "August first [the move date] is an eternity away."

KEEPING SPACE OFF THE CRITICAL PATH

Although they generally were careful about costs, getting the space up in time was the major priority for the facility managers running the Milpitas site. A major source of competitive advantage for Sun was to get the product into the hands of customers faster than their competition could. With product life cycles ever shortening, sometimes only a few months' advantage over the competition could be expected. Delays in assembly and shipping were costly in the short term because of lost sales, but even more costly in the long run because of lost customers. A sign taped to the door of the conference room in the Milpitas facility manager's office said it all:

The Mission of the Facilities Organization Is to Keep Space off the Critical Path to Meeting Our Business Goals. To Ensure That Adequate Space of the Right Type Is Available in the Right Locations at a Reasonable Cost.

Like in Mountain View, the local Milpitas developers knew they had a good thing going with this high-tech sprinter. The Milpitas facility manager explained: "We got a good deal on the first three buildings but as we committed to the site, negotiations got tougher. Sun wasn't too careful with the early leases, but now we're more thorough." Lease lengths ran from five to seven years. By the end of 1988, Sun occupied twelve buildings in Milpitas with more than 1,600 employees located there.

Sun also leased a 100,000 SF building five miles east of the Milpitas site in the spring of 1989 to house customer service operations. An important reason for selecting that site was to show the development world that Sun wasn't locked into the Milpitas location. "Part of real estate is signaling by looking at other properties—state economic development people need to see you looking at other options," explained the facility manager. Some managers also felt the time had come for Sun to expand to other locations: "When you reach one million square feet on a site, it doesn't feel like campus anymore; you have to drive from end to end," remarked a planner back in Mountain View.

Efforts were made to integrate employees at the two sites and to treat them equally. Shuttle service was provided between the two locations and Sun began to alternate its monthly beer bust between the two sites. Still, a human resources manager located in Mountain View noted that "There is a lot of them-versus-us between the two sites and some people won't work in Milpitas."

Sun's second major long-term planning initiative was to gain more control over interior office planning by establishing basic space standards. Gensler and Associates, a large interior planning and architecture firm, was hired in late 1986 to help develop the space and furniture standards. Having standards in place reduced the decision making needed every time Sun occupied a new building. The standard gross square foot per person metric was 250–275 SF with a ratio of two double offices (one closed office shared by two persons) for every single office.

Closed offices were an important part of Sun's approach to office space. While many competing computer companies used open-plan design throughout their offices, several key Sun executives believed that engineers preferred closed offices. They thought the ability to offer closed offices helped give Sun an edge in recruiting and retaining talent. However, some experimentation with open-office planning was found throughout the company, and open-office was used to a much greater extent in Milpitas.

No corporate art collection: All that decorates Sun's lobbies are products and product photos, both in a circa 1988 lobby and in the later corporate headquarters lobby.

Sun's approach to interior design aesthetics was described as "specialized functions in vanilla envelopes—Chevy space." Like many of the companies studied, the founding executive had a great impact on the overall design philosophy. Scott McNealy projected a straightforward, determined, and earnest attitude; he had low tolerance for the trappings of success. An apocryphal story within the company was that he once made a divisional vice president return a set of signed Audubon prints he had purchased to decorate the lobby of his division's office building because McNealy claimed that photographs of the product were all that should decorate the lobbies. A human resources manager confirmed that "Scott has hot buttons about frills."

Growth of the facilities management and real estate function was limited until 1989 as well. The senior manager of facilities, who reported to the vice president of corporate services, was conservative about adding staff and often used temporary staff instead. He attributed his reluctance to add permanent staff to bad experiences at previous employers: "I know what it is like to be fired and to fire my staff, and I didn't want to ever do that again." Figure 4–3 shows the structure of the corporate real estate function in 1987.

SPACE WARS COMPLICATE FACILITY MANAGEMENT TASKS

Rivalries and conflict between the business units often manifested itself when facility issues came to the table. Sun was organized around product lines and frequently reorganized as the company grew and products and competitive conditions changed. Through most of 1988, many autonomous divisions developed their own product strategies in response to competitive changes. "Sun is controlled chaos," remarked a vice president to *Business Week* in the summer of 1988.[3]

There was a lot of competition for space among the divisions. Referred to internally as space wars, divisional vice presidents resisted moving their groups to accommodate the growth of other groups. Since divisions grew at different rates and often reorganized, it was difficult to maintain adjacencies to co-workers. As one planner described the process, "It's like putting together a jigsaw puzzle while the shapes of the pieces are constantly changing."

Figure 4–3
Sun's Corporate Real Estate and Facilities Management Organization,
1987 and 1988

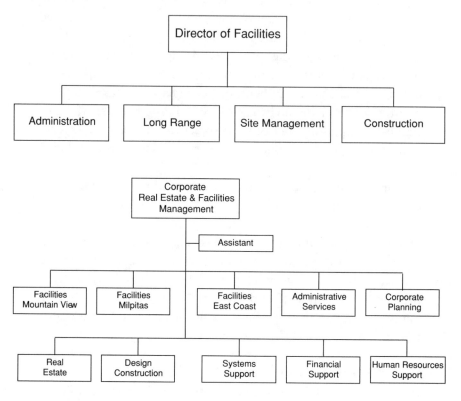

The facility management function at Sun had little formal authority and had to rely on influence and persuasion to coordinate the use of space. The senior manager of facilities explained, "There is some gamesmanship among the vice presidents. They are reluctant to relocate so facilities has to 'market' to get them to move and you have to convince two or more VPs about what needs to be done. The VPs are still positioning by trying to get control over particular buildings" in an effort to build minicampuses within the larger site. The facilities department experimented with several ways of organizing project management, but by 1988 were attempting to assign project managers to certain buildings. A planner remarked that formal site planning was precluded, instead

"We selected a building by taking a quick look at who works with whom in what buildings, what the building does, and compare it to other buildings."

All facility costs (leases, depreciation, asset retirement, staff) were charged back to the divisions on a square-foot-occupied basis, but were allocated based on the costs for the total site rather than individual buildings. In 1988 these costs totaled $11.00/SF in Mountain View and $7.30/SF in Milpitas. There was some consideration of tracking costs by individual buildings to keep managers from spending too much on initial building improvements. However, there was concern that such variances in building costs might subsequently cause people to try moving to less expensive buildings in order to reduce their departmental costs, further complicating facility management. As it was, it was difficult to get the departments to take previously occupied space. A space planner observed, "Each VP wants to recreate what they had at their previous company," so there was some variance by building and function.

ENGINEERS ARE KING

Facilities was expected to take a service-oriented perspective. The Sun culture revolved around the sentiment that engineers are kings here. The vice president for corporate services explained why: "Since the technology changes so fast and the competitors catch up so fast, you must hold on to the top talent in all areas—from the telex operator to the president." Despite McNealy's no nonsense attitude toward office design, accommodating the preferences of the engineers was a clearly understood priority. In fact, a new corporate headquarters building was 98% completed at a cost of $4.2 million for improvements when Sun management suddenly decided to change the use of the building to house a rapidly growing product engineering group at an additional cost of $700,000. Senior management remained in their old cramped quarters while the engineers had the space they needed to keep new products rolling out the door.

Sun's work environment was intense: Managers interviewed for the study reported that working 60 to 65 hours per week was the norm. Frequent references were made to *sunburn,* a term describing exhaustion that began to grow on employees after several months with the company. Sun employees were young; the average age in 1988 was about 30 years. Eighty percent of Sun employees owned shares in the company. These employees, especially the engineers, were outspoken about the company's decision making, and facilities were often a flash point for controversy. Spending so much time at work, there was little that escaped their attention: housekeeping, security, and even landscaping.

Facilities also was charged with managing the important traditions that dated back to the early days of the company and which were highly valued by the young, intense employees. For example, Wednesday morning doughnuts, which were a nice gesture when the company was small, had become a major weekly undertaking for the facilities department. They had to get doughnuts delivered to each building in the space of an hour. Facilities also coordinated the monthly employee beer bust.

WHAT PLANNING?

Formal programming of interior space was rarely done at Sun. "With high change [churn] you can make incremental improvements by watching how people use space," explained a project manager. Internal office planning was complicated by the computer technology at Sun. The physical position of computer users had to be hardwired to their assigned location on the floor. In the period of time between space planning and the actual occupancy of the space, often people were reorganized or reassigned which frequently meant that their physical location also had to be changed.

At the corporate planning level, a tight business plan was articulated for the first year with loose plans for the second. "You can't have a detailed plan when you are growing this fast," explained one corporate officer. "The possible horizon is double your present size—you can't write a plan beyond that. In contrast you can look forward twenty years if you are an oil company, seven years if you are Hewlett-Packard." The corporate strategy committee, consisting of McNealy, the executive vice president, the head of worldwide field operations, the CFO, and the vice president of corporate resources, met weekly. Real estate and facility matters were represented to the committee by the VP for corporate resources. Each division wrote a charter for the coming year, then objectives, then the budget, with extensive reviews (referred to as hacking) at each stage. But despite these efforts, the plan still changed frequently during the year.

CUMULATIVE DISADVANTAGES OF INCREMENTALISM BECOME EVIDENT

The scattered locations of Sun employees made face-to-face communication difficult to coordinate. Informal meetings were as likely to be held in parking lots as in the hallways. Therefore, electronic mail on the computer network played a key role in accommodating communication needs at Sun. "A tremendous amount gets done over E-mail, such as debates with large mailing lists. The E-mail culture is passed on through the bulletin boards and junk mail," explained one human resources manager. E-mail also increased the amount of time Sun employees were tuned into their jobs. Many had home terminals: "You can read E-mail that was written at 1:00 A.M."

One problem arising from Sun's physical configuration into many small buildings was that for security reasons the lobbies could not be opened to the public without a receptionist present. In the spring of 1988 there were 32 full-time receptionists covering 24 buildings. Administrative services also managed food services (which was contracted out for the two cafeterias), moved coordination, and transportation including delivery and shuttle service between buildings in the Mountain View and Milpitas areas.

CHALLENGES TO INCREMENTALISM—A SEARCH FOR A DESIGN IDENTITY

An early corporate design project for a training center revealed the lack of consensus regarding an aesthetic image for Sun. Training at Sun was almost nonexistent during start-up, but began to get more attention in 1987 as staff problems became acute: "People are being asked to grow a tremendous amount in their jobs—we want to improve people rather than hire them bosses." Sun used a combination of customized and generic training programs. Early training programs were held in conference rooms at Sun or at nearby hotels. But as the number of programs increased, there was a need for dedicated space. The manufacturing campus in Milpitas was selected as the site of the training center because space there was less expensive and 23,000 SF was immediately available in an existing building which had some interior improvements already.

Sun hired an architectural firm to design the interior of the training center. It was difficult to reach agreement on the interior aesthetics. The human resources manager for training and development, who was the primary Sun manager of the project, explained: "There were a lot of theories about how to design the space. The architect wanted to create a real state-of-the-art, fun place, rather than boxes. We looked at Apple's center, which has popcorn and bright colors. But Sun has a real lean and mean attitude and image. We didn't want the training center to be lavish while the engineers are being squeezed into two-person offices. There were disagreements over how fun and spacious the center should look." An early design placed the interior walls at a 45-degree angle to the building structure but the VP for corporate resources, who was highly involved in the design approvals, objected because he thought it looked wasteful. In all, it took over nine months and ten design proposals to design the space. McNealy reviewed the design with his usual disdain for frills, asking "Do we really need an oak podium?" Midway through the planning, another 26,000 SF became available in the building which allowed the program to be extended and space to be better utilized. Looking back on the project, a human resources manager sighed, "This is the biggest headache of my career at Sun."

A great deal of effort went into the design of the classrooms. There was a lot of discussion over whether the rooms should have windows. Ultimately most rooms did. No access to electronic mail was included, and only a few pay telephones were installed. The training center facilities were managed by the Milpitas facility staff, with full-time training and development personnel from corporate human resources running the programs within the building.

When a company builds a special purpose facility with an extended horizon of use, it often faces the need to put more thought into facility design—the quick and dirty approach, which can work for generic office space, is no longer appropriate. By the time Sun was ready to purchase and renovate its own headquarters building, the need for value-based decision making was acute. This period of Sun's history is covered in Chapter Seven which describes how real estate strategies change over time.

INCREMENTALISM PREDOMINATES AT MANY START-UP AND HIGH-GROWTH COMPANIES

Many other companies I have studied over the years showed the same incremental decision-making behaviors in their early years and during periods of rapid growth. For example, Digital Equipment Corporation grew its operations from a tiny sublease in an old woolen mill in a sleepy Boston suburb, leasing and renovating old mill space as needed for expansion. Digital purchased the mill property in the mid 1970's and it served as the company's corporate headquarters until DEC was restructured 1994. DEC's first office furniture consisted of household castoffs and lawn furniture tables and chairs.

G-Tech Corporation, which we will examine in greater detail in Chapters Six and Seven, grew during its early years by leasing a part of a floor at a time in a renovated old building in downtown Providence, Rhode Island. Thomson Financial Services, which began in an industrial loft in Boston's old leather district, has rapidly grown its business into a series of nearby retrofitted brick buildings in what is now the hottest area for development in Boston.

Financial services giant Fidelity Investments expanded incrementally into leased space in Boston, and bought several small, older buildings to renovate, during the company's early growth years. We look at Fidelity further in this chapter.

A break with incremental planning and a turn to more value-based approaches occurs when the scale of the company reaches a point where custom-built facilities can be economically and functionally justified, and when the company's strategic environment stabilizes enough to allow more long-range commitments. However, while strategic uncertainty is certainly the major driver behind the use of an incremental strategy, a conservative financial strategy will lead other firms to prefer an incremental approach to real estate and facilities even after they have weathered the highly uncertain stages of start-up and high growth. And as we see later in this chapter, firms experiencing downsizing or other major shifts in their strategies revert to an incremental strategy to dispose of excess space, consolidate operations, or reconfigure for new competitive requirements.

FINANCIALLY DRIVEN INCREMENTALISM

Some companies chose to pursue an incremental strategy even after they are well established in their marketplace. Although they may have reached substantial size relative to their competitors, these companies may still face rapidly changing competitive markets. Their senior management is still intent upon avoiding the risk of additional financial obligations beyond their immediate business forecasts. Two very different companies, midsize high-technology Millipore Corporation and financial services giant Fidelity Investments, continued to pursue real estate strategies dominated by an incremental approach even after they passed the start-up phase, albeit in very different ways.

DEBT WARY—CASH RICH:
CASE STUDY OF MILLIPORE CORPORATION

Although Millipore Corporation, a leading producer of analytic and purification products for industry and scientific research was founded in 1954, it continued to use an incremental approach to its real estate and facility decisions for decades. This incrementalism was driven both by relatively high strategic uncertainty and a strong desire by management to avoid long-term debt. Millipore financed most of its growth out of earnings and in 1987 its debt was less than 2% of total equity. By 1995, that debt to equity ratio had hardly budged. Like most companies with highly specialized manufacturing requirements, Millipore owns its manufacturing facilities and headquarters and usually leases other office space.

Millipore develops, manufactures, and sells a broad range of purification products to the microelectronics manufacturing, biopharmaceutical manufacturing, and analytical laboratory markets. Millipore develops technology in close association with its customers.[4] It serves a range of specialized product niches with rapid product development cycles. Most new market opportunities grow out of responding directly and rapidly to its customers' needs.

A key reason Millipore was able to add facilities incrementally over time is that in the late 1950's the company's founder, Jack

Bush, made a bold, visionary real estate decision and purchased 32 acres of farmland in Bedford, Massachusetts. Today, Bedford is in the heart of the thriving Route 128 corridor, home to many legendary high-technology companies but at the time of Millipore's purchase it was considered the boondocks. Many people thought it was crazy to locate the company so far from Boston. This land parcel allowed Millipore to expand its headquarters location seven separate times over the years, and the site was not filled out until 1988. During that time and since, Millipore was able to lease additional space in the area as needed because much local speculative office and industrial space was built nearby during the past two decades. As a longtime Millipore manager explained in 1988: "These small increments were driven by a reluctance to commit to [what was then thought to be] a crazy growth rate for just a few years, but in the long haul the growth rate was 15% per year in real growth." Millipore made new product development the greatest strategic priority. "We will probably always be a lean corporation with lean staff. The extra is spent on sales, research, and marketing. There is a certain denial of success. People at Millipore don't want to look like too hot of a company," characterized the vice president for human resources during this era. Although there was a lot of churn and frequently a shortage of offices at the Bedford location, as one manager wryly observed of the offices, "People change jobs here so often they don't get sick of their space."[5]

Millipore had a brush with more value-based planning in the late 1980's. At the time, Millipore owned a company called Waters, purchased in 1980, which was the market leader in high-pressure liquid chromatography. Waters's sales were about the same as Millipore's. Integrating the Waters acquisition into Millipore was a daunting task from the beginning. The companies had different technologies, products, customer bases, and cultures. While Millipore was an aggressive marketer, Waters cultivated a few customers over a long product development collaboration. The Waters headquarters was about a one-hour drive away from Bedford. Waters also had added onto its space incrementally five times since 1974 but generally had higher-quality designed facilities than Millipore.

Prior to the late 1980's, little real estate strategic planning was done. The COO of Millipore at the time, who was formerly the president of the Waters division confirmed that: "Previous to 1986, we didn't think about getting any more space until we would run out." But by this time, there was no room for new business groups at either site. A 70,000 SF addition built at Waters in 1986 was already filled. With combined 1988 sales of $622 million and 5,800 employees worldwide (4,000 in the United States), the company was becoming scattered among many leased sites in the greater Boston area, in addition to its multiple international locations. Also the physical distance between the two parts of the company was hampering communication and collaboration. Millipore managers embarked on a search for a third site to accommodate expansion and possibly to serve as a location for a future new corporate headquarters.

To develop a customized design approach while conserving capital and limiting risk, Millipore began to negotiate a build-to-suit deal with a prominent local developer for a site that was roughly equidistant to Bedford and the Waters site in Millford. "We wanted a site that was relatively inconvenient to both existing sites," explained a senior manager, yet one that would not require existing employees to relocate their homes. An architect with significant high-technology laboratory and office design experience was selected by the end of 1988. However, planning for the project got bogged down before the deal was ever finalized. The state of Massachusetts balked at spending $2 million to build an off-ramp that the site required and the accumulating project costs got a bit too rich for Millipore's conservative tastes. Meanwhile, Millipore recognized that the Boston real estate market was softening, particularly in the local outer suburban ring where many computer companies were located. This was the same time that minicomputer companies such as Data General, Wang, and Digital Equipment Corporation were getting clobbered in the marketplace by workstation and personal computer products. Millipore was able to lease space from Digital in Maynard and colocated some Millipore and Waters businesses there. Additional leased space became available in the Bedford area which helped to accommodate the incremental growth of new product areas. In hindsight, Millipore's incremental decision-making style put the company in the position to take advantage of late-breaking opportunities in the local real estate market, resulting in lower real estate costs.

By the early 1990's frustration over the inability to integrate the Waters division had grown and in 1993, the division was put up for sale, eventually resulting in a venture capital supported Waters' management buyout. One could wonder whether the integrated third site would have helped to bring the two companies together more effectively, or whether the company was fortunate not to have committed resources to a site which would have soon become unnecessary. By the mid-1990's Millipore was a leaner, but still high-performing midsize company with an increasing emphasis on international customers and still highly specialized niche markets.

The Millipore story illustrates that some successful companies can remain in an incremental real estate decision-making mode for many years. It is helpful to have a solid core of owned facilities and a good selection of geographically diversified leased space available to enable an incremental strategy over the long haul. With an established home base and an emphasis on locating additional facilities close to the customer, Millipore continues to make opportunistic real estate decisions based upon incremental business opportunities.

FIDELITY INVESTMENTS:
LARGE-SCALE INCREMENTALISM

In the financial services industry, market leader Fidelity Investments has long pursued an incremental real estate strategy in its headquarters operations at a scale that would amaze other similar size companies.[6]

Fidelity Investments was started in 1946 by Boston native Edward Crosby Johnson II. For thirty years the company was a well-respected local investment consulting firm without much growth. In the 1970's the founder's son, Edward "Ned" Johnson III expanded the business by broadening the scope of Fidelity's mutual funds. Ned Johnson was well acquainted with the ups and downs of the stock market, and his entrepreneurial temperament was balanced by a conservatism toward long-term real estate commitments. This conservatism is still reflected in Fidelity's corporate real estate strategy today.

The explosive growth of mutual funds, fueled in part by government policies encouraging individual retirement savings, led to not only Fidelity's rapid growth also but the expansion of the entire financial services industry. From 1987 to 1998 Fidelity's total customer accounts grew from 6.2 million to nearly 40 million. During the mid 1990's the company grew its space by 20% annually, often topping out at over 100,000 new square feet added per year. By the late 1990's, 10% of the New York Stock Exchange's transactions cleared through Fidelity each day. Over seven hundred thousand phone calls were handled daily, and many of the company's operations required electrical, mechanical, and systems redundancy.

During the 1980's Fidelity grew operations in the downtown Boston area at the same time it began to geographically diversify into other regions of the country. By 1987, plans were on the drawing board for Fidelity to build its own corporate headquarters tower in Boston but those plans were dropped after the October 1987 crash. The downtown Boston real estate market had softened considerably. Fidelity instead added space downtown on a building-by-building basis, and was able to take advantage of the late 1980's–early 1990's depression in commercial real estate to either acquire or lease space at attractive prices on very flexible terms. Fidelity's insistence on flexible lease terms, with easy exit options, are also a legacy of Johnson's experience with volatile financial markets. This flexibility was called upon when Fidelity had to shed employees after the downturn in the industry in the late 1980's. As hiring started to ramp up again, Fidelity also renovated some older "class B" buildings into office space. During its remarkable growth in the 1990's Fidelity remained headquartered in downtown Boston and still houses most of its research and administrative operations there. The result today is a corporate headquarters in which the streets of centuries old downtown Boston serve as the aisles. The rapid recovery of the downtown real estate market, and indeed some of the vitality of the city itself, owes a great deal to Fidelity's commitment to Boston. (Figure 4–4 shows how Fidelity's corporate headquarters of streets knits together the urban core of Boston.)

Meanwhile, across the Fort Point channel in Boston, Fidelity developed its own World Trade Center on surplus piers to overlook the Boston waterfront and skyline. Along with an exhibition hall, Fidelity built 480,000 SF of offices and trading floors. At the time, this location was thought to be remote; years later, this newly renamed Seaport district is poised as the next major area for intense real estate development in the

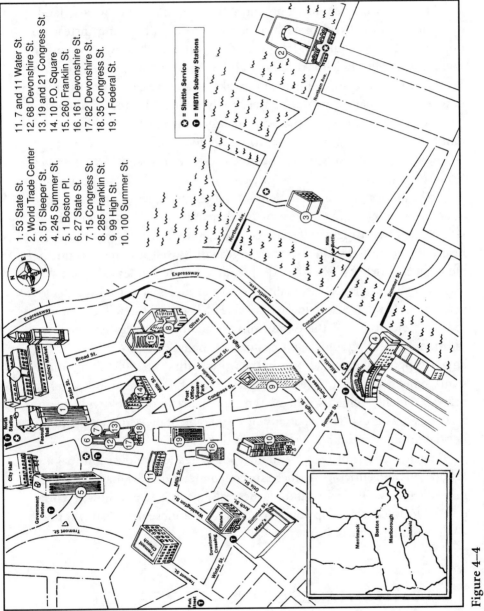

1. 53 State St.
2. World Trade Center
3. 51 Sleeper St.
4. 245 Summer St.
5. 1 Boston Pl.
6. 27 State St.
7. 15 Congress St.
8. 285 Franklin St.
9. 99 High St.
10. 100 Summer St.
11. 7 and 11 Water St.
12. 68 Devonshire St.
13. 19 and 21 Congress St.
14. 10 P.O. Square
15. 260 Franklin St.
16. 161 Devonshire St.
17. 82 Devonshire St.
18. 35 Congress St.
19. 1 Federal St.

✪ = Shuttle Service
Ⓣ = MBTA Subway Stations

Figure 4–4
Fidelity Downtown Boston

city. In 1998, a real estate development subsidiary of Fidelity opened a 427-room hotel next door, broke ground for an adjacent 17-story office building, and announced an additional 500,000 SF office tower for the site.

Despite its intense development activity, Fidelity still avoids developing a traditional corporate headquarters tower, preferring instead to opportunistically acquire and dispose of properties in the downtown office market. By 1998, Fidelity occupied about 10% of the class A space in Boston's financial district. Reluctant to take on any greater commitment to downtown for fear of disrupting the supply-demand balance in the market, Fidelity continues to send jobs to other sites in the Northeast and nationwide, as the company's core continues to grow.

Along with its downtown Boston presence, the company operates from seven other regions across the country in a total of over forty-four major buildings. At these sites, much larger increments of space were added, especially to handle the growing demands of back-office and phone service facilities. In late 1998, the company purchased 314 acres of land near Fort Worth, Texas, to assist future growth, as well as to more immediately house Fidelity's Texas-based operations located in leased space that was about to expire. Additionally, Fidelity occupies about 80 retail sites across the United States located near Fidelity's best retail customers. Fidelity holds most of these locations with short-term leases, changing locations as demographics and customers change. Despite its size as the largest supplier of mutual funds in the world with over $900 billion under management, and as the second largest retail brokerage company after Schwab, Fidelity remains a highly entrepreneurial company with nearly forty business units. The flexibility of its incrementally acquired portfolio helps it to act upon unfolding opportunities.

The attractions of incremental corporate real estate decision making are obvious and enticing. Yet there are concomitant disadvantages to incrementalism as well. Understanding these disadvantages, and how to compensate for them, can help you take advantage of incrementalism's appeal, while avoiding some of its pitfalls.

ADVANTAGES OF INCREMENTALISM

Companies often prefer to approach real estate decisions incrementally for a number of quite sensible reasons.

Figure 4–5
Incrementalism's Balancing Act

Advantages	Shortcomings
Can wait for more information	Location is still a long-term commitment
Shorten the forecasting horizon	Cumulative financial disadvantages
Symbolize "lean and mean" culture	Functional adjacencies suffer
	Policies are still difficult to change later

CAN WAIT FOR MORE INFORMATION

The most compelling reason why companies make incremental decisions is their desire to wait until more or better information about the future becomes available. This is true of not only real estate strategy but also business strategy in general. In his broad study of corporate strategy setting, James Brian Quinn used the term *logical incrementalism* to describe the way strategy was set at the nine Fortune 100-size firms he studied.[7] By terming the behavior he observed logical incrementalism, Quinn emphasized that although a company's strategic decision-making process may look capricious to outsiders, its managers consciously delay making final decisions as long as possible. They may want to obtain more information about their options and possible outcomes or they are trying to get greater participation in the decision-making process or they are still trying to sell the idea within the organization. Over time, such incremental, yet generally logical decision making enabled the companies Quinn studied to better react to unexpected events, to learn from their earlier actions along the way, and to allow more experimentation within the company. Incrementalism was particularly useful when a major change in competitive strategy was underway.

When you consider the difficulty of setting any long-range strategy or set of policies in an uncertain strategic environment, it is not surprising that senior management particularly loathes making real estate and facilities decisions which require a highly visible commitment to location and daunting long-term financial obligations.

SHORTENS THE FORECASTING HORIZON

Incrementalism permits organizations to shorten the time horizon in which they must forecast facility requirements. Companies incrementalize their real estate by taking short-term leases on space (Molecular Devices) or not committing to more space until current working conditions are overcrowded (Sun). They can incrementalize their facility development by avoiding expenditures on on-site employee amenities, by purchasing used furnishings, by leasing furniture, or by substituting lower cost materials for typical office furnishings (such as DEC's used lawn furniture in its first offices.) If managers in the organization find they have made erroneous decisions, either through a misinterpretation of requirements or a change in requirements, they perceive that there is less sunk cost at stake. Through incrementalism, they may more flexibly and quickly change their physical setting to meet new requirements than if they have taken a long-term commitment to space with a large capital investment that must be depreciated.

In a positive light, incrementalism allows managers to make quick adjustments to new competitive conditions, such as Sun's last-minute conversion of its corporate offices to R&D. A more cynical interpretation is that managers prefer incrementalism because they want to avoid being held responsible for making the wrong decision. Line managers who are frequently rotated through various business units are notorious for making short-term commitments which may have an immediate benefit to their performance evaluation and bonuses, but in the longer term are damaging to the strategic or cost position of the firm.

Incrementalism helped Sun to wait until future business requirements became more certain before the company made a commitment to develop a campus to fit its future needs as a major industry player, as we show in Chapter Seven. By waiting to build, Sun benefited from a favorable decrease in local land prices during the early 1990's recession. On the other hand, when Molecular Devices did attempt to do more long-range planning, the start-up got into financial trouble. The company overestimated the rapidity by which it could ramp-up production and was faced with expensive underutilized office space. Like any major strategic decision, if the future plays out in a way that coincides with your decisions, you look like a genius—if not, you look like a fool. The highly visible nature of corporate real estate and facility decisions raises the stakes even higher.

INCREMENTALISM SYMBOLIZES A
LEAN AND MEAN ATTITUDE

Incrementalism also is preferred by some senior managers for its symbolic value. The no-frills work environment which is characteristic of interior design at incremental companies sends an important message to employees. These managers do not always use an incremental strategy out of purely financial necessity. They often are aware of the important symbolic messages that the work environment sends to employees and to outsiders alike. As the cofounder of a software sales support company explained: "We can afford to take more space right now, and we'll need more soon, but I want people to remember that they are in a start-up. If things start to look too luxurious they may forget that we have still not consistently produced quarterly profits, and that they have to watch expenses very carefully." She was constantly balancing the need to provide people with the right tools to do their job—in this case phone support—with the desire to maintain the esprit de corps and attitude of a start-up.[8] Molecular Devices was concerned that the expansion space they leased would look extravagant to their venture backers so they walled off the excess space from view.

This incremental look may later become a symbol of the values of the company and be part of a more carefully considered value-based approach to decision making as discussed in Chapter Six. Long after Digital was a financially secure market leader with strict worldwide facility design standards, the company was still taking additional space in former grocery stores, and outfitting its offices with folding tables, in a deliberate effort to retain a down-to-earth atmosphere reminiscent of the company's roots. Even Sun Microsystems still avoids displaying real art on its walls—well-lit photographs of Sun products remain the decoration of choice.

DISADVANTAGES OF AN
INCREMENTAL STRATEGY

The simplicity of incremental decision making can be very deceptive. Although managers may think they are retaining more long-term flexibility with an incremental strategy, any sort of physical commitment, even one that appears to be short term, can be difficult and costly to change later on. Many facility decisions made while a company is starting in the garage set in place policies and practices that then persist at later stages even though they are no longer appropriate. These practices may make it more difficult for the organization to change its workplace to meet new competitive requirements.

LOCATION IS STILL A LONG-TERM COMMITMENT

When a company is starting up, often it is located close to the founder's home and its nascent base of business operations. Entrepreneurial spin-offs usually locate nearby their parent companies. The tendency for founders to remain close to home is a major factor in why industries tend to develop geographical concentration, even when access to raw materials is not a major factor.

The early location decision is critical. Most important, it determines the type of human resources easily available to a company in the local labor markets, as well as availability and relative quality of external professional support such as legal, accounting, and advertising talent. Companies then get locked into their location because once a critical mass of employees is hired from a local area, or transferees are relocated, it is very difficult to later move these employees to a location with more favorable labor market or real estate conditions. Skilled professionals in a tight labor market, such as engineers, have the power to resist relocation. If the company is located in a high-priced residential real estate market, it can both make it more difficult for the company to attract talent from other parts of the country and it can raise labor costs in comparison to those of competitors who locate their employees near cheaper residential real estate. A major reason why Sun Microsystems established a second base of operations for certain product lines in Massachusetts was to be close to the pool of computer talent being laid off by the many local minicomputer companies. Many of these engineers were not willing, or could not afford, to relocate out of the Northeast to the more expensive housing of the Bay Area. By 1998 Sun also had begun development of a major site in Colorado, in part to take advantage of comparably lower living costs.

Real estate disadvantages also can add up with an incremental strategy. Even though a company may view leasing property one parcel at a time as a more flexible approach, it is still really a long-term commitment since most leases are for a minimum of five years and any building improvements made must be paid for. The type of space available for occupancy from the local real estate market may not be the most optimum for the company's needs. More or less space than is needed may have to be acquired. While developers may be eager to lease space to a start-up on favorable terms, this capture strategy can eventually trap companies into unsuitable, costly space. Sun found itself spread out into dozens of 50–60,000-square-foot leased buildings with lease renewals priced at top market rates; it is still working on consolidating its Silicon Valley locations into more manageable clusters.

CUMULATIVE FINANCIAL DISADVANTAGES

The cumulative inflexibility of incrementalism has negative financial consequences as well. In Sun's early years, its managers were too preoccupied with navigating their turbulent competitive environment and their exploding growth to think about relocating. Sun was then held captive to above-market rent rates in Mountain View because the developers knew from other sources within the company that Sun was desperate for the space and accordingly charged Sun premium prices.

Coordinating between a large number of locations also adds both direct and hard-to-track costs. Sun was required to maintain building security in each of the twenty-five plus buildings it occupied in the Bay Area which meant each building had to be assigned full-time coverage by a receptionist. This resulted in a staff of nearly 40 receptionists. Sun even developed a career path program for receptionists! While the cost of shuttle buses and messenger services can be tracked, the lost productivity of employees driving from building to building or meeting in parking lots instead of conference rooms is a potentially much larger indirect cost that is seldom quantified.

Fidelity Investments used so many taxi cabs and shuttle buses to move employees and visitors among its various Boston area locations, that the chairman insisted they start their own limousine service. The resulting company, Boston Coach, is now the largest limousine service in New England and is expanding nationwide.

Although Millipore's founder had the foresight to purchase a large tract of land upon which to grow the company's facilities, the actual planning and construction of these additions were done in such a way that they eventually compromised the effective use of the site, making the later additions more difficult to place on the site and more costly to build.

When an organization resists equipping its employees with the proper workplace support (space and equipment), it may impede productivity at a time most critical for the organization's survival. How productive were those 10% of new Sun employees who did not have a physical place to work when they first joined the company? High growth can cover up a lot of mistakes. Real estate inefficiencies only become evident when the growth slows or margins erode.

ADJACENCIES SUFFER

Another disadvantage to incrementalism is that when space needs become acute, the organization's facility choices are limited to whatever buildings are available in the local real estate market at that time. By waiting until the last minute to obtain more space, the organization is forced to conform its workplace design and departmental adjacencies in a way that might not fit or complement its organizational structure. When space is not available adjacent to existing facilities, the business must decide which group will be moved off site, often with painful internal political struggles over who will go and who will stay.

The desire to colocate employees and share more common resources across facilities are the major drivers of company headquarters and operations consolidations. The need to consolidate to a larger, custom-designed site is often the catalyst for using the value-based decision-making strategy which is discussed in Chapter Six.

POLICIES ARE STILL HARD TO CHANGE LATER ON

Although one of the major reasons to make decisions incrementally is to retain flexibility, experience shows behaviors that emerge during the early years of a company, such as how space is allocated and used and the ways individuals interact within that space, are hard to change once established. Managers who do not think through the longer-term implications of a policy may find it more difficult to make needed changes later on. Early precedent also influences the way subsequent opportunities for change are identified and evaluated. The phrase, *We've always done it this way,* emerges remarkably early in a company's life. Since spatial relationships within the organization influence the development of informal personal networks and over time help influence the company's culture, companies must use this powerful tool carefully and deliberately. Incremental decision making rarely encourages such thoughtfulness.

An incremental strategy that locates organizational units in separate facilities may make it more difficult to subsequently integrate those units later on. Groups formerly located off-site may have difficulty adjusting to the increased visibility and supervision once they are brought back into the fold and colocated with the rest of the company.

MAKING INCREMENTALISM LOGICAL

Despite the inherent disadvantages, many companies have no choice but to make many real estate and facility decisions incrementally. Certainly the start-up or the high-growth company has neither the financial resources nor the management time to make longer-term commitments. They are genuinely unable to see their future. In a rapidly changing, highly competitive environment, it is difficult for a company to invest many resources into real estate and facilities because developing the market and the product consumes all available capital. The main role of the corporate real estate and facility management function is to support and enable the growth and development of the company, while allowing as many contingencies as possible for unforeseen outcomes. However, a great many lessons can be learned from studying the incremental strategies of previous start-up and high-growth companies and seeing how an overall logic for making incremental real estate decisions can be established which sets the company in the right direction in preparation for the time when more long-range planning and commitments can occur.

How can a start-up company enjoy the benefits of incrementalism, while still positioning itself for the greatest advantages in the future? Based upon the experiences of the companies profiled in our research, here are some suggestions for using incrementalism to enable competitive advantage:

MAKE TOUGH LOCATION DECISIONS EARLY

Start-up and high-growth companies need to realize that the general geographic location in which they start and grow their businesses will be very difficult to change in the future.

Early in each firm's history both Millipore and DEC made bold location choices which placed them in a favorable real estate position for many years. By purchasing a large tract of land early on, Millipore was able to expand incrementally in a series of building additions allowing them to keep employees together and utilizing common facilities, such as a cafeteria. Incremental construction was funded by working capital rather than debt. Digital, realizing the potential of a large mill complex that was obsolete for its original use, also was able to renovate the space incrementally and in the end, ultimately created a handsome and meaningful corporate home. Although Millipore's final building configuration was not optimal and DEC still required substantial expansion space beyond the mill complex, both companies avoided two of the major pitfalls faced by companies in uncertain competitive environments—too much of the wrong space at the wrong time, or not enough space of the right kind when its needed. Although still retaining proximity to Boston and its area research labs, both companies located further out in what were considered the exurbs, where commercial land and employee housing were less costly.

ARTICULATE YOUR CORPORATE VALUES AND THOSE SYMBOLS WHICH HOLD MEANING FOR YOUR ORGANIZATION

Most founders have strong beliefs not only about the kind of products they want to sell but also about the kind of company they want to build. Rather than assume that workplace design is something that can be dealt with later when the company is more established, it is helpful to at least set out some basic principles to guide decisions. Sun's no frills decor, while updated with an emphasis on encouraging interaction, has always focused on glorifying the firm's products. Silicon Graphics corporate color, purple, was featured early and prominently in its interior design. Cisco Systems's emphasis on an egalitarian culture was expressed in its earliest facilities by not placing any closed offices on perimeter walls, a policy that prevails in the millions of square feet occupied by the company today. These articulated values also aid in longer-term decision making, which the following chapter discusses at length.

FIND CREATIVE WAYS TO OBTAIN SHORT-TERM SPACE

Start-ups rely on a variety of creative ways to get the space they need in the short term. It helps to be part of an informal network of start-ups.

Incubators have developed in many parts of the country to help encourage the development of new businesses. It is an especially popular approach in the Silicon Valley where office space is often scarce and expensive. One incubator, created by NASA in 1993 to help develop businesses based on technologies spun off by the space agency, has become so well-respected that just getting admitted to the incubator and allocated space is seen in the Valley as a sign that a business has high potential. Some venture capitalists sponsor their own incubator space. Incubators usually provide office equipment, some central administrative services, and most important the presence of the other entrepreneurs with whom to commiserate and conspire.[9]

As small businesses grow—or as is often the case—die, other start-ups can gobble up their space. Molecular Devices relied on the scaling back of a research institute and were able to expand room-by-room in their first location.

These days an increasingly large number of entrepreneurs in service industries are forgoing formal offices to work out of their homes and even build in space for a few employees. Office suites also can be rented on a monthly basis. Although this kind of rental space can be costly on a square-foot basis, it may provide the small amount of front office space needed for meeting with clients.

Holding meetings in hotels and restaurants is an obvious option for very short-term space needs, but rarely thought of as a deliberate incrementalizing strategy. One start-up had monthly meetings that all employees attended. Rather than include a large conference room in their own offices, they worked out a good deal with a nearby hotel to meet there, obtaining a substantial discount because they committed to several months worth of business at once.

Senior managers' homes often become swing space for the conferencing needs of the start-up. The president of one start-up held regular Friday afternoon staff meetings poolside at his nearby home; such meetings often progressed into informal evening cook-outs.[10] Entertaining employees in the home can help break down barriers between people and build team spirit. However, sensitivity should be exercised if the senior manager's home is much more opulent than those of other members of the start-up. On the other hand, in some service businesses where partnership is a coveted goal, showcasing a partner's fine home is seen as a way of building ambition in new employees—one management consulting firm refers to this as the all-this-can-be-yours-someday motivational approach.

PARTNER WITH A DEVELOPER WHO WILL
SUPPORT INCREMENTAL OCCUPANCY

Incremental strategies often are made possible because some developers are amenable to making deals such as the one made for Molecular Devices's expansion into its Menlo Park headquarters. The developer was willing to let MD incrementally occupy the space and pay a less-than-market-rate rent because he knew that if the company were to prosper, it would have the potential of moving into one of the additional buildings he planned to construct on his property.

Some developers recognize the upside potential of providing space to a company during its start-up and offer their own sorts of incubators. They may provide office services, such as clerical support and copying facilities with other amenities that a corporate campus might offer, such as on-site day care, food services, athletic facilities, and shopping. By clustering companies that are operating in similar markets (e.g., software) and colocating companies that offer support services, such as advertising or accounting, small companies can enjoy the benefits of proximate services and the ability to build relationships with a responsive network of suppliers. One example of such a cluster is the Prospect Hill office park development in Waltham, Massachusetts. This "super park" of nearly twenty office buildings is home to many high-technology companies; it includes a 350-room hotel, fitness center, child-care facility, heliport, and stores. The park also houses an entrepreneurs center where small businesses can share resources with each other, thereby lowering their overhead. This arrangement provides a competitive advantage to the development's owner; businesses which succeed and grow out of the incubator often look to the Prospect Hill complex for new office space.

Companies taking temporary space should remember that they still need to feel confident that the overall location they select is where they would like to be in the future. As the employment base of the company grows and more employees buy homes close to work, the more difficult and costly it will be to get them to move to a different location later on.

PAY MORE NOW TO HAVE GREATER FLEXIBILITY LATER

As DEC expanded, the firm often obtained options on land or purchased it outright. Managers did the necessary permitting and site development studies, sometimes even designing the building. Then, they would hold this property in inventory until the need for space was clearly identified in their business plan. It would only take a short while to ramp-up to building construction, compared with the time it would have taken if they had waited to look for a site after the need for space had been concretely documented. This strategy is shown graphically in Figure 9–1.

While holding land can be costly over time and lease options also add cost and risk, those costs must be considered in light of not only real estate cost savings further down the line if the local market is improving but more important is the time saved if additional space is needed quickly. In today's change-on-a-dime competitive environments, speed and responsiveness are equal metrics to dollars.

We began our discussion of corporate real estate strategy with the observation that people in organizations hate making decisions. It is no surprise then that incrementalism—holding off commitments until the last possible minute—is so inherently attractive. If properly designed space in the perfect location at a cheap price could be obtained at the very minute it is needed, with infinite opportunities for disposal once it is no longer required, no one would ever consider any other strategy. However, the reality is that space takes a long time to acquire and build, that it costs a lot of money, and that it is difficult to easily change the design—much less the location of the space—at a later time as requirements change. Companies need ways to both plan for certainty and to be flexible in the face of uncertainty, all the while getting the most while spending the least on real estate and facilities. Two other approaches to real estate decision making are available to take advantage of learning and economies of scale, and to provide a home which supports the strategic goals and the cultural values of the organization. We will explore these other two approaches in the following chapters.

CHAPTER FIVE

STANDARDIZATION

A standardization strategy attempts to control and coordinate facility design and real estate operations across the entire organization. Standards are set centrally and applied throughout the company. These standards may specify design, such as the size, color, materials, and manufacturer of everything from chairs to interior offices to exterior construction materials. Standards also may be used to control administrative processes which direct the allocation, development, and administration of real estate and facilities. Standards usually are established as written policy and integrated into the formal management processes within the organization. Company managers are not free to obtain office space or furnishings whenever they wish; they must conform to a process of requesting, justifying, and receiving these resources. When a real estate or facility management decision is needed, the standards are consulted. Standards can be presented as general guidelines or they can be strictly enforced.

In this chapter we discuss the use of *standardization in the decision-making process* not the implementation of design or operating standards per se. We examine the origins of standardization, its impact on how we occupy Place, and the advantages and disadvantages of a standardized approach. Under what conditions can a standardization strategy enable the organization to achieve and sustain competitive advantage?

In order to standardize real estate and facilities decision making, a company must be able to make some confident predictions about its future facility requirements. An extensive use of a standardization strategy often is found at companies which occupy a great deal of real estate, have a fairly predictable use of these assets based upon function, and place a priority on control and efficiency. In general, the older and larger a company is, the more likely both design and operating standards will be found.

Standardization is illustrated by comments such as:

There are three prototypical open office layouts and over 6,000 employees at the facility.

Architect, Regional telecommunications company

Ninety percent of the company occupies a 10' x 10' sized office.

Director of Facility Planning, High-technology company

Exterior design standards are so set that you need special permission to put more than one flagpole outside a new building.

Project Manager, High-technology company

Each level of corporate real estate expenditure is formally reviewed at a corresponding level of senior management.

Real estate planner, Financial services company

Standardization is all about control. Cost control is the most obvious, but control over behavior within the organization also is sought. Standardization reduces conflict over resource allocations and helps promote uniformity across locations. Let's examine these reasons in closer detail.

Cost control is the most common reason for implementing both design standards and process standards. Control may be needed to limit the amount of discretion line managers can exercise over long-term financial commitments for the organization. The savings can be substantial: costs can be lowered through economies of scale when purchasing furnishings and equipment for the entire organization. Furnishings can be moved from one facility to another without requiring new interior design. Further, by standardizing, the company does not have to reinvent the wheel every time a new facility is built or an office is planned, and projects can be completed more quickly at lower cost.

Control over behavior within the organization also can be a goal of a standardization strategy. Standards may be put into place to encourage similar individual behaviors across dispersed locations, by providing the same environmental symbols and cues in all of the company's facilities. Often, the standardization of real estate decision-making processes is used to control managerial actions far beyond the scope of real estate and facility issues. By using a formal, bureaucratic process for gaining access to or changing space, a company can indirectly control its head count or limit the number of new products in the development pipeline.

Standardization ostensibly reduces conflict over facility allocations and promotes uniformity throughout the organization. In particular, standards set at the corporate level can not only help reduce competition and conflict between business units but also discourage unnecessary purchases which might add to corporate overhead. Maintaining a uniform look for the company's facilities in different locations gives visiting and transferred employees a stronger sense of place. Facility managers push for standards because it simplifies their job and gives them a basis for resolving disputes between competing subunits within the organization. Senior management favors standards because they do not have to communicate values for every single design project the company undertakes.

Standards, or policies set down on paper, differ from norms, which are unwritten and sometimes even unarticulated guides for behavior within the organization. Even if formal standards exist, they may not necessarily be followed throughout the company. Having standards does not guarantee they will be followed, unless there are some administrative processes in place to enforce the standards.

IDENTIFYING STANDARDIZATION

What does a standardized decision-making strategy look like? Standardization becomes a method of strategic decision making when established standards are used to guide real estate and facility decisions. A new project is planned using established procedures and designed according to existing design standards. The need for decision making may be initiated by real estate and facility requirements such as the acquisition of new space or the redesign or reassignment of existing space, or it may be in response to changes in real estate or facilities such as lease expirations or new office technology. When the need occurs, managers within the company turn to established procedures and design guidelines to help guide their decision.

While companies that are either incremental or value-based in their approach to real estate decision making also may use design standards when planning a new facility, this does not necessarily mean that they are using a standardization strategy. Incremental companies may have some design or space standards in place, but the acquisition and planning of each new project is undertaken one at a time, with little future planning and not much concern for following standard procedures. As a company matures and grows, later it may view standardization as an antidote for incrementalism by minimizing the number of decisions to be made whenever new facilities or a move is anticipated. It is an effort to capture learning from previous experience. A value-based strategy considers the specific needs of each project within the context of the organization's physical requirements and its culture and values, as further discussed in the following chapter. Under a value-based real estate decision-making strategy, design and operating standards may help the company to handle the complexities of a large project, but they do not drive the outcome of the project.

THE RELATIONSHIP BETWEEN STANDARDIZATION AND LOW STRATEGIC UNCERTAINTY

A standardization approach to real estate and facility decisions is most appropriate for companies operating in relatively stable competitive environments. Companies in more predictable competitive environments usually have predictable patterns of inputs and outputs. Stable markets often pressure these companies to compete as low-cost producers, so the cost controlling aspects of standardization's scale economies can help sustain cost advantages. Standards are easier to implement since much of the company's product development and production can be routinized. Further, businesses which can anticipate the bulk of their future facility needs are able to make longer-term commitments and do so in larger increments than firms facing greater competitive uncertainty.

Figure 5–1 illustrates the role of standardized decision making under conditions of low environmental uncertainty. For example, the insurance industry can commit to longer-range facility plans than most companies because part of their business is based upon long-lived financial commitments from their customers. While insurance is certainly not a low-risk industry in terms of profitability, at least part of its daily operations can be forecast with a relatively high degree of confidence. The processing of documents and claims is highly routinized and only changes when new enabling technologies are developed.[1]

Figure 5–1
Standardized Decision-Making Model Under Conditions of Low
Environmental Uncertainty

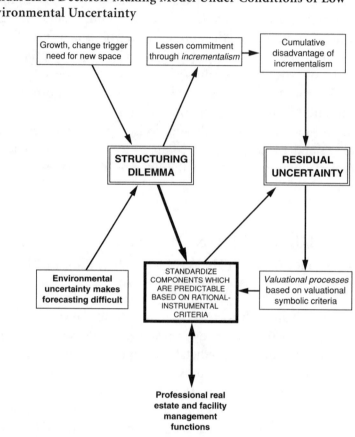

The ability to take a long-term perspective when planning facilities, and the financial stability that often accompanies such a secure position, might lead us to wonder why firms in low strategic uncertainty environments don't demonstrate even more value-based behavior than firms in less certain environments. Don't these stable companies have the luxury of resources and predictability to do so? While value-based statements certainly are made on major projects by companies operating in relatively predictable environments, great pressures exist both within and outside the organization to heavily standardize both design and policy. These companies tend to be older and have long histories, with much tradition. Their senior managers usually have been with the company for a long time and may be less open to new ideas. The stability of the industry also may be accompanied by strong industry and regulatory standards and extensive benchmarking, which encourage standardization of both design and operations. As industries mature, product margins often erode so that the cost control benefits of standardization become increasingly attractive.

Before discussing the advantages and disadvantages of standardization in the decision-making process, it is helpful to clarify the different ways design standards and operating standards are used in practice.

Sidebar 5—1
THE ORIGIN OF THE PERSON-PLACE STANDARD

The custom of representing job positions by the quantity and design of space assigned to the person occupying that position is a basic principle of the bureaucratic form of organizing. To Max Weber, the noted German sociologist who provided the seminal definition of the bureaucratic form in the late 1920's, the physical office was the fundamental symbolic representation of a position within the company. A person occupied an office and this was assumed to be a place, as well as a job position.[2]

In the early part of this century, scientific management principles based on manufacturing processes were applied to the office and analyzed work by the tasks performed. Equipment and places were then assigned according to both these tasks and the supervision that the employee required.[3] As office buildings grew larger and the management of operations more complex, standards helped simplify planning, purchasing, and daily operations for maximum efficiency. The office was viewed as another sort of factory where clerical work, much of it repetitious, was routinized.

DESIGN STANDARDS

Design standards define many aspects of the workplace; they may focus only on issues of interior space design. Or, for multisite companies they may extend to detailed design specifications for building architecture and exterior finish materials. These standards are documented in writing, usually as operating manuals or some other method of recording managerial policy. Responsibility for enforcing compliance to standards usually is assigned to real estate and facility managers whose authority is backed up by the senior officer of the company to whom their function reports.

The most rudimentary form of design standards is the space standard which allocates a certain amount of floor space to a given job function or position within the organization's hierarchy. Basic space standards are essential to the planning of any facility of significant size. A standard amount of space allocated by job position helps companies to calculate the amount of space they will need as their head count changes, or as job functions change within the company. However, for many companies, space and design standards are only the beginning of a standardization approach to decision making.

Nearly every organization sets up some office space standards early in its life. Even at small start-up companies, rules for who gets what appear very early in the company either formally or informally. Basic design standards, especially the use of open or closed wall offices, are established. However, space standards at start-ups tend to be flexible based upon the existing space available for occupancy. Entrepreneurs are often highly influenced by their previous job experiences. Some try to recreate the look and feel of their old companies by implementing similar design standards—others purposely try to define their new company by defying their old office standards. For instance, Sun Microsystems purposely used a closed office design standard for its engineers in deliberate response to the open plan standards in place at competitors HP and DEC.

A major change or crisis in the organization's real estate and facilities often precipitates the establishment of standards, or the development of new standards. This crisis may be precipitated by a change in the property portfolio, or by an acquisition or merger. Originally standards may have been developed to assist in space planning for a new headquarters or another major building project and then later applied at other locations. Or they may evolve as part of an overall change in the facility management strategy in the organization, possibly brought about by a reengineering effort. There also may be a lot of reliance on benchmark information to compare the standards to what other companies in the same industry are using.

Sidebar 5–2
BENCHMARKING

The benchmarking of facility management practices and performance has become an increasingly popular way to demonstrate the achievements of the corporate real estate and facility management functions within organizations. Benchmarking is the systematic comparison of management practices, work processes and performance along established metrics between your company and other companies, usually those in the same industry. Benchmarking is an integral part of total quality management programs—without some ideal of where you stand, improvement cannot be measured either internally or relative to your competitors. It also helps establish baseline performance as part of a re-engineering effort.

Corporate real estate benchmarking was inspired by the benchmarking of other business processes. Corporate real estate and facility managers often institute benchmarking efforts as a way to demonstrate to senior management how they can help enhance the corporation's performance and to document their own improvements over time, particularly in response to the threat of outsourcing. Consultants have also promoted benchmarking as a way of encouraging their clients to improve their real estate and facility operations—with the consultant's help, of course!

When benchmarking is applied to corporate real estate and facility management, the focus is usually upon reducing occupancy costs and gaining more value for the money spent on real estate and facilities. Benchmarks may be assessed internally and externally as part of the process of setting corporate facility design and management standards. Other common goals include operational improvements to increase internal customer satisfaction and greater productivity of the real estate and facility staffs.

A company may simply want to compare its performance on some simple metrics such as occupancy costs or space per employee and compare these to financial performance measures, or it may want to fully operationalize its perfromance parameters in detail such as the time it takes to negotiate a lease, build a facility, or provide a service to a customer. At some point, benchmarking requires the cooperation of other companies in sharing performance data to establish meaningful goals for improvement.

While benchmarking can provide valuable performance information and help spur operational improvements, it also can be dangerous if carried to an extreme. What is being measured must show a direct relationship to the well being of the business enterprise, not just be measured for the sake of counting something. It can be difficult to accurately compare across companies so make sure you are measuring the same things such as what spaces get included in square foot per person metrics, and exactly what costs are included in real estate and facility costs.

By limiting your benchmarking comparisons to just companies within your own industry, you may miss opportunities to discover advantages over these competitors. You should also look at the characteristics of companies you admire or want to emulate. For example, a telecommunications company might want to benchmark against a cable operator or a software company. Above all remember that quality work environments go beyond the numbers and that the qualitative elements of your approach to Place are as critical as those which can be quantified.

Some companies use the same general design standards for both headquarters and field locations. Some even standardize down to a corporatewide selection of office furniture systems (chairs, and other furnishings) by specifying colors, fabrics, and finishes. Others have broader standards, specifying square footage and the type of furnishings, but allowing more regional or local autonomy in the choice of styles or manufacturers.

Corporate design standards are used to minimize the amount of discussion and controversy that a new facility may generate, especially if it is located away from the headquarters. As one manager in charge of field office relocation at a telecommunications company explained: "Design standards are centrally set here. You can't design by consensus. There are too many parties involved, so there is a lot of reliance on standards."[4]

Standards usually are developed with the help of office interior design consultants. The standards may be based upon information gathered through interviews and observations of people on the job, or by using written surveys. Studies of office layout efficiency based upon the way the organization works on a daily basis also may be conducted. Examination of work processes is discussed in Part Three.

Design standards have been promoted widely for the past twenty years by office furniture manufacturing companies. The use of systems furniture, the combinations of fabric-covered panels and furniture components which attach to the panels, encourages standardization by using a limited number of component parts capable of being rearranged as requirements change. In practice, such systems often are used to develop a minimum number of workstation types usually keyed to managerial position, which makes the space planning and interior layout processes easier. Standards based upon their company's products help furniture companies to raise switching costs for their customers—those corporations that use their open office products. By convincing a company to standardize its office interiors based upon their furniture system, the manufacturer has locked in a customer for many years to come. Setting design standards based upon systems furniture then leads to the implementation of operating standards to control the ordering and installation of furniture.

Institutional isomorphism—the tendency for companies in an industry to look more and more like each other over time—is also at work in the drive for standardization.[5] As facility management has become increasingly professionalized, there has been a great deal of discussion regarding the best practices for managing real estate and facilities functions. Companies look to each other and to outside experts such as interior designers for guidance; based upon the experience of other companies, they find a frequent recommendation is to standardize more outcomes and processes. Interest in cross-industry benchmarking, fueled by the reengineering movement, also has led to greater use of standards.

While standards might be specified companywide, the actual use of those standards might be put into place incrementally over time. For example, as part of their overall effort to reduce occupancy costs, Merrill Lynch developed new standards for its office space in downtown Manhattan. When a department or floor is reorganized and the space must be redesigned, the new standards are implemented, reusing as many of the existing furnishings as possible. Over time, with normal churn within the buildings, Merrill Lynch will have reduced its space per employee, while avoiding a costly, disruptive replanning of their New York City locations.

Design standards are used more often to guide interior design but can be applied to entire building programs as well. Here are some examples of standardization in action:

DESIGN STANDARDS AS PART
OF A MAJOR PROJECT AT PACIFIC TELESIS

The operating headquarters for Pacific Telesis (now a part of Southwestern Bell), located in San Ramon (the east bay area of northern California) is an example of an extreme move to standardization. This 2 million-square-foot building comprised of four wings and four floors was divided into 50,000 SF planning modules (two per floor per wing). When it was originally occupied, 95% of its 6,000 office workers were housed in just three prototypical open office workstation types: general office, software programming, and engineering. Closed offices, of which there were initially very few, were either 8' x 8' or 8' x 10'. Since the building was being planned during the telecommunications industry's divestiture process, there was a great deal of uncertainty over exactly which functions would eventually be located in the building. The present organization and space needs of ten typical districts were examined and used as the basis for developing the space and interior furnishing standards. At first it was thought to be largely a clerical facility, but over time an increasing number of managers in more senior positions were located there. Departments that occupied the space were given a menu from which they could choose the orientation of their layout (on the grid or on the diagonal), the height of the panels, and the location of electrical outlets. To help orient people in the space, different color schemes were used on each floor.

For many years the building served as the office home of a software programmer named Scott Adams, who enjoyed drawing cartoons illustrating the foibles of the modern workplace. Now famous for his creations

Turn left at the purple baloon: Although standardization simplifies planning and reconfiguration, it also conduces anonymity.

Dilbert, Dogbert, and Ratbert, the cubicle-land vilified by Adams was none other than the San Ramon facility.

ARCHITECTURAL AND BUILDING QUALITY DESIGN STANDARDS

Corporate design standards do not stop at the inside walls of the building. Companies operating in multiple locations may have standards for building architecture and may even apply those standards to international projects. During DEC's high-growth years, building design standards were strictly enforced. According to a real estate project manager who developed a new facility for DEC, "We had to use a brick skin even in locations where marble was cheaper." Worldwide, Procter & Gamble (P&G) has three basic building types for local operations depending upon their use and the level of investment the company plans to make. This standardization helps P&G to coordinate a global portfolio of development projects with a very small in-house staff.

STANDARDIZATION OF MANAGEMENT POLICIES AND OPERATIONS

The management processes and practices by which space is acquired, allocated, managed, and eventually disposed of also are subject to standardized policies. Of course, having corporate policies in place is integral to every support function within any organization, and real estate is no exception. Standard office design and process standards may be an extension of human resource policies. Whatever its origin, it is critical that the company is clear about why the particular policy is in place and how it directly contributes to enabling competitive advantage.

Standardizing corporate real estate management processes and practices across the organization has several strategic objectives and some are similar to those for design standards. Along with closer control over costs, more uniform resource allocation across the company, and greater efficiency for routine decision making, standardized practices also provide better and more timely real estate information.

Standardized practices tend to be accompanied by more sophisticated information systems to track such things as facility costs, balance sheet effects, property maintenance, and lease expirations. Accurate, current information is essential to improved long-range planning.

The amount of discretion local operating managers have over facility operations, moves within the building envelope, and other minor decisions usually are based upon specified levels of expenditures. Companies in multiple locations or those that must manage many projects at a time often allow local control over minor expenditures. As the decisions at stake involve greater costs, risks, or strategic importance, they are made higher up in the company. The amount where the dividing line is drawn depends upon the company's overall profitability, its bias toward centralized or decentralized control, and its culture. Companies which centralize the costs of their real estate and then charge back a rate based upon a blending of costs across buildings to their business units tend to retain more centralized control than those whose business units are directly responsible for paying for their own facility-related expenditures.

Outsourcing day-to-day facility operations also leads to greater standardization of policies and operations. Major vendors for outsourced services, such as Johnson Controls, CB/Richard Ellis, and United Systems Integrators—to name a few—operate on a national basis and compete on their ability to lower costs and improve service through scale efficiencies and focus.

ADVANTAGES OF STANDARDIZATION

Using a standardization approach for some corporate real estate decisions provides several advantages. Standardizing routine decisions frees up management time to focus on more challenging and strategically significant issues. Thoughtfully applied, standardization can enable better control over the allocation of resources, create economies of scale in purchasing, simplify the management of repetitive projects, and reinforce the organization's culture through design uniformity across facilities. These controls can save time and cost and help to share learning across the organization— all factors enabling competitive advantage. The key is to remain aware of your company's competitive situation so you can recognize when changes to standards are needed. You also must be flexible enough to overrule the standards when they do not fit the requirements of particular situation.

BETTER CONTROL OVER
THE ALLOCATION OF RESOURCES

Standardized resource allocation procedures can help to reduce overt conflict between operating units. By standardizing design, one location doesn't look more favored than another. It is easier to enforce standardization across the company if real estate and facility costs are aggregated at the corporate level and then allocated to the various parts of the company based upon the amount and type of space they occupy.

Better controls can help build cost advantages. Controlling who makes decisions such as the leasing of field facilities can frequently lead to cost savings in the overall portfolio. For example, a local manager who is in charge of selecting office space for a branch location may not be very knowledgeable about real estate transactions. The manager may choose a location out of convenience, or because of personal ties to a local developer or broker, without fully exploring other options in the marketplace which might be less costly or more flexible. The manager may not fully understand the terms of the lease and lock the company into an inflexible deal. Many of the corporate real estate managers I interviewed complained that the branch managers believe they know a great deal about real estate since most have purchased a home, even though a business lease transaction is far more complex. An early warning system can be put into place when leases are tracked and managed centrally. This allows adequate time to develop alternatives which can strengthen the company's renegotiations with an existing landlord. Standardized real estate processes and centralized lease negotiations also relieve the local manager of the burden of monitoring real estate issues which can take attention away from the real mission of the company—to sell products and serve customers.

Such standard real estate activities can be serviced either by the corporate real estate staff, or by outsourcing to real estate brokers or property management professionals.

ECONOMIES OF SCALE IN PURCHASING

Design standards, particularly furniture specifications, provide economies-of-scale in purchasing by using greater leverage over suppliers. New England Telephone (now Bell Atlantic) was, in some years, the largest single purchaser of office furniture in New England. Prior to standardization, each office location throughout the telephone service area managed its own furniture selection and purchasing, and often bought from small local dealers with higher margins. By standardizing items and centralizing furniture purchasing in the late 1980's, the company was able to lower its annual cost of office furnishings from about $25 million to about $9 million while obtaining similar quantities—a cost reduction of 70%.

Uniform furniture specifications also help to reuse and readapt furnishings more easily when moves, particularly space consolidations that combine facilities, take place.

SIMPLIFY MANAGEMENT OF LARGE-SCALE AND REPETITIVE PROJECTS

Standardization helps capture learning across the portfolio, saving time and expense planning for large single projects or a number of similar subsequent projects.

Design standards form the basic building block of any headquarters planning project because they help to determine the optimal module upon which the construction of the building is based. Simplifying the relative sizes of closed offices to conform with the major structural elements of the building such as window spacing and ceiling and floor service access grids facilitates not only interior construction but also later alterations. When a great deal of standardization is used, the entire design and construction process can be simplified and projects completed at a faster pace. Cisco Systems, discussed in Chapter Seven, is able to add buildings in the Silicon Valley at a very fast pace because many design elements, both interior and exterior, are standardized.

As the space allocation and development process becomes more standardized, decisions can be made at lower levels in the organization. Standards help field operations keep focused on the important tasks of selling products and serving customers because they do not have to start from scratch on every new project.

For companies which must construct a lot of facilities at the same time, or get facilities on line very quickly, standardization reduces the complexity of decision making. Design standards reduce the number of decisions which have to be made every time a new project is built. A high degree of standardization in its field operations allows G-Tech Corporation to have a lottery system up and running only eight weeks after the state awards the contract. As Paul Donnelly of G-Tech explained, "My job is to crash through a very standardized program for 15 to 20 contracts a year and in each instance we have all the engineering done up front. All the architecture done up front, we have preordered almost every piece of equipment you can preorder and it is all sitting in a warehouse very close to where we want to be. The day we get the award, the contractor has to begin to build. . . . Whether or not we make money on that five- or seven-year lottery contract is partially reflected in how good we are at doing what we do."[6]

STANDARDS REINFORCE THE CULTURE ACROSS THE ORGANIZATION

Some senior managers insist that company facilities look similar no matter where they are located. By providing the same type of working environment in all the company's locations, consistent messages are sent to the employees working there, helping to reinforce a common culture and set of values across the company. In retailing, a common appearance promotes trust and brand loyalty in customers. In an office setting, a common visual identity is more meaningful to employees who move from facility to facility than to customers and suppliers in the local area who go to only one location. Managers must consider which approach conveys greater advantages—uniformity across locations or customization to fit local needs and tastes.

DISADVANTAGES OF A STANDARDIZED STRATEGY

Although the organizational pressures to standardize decision making are great, standards can become dysfunctional over time if they no longer serve the strategic or organizational needs of the company. In today's rapidly changing competitive environments, a highly standardized decision-making process may overlook vital opportunities to improve the effectiveness of the company's operations.

STANDARDS INHIBIT ADAPTATION TO
CHANGING REQUIREMENTS

Standards set at one point in the company's history may make functional sense at that time but not serve the company under new competitive conditions. As management theorist Karl Weick once observed, adaptation precludes adaptability.[7] Once we adapt, we find it difficult to subsequently change again. Design standards freeze an organization in space and time because they represent the structure and hierarchy that existed in the organization during the period the standards were developed. When a building or its interiors are based upon these standards, it may be difficult to change the facility later. As the competitive environment changes, a company also may need to change its operating methods, its structure, even its culture. If a facility still looks functional, the company may be reluctant to spend time and money to change it, even if the work systems or the behaviors it was designed to support need modification.

For example, at Pacific Telesis's operating headquarters—which earlier served as our example of standardization on a grand scale—many problems were encountered as the demographics of their organization changed. The original building and interior design called for only 5% closed offices because most of the employees there were either clerical or low- or middle-level managers who qualified for only open cubicles with fabric partitions. Over time, as technology enabled the elimination of a lot of lower-level information processing jobs and new competition in the telecommunications industry demanded more experienced senior managers with industry expertise, the percentage of senior managers in San Ramon rose to over 10%. The facility ran out of places to build closed offices since the design of the interior was predicated upon lots of open window space with large floor plates. Also, the company was reluctant to change the managerial levels that qualified for closed offices because that would require moving some managers out of their already occupied closed offices into the open plan. This pressure led them to convert conference rooms to private offices even though the general trend is to try to increase the amount of group work space. Pacific Telesis standards also forced the company to build interior offices, breaking up the broad visual expanse from window to window that the original building design intended.

The large floor plates of the building also had other unintended consequences limiting later flexibility. Large floors, which are useful for housing large populations of people doing the same kind of work, are not as suitable for smaller work groups that rapidly change in size. As the company both downsized and reorganized to meet increased competition in the telecommunications industry, "holes" were left all over the floors which made the overall space per employee rise. This space was hard to recapture because an entire floor would have to be replanned to move all the holes together in one place.

Telesis also ran into problems among workers at the same level, as the work to be performed changed from routine information processes tasks to computer programming and other creative work. The open-plan office that was designed for easy supervision of clerical employees was too distracting to the computer programmers who needed to be shielded from distractions. A compromise was eventually reached by having Knoll custom-manufacture special fabric panel doors to hang on the openings of the programmers' workstations. This solution limited visual interruptions, but did little to ameliorate sound disturbance, which easily travels over and through the 60" high doors.

A great reliance on furniture standards makes it hard to alter and change furnishings, even when a better product becomes available. Companies are especially loath to change their furnishing standards when the existing inventory has not been fully depreciated. New England Telephone's real estate managers had difficult time convincing senior management that a different open office furnishings provided a much better solution to the new headquarters' interior layout requirements because the company had already made a substantial investment in another open office system. Although the St. Paul Companies was able to refurbish and reuse some of its existing inventory of open systems furniture when it doubled the size of its headquarters, reuse of the existing system greatly limited the design alternatives that could be considered. DEC clung to its 10' x 10' office standard even after numerous studies showed it to be an inefficient dimension, because senior management thought the 10' x 10' office was an important tradition to be upheld. It was only after the company had to make severe cuts in operating costs that the standard was changed to more space-efficient dimensions.

FOLLOWING THE PROCESS BECOMES MORE IMPORTANT THAN ACHIEVING THE BEST OUTCOME

When the approach to allocating facilities is highly formalized, it may start to function as part of the organization's management control system. Some companies pose numerous obstacles for managers to overcome whenever they need to have more space for people or new projects—hurdles which require persistence and politics to overcome. During the late 1980's at Digital, property and plant decisions were made separately from business planning decisions. A complicated procedure for justifying the allocation of new space meant that the real estate approval process became the first place in the organization which could say no to a new idea. Ideas were justified less on the merits of the product in the marketplace than on whether the proposing manager's operating plan was sensible. The company acknowledged that space was used as the control mechanism over uncontrolled expansion by the business units. DEC is not the only high-technology company I have seen with this approach to controlling business unit expansion. At another company coping with fast, somewhat out-of-control business growth, the real estate approval process was deliberately used to slow down growth. As one manager explained, "It's easier to control space than head count."

Although controlling space does have the side effect of controlling growth, it is a backward approach to confronting real decisions. Senior managers who have difficulty saying no to new ideas or to business expansion can simply say, "Sorry, we don't have any room for it," to avoid being held directly responsible for killing a potentially profitable idea. Some companies I have observed do not want to stifle innovation, so they use bureaucratic hurdles instead, in a Darwinian survival-of-the-fittest mentality. They assume the best ideas will have the most well-thought-out facility plans. The problem is that the managers who work the system best may be those who succeed in getting facilities allocated—not necessarily those with the best new product idea. Senior managers who avoid having to pass judgment on the business merits of a proposal by blaming the supply of corporate real estate should instead question whether the space is needed in the first place, or whether alternative office approaches can be used to reduce, eliminate, or change the design of space needed for new or experimental operations.

STANDARDS ARE SYMBOLS, TOO

Since standards allocate space and amenities as well as decision-making power, they are emblematic of the values of the company. The manager who gets the resource of space is a highly visible reminder of who has power in the organization; this is the person the company is betting its future on. Once they have it, managers are loath to give up space. To maintain existing power relationships organizations may cling to outmoded standards. To use the elements of the physical setting that are standardized to their utmost utility, the symbolic content of those standards should be examined on a regular basis and updated according to the value-based processes described in the next chapter.

ARE STANDARDS REALLY NEEDED?

Standards assume everyone everywhere works in more or less the same way in all parts of the company; they also infer that all real estate markets are pretty similar. Frequently there is a great deal of variance in both company operations and in the real estate markets where they are located.

In order to simplify the management of the real estate portfolio, as well as to accommodate high rates of churn, some companies use a universal approach to office design by minimizing the differences between workstations and other spaces. However, this approach overlooks the different needs of various groups within the company. No one knows better what they physically need to do their job than the person who does that job. Design standards tend to homogenize a lot of job categories. Process standards leave little flexibility in what local managers can do with their facilities. At one financial services company, there was an acute need for a day-care facility at its remote suburban site, since there were no local providers in the area; however, the company had a policy of not providing on-site day care. The suburban site kept experiencing high turnover, in part due to a lack of day-care options in its location.

Andersen Worldwide, which until 1998 provided administrative support to both the consulting and public accounting parts of the company, has no specific design standards for branch offices. The Andersen philosophy is that each office knows its requirements best, and that these requirements vary geographically depending upon the client base, the demographics of the office, and the local real estate markets. When a location needs new space, the project starts out with a visioning session with the office's senior management. During the early stages there is also a programming effort using observation studies of office occupancy patterns and surveys of preferences. The information gathered then is used to evaluate potential properties. Although the use of alternative office approaches is encouraged, there is no strict policy enforcing its use. The company also keeps a database of best practices collected from its offices.[8] Even with this flexibility, Andersen has been a leader in experimenting with and implementing alternative office approaches. In Andersen Consulting's first U.S. office of the future located in the Boston area, most of the employees use hotelling, while a full-time office concierge provides further customization of services geared to local needs.[9]

Real estate markets also can vary greatly by location. Even in a healthy economy, some locations are booming and require overnight decision making simply to acquire any property, while other locations have an oversupply and offer significant savings from careful shopping around. Standardization often can slow the decision-making process, making it harder to react quickly. It may make the process so rigid that true market opportunities are overlooked. To get better intelligence on local markets, some companies enhance their standardized corporate real estate acquisition and disposal processes by entering into strategic alliances with national real estate brokerage firms that have strong presence in key local markets.

USING STANDARDIZATION TO GAIN COMPETITIVE ADVANTAGE

How can some of the benefits of standardization be achieved while retaining flexibility for future change and the ability to express values?

To begin, you must understand how standardization supports your competitive strategy. Questions to be considered when approaching real estate decisions using a standardization approach include: Are we likely to save money or time by standardizing? At what levels do we control other expenditures in the organization? How much direct responsibility do individual business units or products have for their real estate expenditures? Will we actually move furniture from location to location over time? Are there strong regional preferences or tastes across the company? Do lower real estate costs in some parts of the country allow for more generous space allocations than in high-cost areas? Do we have the staff available to administer and monitor the standards? Do the savings from standardization justify their costs?

Some companies are trying to combine incrementalism and standardization through the development of modular designs which can be adapted later to different functions. For example, for space to easily adapt to future office technologies, some companies are willing to invest additional money during construction to include more comprehensive building systems such as raised floors.

One way to gain the benefits of standardization without its rigidity is to avoid setting physical design or operations standards, and instead set performance standards. Specifications for property, building design, interior design, and furnishings set out cost and functional guidelines, rather than a menu of specific choices. Benchmarking costs and performance across the organization can allow for more local customization within a basic set of requirements.

The essential factor influencing the extent standardization is used in corporate real estate decision making is centralization versus decentralization across the entire organization. Keep in mind that many companies fluctuate between centralization and decentralization as competitive conditions, and internal politics, change. Standardization can be an approach to attain control for control's sake, or merely a way to more easily manage corporate real estate or facilities. It should be used when it leads to true competitive advantages: greater cost efficiencies, faster reaction time, and the design of a work setting that both enhances work processes and expresses the corporation's core values. We examine how values and symbols are incorporated into real estate decision making in the following chapter.

CHAPTER SIX

VALUE-BASED STRATEGY

A value-based strategy deliberately expresses the values and strategic direction of the company in the real estate decision-making process. It uses Place as an enabler of competitive strategy. Both the functional and the symbolic roles of the workplace are addressed.

When a value-based strategy is followed, people not only speak of the building's function but also highlight its meaning to the organization. These quotes illustrate how the power of Place is used to symbolize strategic intent:

> The building must look like an advancement for us and send the message that the company will be around for a long time. It should be seen as open and honest but with some mystery.
>
> CEO, midsize company[1]

> Our business was becoming more competitive after deregulation and we wanted to send a message to our employees that we were no longer part of the telephone company culture, but needed to be more competitive, customer oriented, and sophisticated.
>
> Facility Manager, regional telecom company[2]

> The new site is a catalyst for a reexamination of the company which we know we need to make.
>
> COO, biomedical products company[3]

> The buildings are a visual statement of who we are. When you walk through here, you intuitively grasp 60% of our culture.
>
> Chairman and CEO, mutual fund management company[4]

A value-based approach recognizes that people construct social meaning out of their physical environment. Whether we plan for a space to convey a certain impression or not, our human inclination is to infer symbolism, to search for meaning in our environment.[5] A value-based strategy actively celebrates this innate human behavior. It seeks to create work environments which reinforce those behaviors most likely to help the company build and maintain competitive advantage. A value-based strategy embraces what *Place* means to the organization and uses that *Place* to support its goals. The workplace embodies the culture. It is a tool for implementing the strategic mindset because it sets a coherent and consistent direction when costly spatial resources are allocated. It establishes a basis for prioritizing expenditures when there is uncertainty over specific future requirements.

In this chapter, we define value-based strategy and examine how it is applied in organizations. In Part Three, we further suggest ways to fit the design and management of the workplace to the work processes, demographics, and culture of a company.

As discussed in the previous chapter on standardization, the design of the workplace often reflects people's position in the organization's structure and hierarchy. The office is seen as a symbol of the organization because we deliberately design it according to our systems of work, and we spend money on those things the organization values most highly. Whether we deliberately intend to symbolize our organizations or whether what we portray is inadvertently expressed, the outcome is still the same. Our understanding of our organization, and our importance to it, is largely demonstrated by the resources we control and is signified by the space we occupy.

Real estate and facilities—who gets what—can be the most emotional battleground in a company. Why is this so? Real estate is power made visible. It is physical and tangible. The occupancy of high-status real estate—the quality and amount we possess or are assigned—says to the world that we are important. The ability to allocate high status real estate to others gives us power over them. The value-based approach is proactive about using the inherent power of the physical setting to symbolize values and influence behavior. It embraces and utilizes the setting's communicative powers to the organization's advantage.

Value-based corporate real estate and facility management decision making can be applied to all sorts of projects, with varying scopes and budgets. A value-based strategy can be used to make design decisions about both the outside and the inside of buildings. It also can be applied to management processes from the initial design stage and through the ongoing management of Place.

Figure 6–1 shows the value-based decision-making process found under conditions of moderate strategic uncertainty.

IDENTIFYING THE VALUE-BASED APPROACH

You can detect a value-based approach in action when organization members speak about what their work environment means to the organization

Figure 6–1
Model Under Conditions of Moderate Strategic Uncertainty

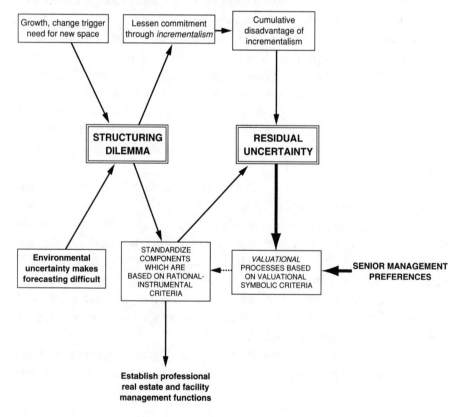

in noneconomic terms. During its planning and development, time and expense are spent thinking about the organization's identity and mission, its history and its future direction. The ways in which the workplace symbolizes the company's values and corporate culture are an active topic of discussion. The value-based approach considers the company's relationship with its customers, employees, and the community. Aesthetics—the visual appeal of the place—is considered important. But the aesthetic quality represents the occupants' taste, not just some outside design authority or the latest fashion.

Value-based decision making can be used in conjunction with other strategic approaches, or applied only to certain aspects of a project. For example, a project's goals may be conceived using value-based decision-making criteria, and then those guidelines can be used to develop standards for the programming and design of workstations.

The level of direct employee participation in value-based real estate and facility management decisions can vary. Some companies use a very open process to solicit employee opinions and involvement, others harbor decision making within the confines of senior management. We will look at examples of both approaches.

HOW A VALUE-BASED APPROACH HELPS MANAGE MODERATE STRATEGIC UNCERTAINTY

Strategic uncertainty is moderate when a company is well-established in its marketplace, but still has difficulty foreseeing future competitive conditions. The sources of this uncertainty may be fast product life cycles, fickle customers, aggressive competitors, or changing technology, to name just some causes. The company also may be large enough, in terms of sales or numbers of employees working in offices or factories, to benefit from larger-scale real estate commitments. It may have a healthy base of customers and some sustainable competitive advantages such as superior technology, advanced work systems, or an especially effective corporate culture. These attributes give senior management the confidence to undertake larger projects and to spend more time on planning for the future.

Companies in moderately uncertain competitive environments have access to financial resources to allow a more substantial commitment to real estate, but still have difficulty establishing specific long-term space and facility design requirements. Yet incrementalism no longer works as the strategy of choice. Firms want to claim the advantages that longer-term and larger-scale commitments entail: more colocation of employees in one place; the opportunity to design more suitable, customized facilities; and lower overall real estate and facility costs through leverage and scale.

The model in Figure 6–1 illustrates how the use of value-based criteria typically is incorporated into the real estate decision-making process.

WHEN DOES VALUE-BASED DECISION MAKING PREDOMINATE?

Once a company establishes more confidence about its future success and reaches a size where incremental decision making has more disadvantages than advantages, value-based decision making gets more emphasis. This can coincide with certain thresholds of size, such as $500 million sales or the occupancy of 500,000 or more square feet of space.[6] It also can be precipitated by a crisis such as the lack of nearby expansion space, or when the high cumulative costs of incrementalism become obvious to senior management.

At one high-growth company, the corporate real estate executive wryly noted, "Once you occupy more than a half-million square feet, you're in the real estate business whether you like it or not." The issues size raises at this point are more a matter of long-term strategy than short-term tactics. Questions which require answers include:

- In what location or locations do we want to grow our business?
- Do we want to custom design our own facility?
- Do we want to lease or own our major properties?
- What kinds of workplace amenities do we want to provide employees?
- How can we best support work processes in the design of the facility?
- Will the organization's structure and work systems remain stable?
- How can we plan for, and cope with, changing requirements?
- What is our need for flexibility in the future?
- How will we allocate space to the businesses?
- How will we charge for the use of facilities by the various businesses?
- How and who will select the layout, furnishings, and decoration of the space?
- And eventually, what design features, colors, and materials are preferred?

The manner by which these decisions are made, as well as the substance of the decisions, all communicate values and priorities. Intended or not, the choices indicate where the power resides in the organization and define what sorts of behaviors are appropriate. A new facility offers the opportunity to proactively shape the organization's culture and to direct a message to customers and competitors outside of the company.

External forces may all press for a clear statement of corporate values when a major real estate and facility commitment is made. In particular, a company embarking on its first major real estate project attracts lots of attention from all its stakeholders—employees, customers, the capital markets, and the local community. The project may represent the company's first major commitment of capital that requires a leap of faith beyond the immediate business forecast. There may be pressure upon senior management to clearly articulate reasons for the project and the longer-term strategic benefits to the company. At this point, senior management is willing to pay closer attention to the process and sees the project as an opportunity to influence the development of the organization's culture and identity.

Let's look at some ways a value-based approach to setting corporate real estate strategy can be applied to both design outcomes and everyday facility management processes.

HOW VALUES ARE EXPRESSED THROUGH DESIGN

EXTERIOR ARCHITECTURE

Using the image of a building to express meaning and represent the owner's aspirations is a timeless fundamental role of architecture.[7] Exterior architecture has the greatest opportunity to be value-based when a company designs and builds its own facility.[8] The appearance of the building is used to send a very public message about a company.[9] Some companies use their buildings as literal billboards to increase consumer awareness of their existence. When some cities outlawed signage at the top of buildings, as Boston did in 1973, the design of the building's profile and especially its top, received more emphasis and identity. The Transamerica Pyramid in San Francisco, the slope of the Citicorp Center in New York

City, the glass sliver of Boston's John Hancock Tower in tony Back Bay are a few notable examples. It's not a new idea. The much beloved Chrysler Building's evocation of a radiator grille at the top of its midtown New York City marvel is one early example.

A building may be deliberately designed or selected to convey a certain image. The CEO of G-Tech wanted the building to be the physical embodiment of the organization's culture. The company's emphasis on international markets is symbolized at its entrance with a long promenade lined with flags of every country where G-Tech has a presence. Every time G-Tech added a country to its client roster, it celebrated with a flag-raising ceremony for all the headquarters employees. Pacific Bell was concerned that its mammoth operating headquarters in San Ramon, California, be a

Celebrating globalism: The entrance to G-Tech's corporate headquarters is lined with flags from every country G-Tech serves. Photo courtesy of G-Tech.

good visual neighbor to the surrounding community. Its low profile echoes the surrounding rolling hills, and its modern lines convey the image of a company poised for the next century. Pacific Bell Directory chose to lease space in a renovated historic structure in part to show its support for the revival of the south of Market neighborhood in San Francisco.

A building's design also may come to embody unintended meanings. Architect Michael Graves decorated Disney's corporate headquarters with large iconic figures of Disney characters. While this also could be interpreted as a homage to the company's heritage, the overtly stylistic building is seen by some as embodying the company's internally competitive, heavy-handed corporate culture. Accordingly, employees have been known to refer to the building as the "Mouseoleum."[10]

Despite their unique exteriors, the interior workplace planning within most of these edifices is standard high-rise modular planning. In contrast, some companies occupy buildings that are plain Janes on the outside, but special on the inside. Here, the emphasis on design is aimed at employees, not outsiders.

INTERIOR AND WORKSTATION DESIGN

Interior design is the most common application of value-based decision-making processes. Symbols regarding hierarchy are a frequent target. Companies try to emphasize equality and collaboration across management levels by reducing the obvious differences between the amount and quality of space assigned to employees of different rank within the company.

Access to natural light is one common use of symbolism. Rather than placing closed wall offices housing senior level managers along the window wall, blocking access to natural light to those persons working in the interior of the building, offices are placed near the core, and the widow area is exposed to the open office areas. To compensate, interior offices are usually given glass walls facing the exterior. For instance, Cisco Systems has no enclosed window space in any of its corporate developed buildings. Even the CEO of the company sits in the same-size interior office as all the other managers. Cisco employees are very proud of this fact, and cite it as an example of the open, egalitarian culture of this fast-growth company. Intel, which commands more than 75% of the microprocessor market, also uses open offices as a symbol of its lean, aggressive, engineering-oriented culture. Senior management perks are rare at Intel. Gordon Moore and Andy

Grove, the moving forces behind the success of Intel, always worked in open plan cubicles the same as other Intel employees.[11]

Companies which are loath to give up window offices try to compromise by using glass walls instead of solid ones, to allow some light and visual access to filter through. Others try to give common areas such as conference rooms and lunchrooms the best exterior views.

Other ways of reducing symbols of hierarchy in the workplace include giving everyone, or nearly everyone, the same-size workstation or office; eliminating executive perks such as reserved parking or private dining; and providing amenities, such as health clubs, that are available to everyone in the company.

An emphasis on comfortable and attractive design and the use of decorative amenities such as art and plants have different meanings at different companies. G-Tech's senior management believed that high-quality interior design conveyed a sense of how highly the company valued its employees. Pacific Bell Directory deliberately sought a much better quality design in its new corporate headquarters to remind its employees that they were now competing with sophisticated marketing companies and they must respond with new and more aggressive strategies. Some companies pride themselves on their art collections and see them as a way of enlivening the workplace and sending the message that the employees are important.[12]

However at other companies, a Spartan approach to decor is sometimes used to emphasize a no-nonsense culture. As discussed in the chapter on incrementalism, this is especially common at high-tech companies in their start-up phase. Companies with high levels of employee ownership also tend to prefer modest offices to demonstrate that profits are either invested back into the company or distributed to the employee-owners.

It is often difficult to identify when a value-based approach is used for workstation design because of the way systems furniture encourages workstation standardization, as discussed in Chapter Five. Corporate values can be expressed in the amount of customization and personalization allowed work groups and individuals. Companies that place a high premium on individualism may afford office workers or their local managers more personal discretion on the layout and furnishings of their workspace. However, uniformity across all workstations also can be used to express values as noted earlier. Again, it is not the design outcome per se but the way the design was developed that signals a value-based approach. Values often are expressed more through the way decisions are made and the things that are done, not just by the appearance of the workplace.

VALUE-BASED DECISION-MAKING PROCESSES IN ACTION

Companies approach value-based decision making in many different ways. The way they make real estate decisions also expresses their corporate values. These approaches vary by the amount of direct employee participation in searching for alternatives and testing ideas, the level of CEO and other senior leadership involvement, and whether they are more concerned with the physical aspects of the workplace or in the daily management of that space.

Some companies use a consistent process every time a project is undertaken. Others only undertake a highly value-based process when a major move, such as a corporate headquarters is underway. Many senior executives today recognize that the work environment is a critical component of their company's competitive strategy. However, they may chose very different ways of managing its planning and design. Some prefer to delegate most decisions to their corporate real estate and facility management professionals, others prefer a very close, hands-on approach to design decisions. We explore the different ways these managerial preferences manifest themselves and their impact on corporate real estate strategy in Chapter Eleven. Here we will discuss the various ways senior management gets involved in value-based decision-making processes.

There are several ways that companies implement a value-based decision-making process.

CLOSELY HELD BY A SMALL TEAM

Some senior managers are very interested in the design and management of the workplace. They like to have a high degree of involvement in not only the financial decisions but also the aesthetic design of the space and in the selection and delivery of employee amenities. These executives see a major real estate project as an opportunity to personally shape their company's culture and to make a direct connection with their employees. The discussion of the company's values and future direction, and how they are to be represented by the facilities, is closely held by a small team of senior managers, with varying levels of participation by the corporate real estate staff and by outside design consultants.

At G-Tech, Guy Snowden the company's founder and then CEO was closely involved in every major design and facility management decision regarding the company's World Technology Center. He was concerned not only with increasing communication between the manufacturing and the engineering functions but also with how the facility represented G-Tech to outsiders.

For the planning of the revitalized and expanded corporate headquarters of the St. Paul Companies in downtown St. Paul, it was the architect, Bill Pederson, a St. Paul native son, who championed a value-based approach. Along with a small team of corporate real estate representatives and an external consultant, recommendations were formed and then presented to senior management for approval. Although the decision-making process was closely held within the team, they did use a variety of methods, including surveys, interviews, and observations, to learn more about the company's facilities needs and work processes.

BROADEN EMPLOYEE PARTICIPATION

Other companies seek employee preferences before making value-based decisions. A variety of methods adapted from the social sciences can be used to gain broad employee participation in the planning of a new workplace.[13] Surveys, interviews, and observation can all be used to collect data from employees. These information gathering efforts can be formalized, perhaps using outside consultants to aid in data collection and analysis; or more informal approaches can be used, such as focus or discussion groups led by corporate real estate managers. Companies considering new workstation designs often set up a prototype in the existing facility and test the design on employees. Others set up alternative designs and let the employees voice their preferences.

Employee participation in workplace design decisions can backfire if employees do not receive feedback on what decisions were made and why. This can result in even lower morale and greater resistance to the new workplace than if the employees were not involved in the planning in the first place. When people are asked their opinion, they expect to be heard. If

We had a hand in it: Employees who participated in planning Pacific Bell Directory's new offices placed their handprints in plaster, painted it gold, and hung it in the lobby.

their ideas are not used, they need to be told why. Failure to provide this feedback, either through avoidance or oversight, is the biggest reason why many of the instances of employee participation in the design process eventually failed to live up to expectations.

Companies can greatly benefit from using the facility planning process as a way of learning about and improving the work process within the organization. We explore this further in Chapter 10.

LISTENING AND LEARNING FROM EXPERIENCE

Another approach to planning that can be used in concert with the approaches just described is to study the company's existing spaces and operations with the goal of retaining what works and making improvements where needed.

Early in the planning of its new, built-to-suit headquarters building, the Monitor Company, a strategic consulting firm based in Cambridge, Massachusetts, used its existing offices as a laboratory for different workplace designs that were under consideration. Monitor's employees, many of whom are graduates of the country's top colleges and business schools, are used to having their opinions heard; they also have individually idio-syncratic work styles. To develop a space that would be both functional and represent the firm's values, Monitor's facility planning team designed a programming process that fit with the firm's culture and approached the design of the new space in the same manner as a consulting engagement. They first conducted a broad employee survey of current functional and physical needs, and further fleshed this information out with a series of cross-organizational face-to-face interviews. This gave the team a view of current needs. Since Monitor consultants are used to thinking in terms of cases and respect hard data, the second phase of inquiry used a visual pref-erence survey method to help define the interior design scheme. Showing people photographs of a wide range of office designs, they asked them to comment on what best represented their vision of Monitor, not necessarily what they would personally prefer. To advance thinking about future facil-ity needs, the senior management team articulated a future vision of the company, especially how clients would be served and projects would be managed. These efforts yielded clear design alternatives that were then pre-sented to the CEO and board of directors who made the final decisions and communicated these decisions back to the employees.

The St. Paul Companies constructed its corporate headquarters in two phases, first new construction and then renovation of their existing facility. After the first phase was evaluated using surveys, interviews, and observa-tions, improvements to the design were made in the second phase. Later, improvements based upon continual learning also were made to the first phase as churn occurred.

ADVANTAGES OF A VALUE-BASED STRATEGY

A value-based approach to making corporate real estate decisions can help a company position itself for future success. It can promote communica-tion between line employees and senior management—crystallizing a vision of the company shared throughout the organization. It uses the power of symbols to represent the organization's goals and values in ways that are most meaningful to the employees. Most important, it can help the organization adapt to changing competitive conditions by promoting experimentation and a questioning of the status quo.

ENCOURAGES IMPORTANT DIALOGUE
ABOUT THE COMPANY'S FUTURE

The process of making decisions about the design and management of the workplace encourages dialogue about the organization itself. The goal of designing a workplace which best fits the current and future needs of the company initiates dialogue about those needs—critical issues which often get lost in the day-to-day operating routine. Since much of what we understand about the world around us is developed through discussions with others about what we are seeing, listening to other people's points of view help us to see the world differently, and perhaps better. Increased communication reduces equivocality and therefore helps the organization in its effort to interpret and understand its environment. The reality of a long-term commitment forces the company to make projections about the future. Organizations trying to balance uncertainty about future competitive conditions with the need for long-term commitments to location, facilities, and other capital investments can benefit greatly from an active discussion. This is especially true for those companies which in the past have thrived on dealing with short time horizons and rapidly changing conditions, but now may not have the internal processes in place to facilitate longer-term decision making. Yet such a discussion is critical if the company is going to evolve and mature.

HARNESSES THE POWER OF SYMBOLS

The appearance of a place, its use of space and decoration, even its temperature and smell, all convey meanings which tend to have broad agreement within a particular cultural context. The Taj Mahal is perceived differently and makes a different statement about its occupants than a summer cottage on the Maine coast. Indeed, the history of architecture is the history of symbolic construction.

The design of the workplace is a tangible reminder of the values of the organization. By giving the best space and the most amenities to particular individuals or groups, the organization sends out a message about what—and who—is most important. Sun Microsystems gave up its first headquarters building when the facility was needed by a product engineering group, sending the message that product development was more critical to the company's success than a nice building for senior management. The most attractive space in the new Molecular Devices building was given to the laboratory scientists. Digital housed new product development in its coveted and highly symbolic Mill space; most administrative support functions (including the facility department) were located in less prestigious leased space nearby. Cisco Systems gives its rank and file engineering and administrative employees, instead of executives, the best access to natural light.

When a major change is needed, sometimes an entire project is used as a symbol. Northern Telecom (now known as Nortel Networks) used its massive renovation of an old factory building in Brampton, Ontario, into a new corporate headquarters facility to symbolize the major strategic and cultural changes Nortel was experiencing. Once the research and development arm of the Canadian telephone system, Nortel was now a global competitor in the fast changing and turbulent telecommunications equipment industry. New competitors included not only other telephone equipment providers, but computer hardware and software companies as well. Nortel needed to respond with a culture and workforce that could produce innovative products rapidly and cost effectively.

Nortel had previously leased space in three office towers in the Toronto vicinity, but was finding that the design and location of these buildings could not accommodate the company's fast growth and made it difficult to reorganize the company's 3,000 local employees into teams. The challenge was to find a space that the company could occupy quickly and within tight budget limitations. They only had to look in their own corporate backyard—to an outmoded factory outside the city.

The old Brampton factory held meaning for the company. It was the site where some of Nortel's most innovative products had been developed over the years. The facility is over 500,000 square feet on one floor. Using city planning methods as a metaphor for dividing up, designing, and labeling the space into neighborhoods, the company set out to deliberately reflect the company's changing culture, work processes, and products. Employees choose the configuration of their workspace from a menu and teams can custom design their group and individual spaces. The office also supports a variety of alternative work settings such as telecommuting and hotelling. Broad avenues on two axes are punctuated by cafes and shared meeting areas, as well as support facilities, which are distributed throughout the space. Nineteen skylights bring in the sun through the 30-foot-high sky blue ceiling.

Occupied less than a year from the start of construction, the Nortel Brampton Centre project won the 1997 Business Week/Architectural Record award for best corporate facility. This award program to recognize excellence in business facility design was first established in 1997.[14]

By using symbols in the workplace to communicate values and meaning to the organization, we are constantly reminding its occupants of those values. Internalizing a company's mission and values is especially important when the nature of the work performed in the organization cannot be defined in advance within strict operating guidelines. In many knowledge- and service-based businesses, front line employees must exercise a great deal of individual discretion in their day-to-day work.[15] By sending strong reminders about what is most important to the organization, Place helps set the context by which the right decision can be made.

PROACTIVELY USES DESIGN TO SHAPE BEHAVIOR

More overtly, the design of a workplace can unobtrusively control behavior directly through the way it is designed and managed.[16] This does not have to be as reminiscent of Big Brother as it sounds. Factories long have been designed to maximize the productivity of human labor as well as investment capital. Office design should be based on information flow and the level of interaction required to encourage creativity and new ideas. It also should provide enough quiet and privacy to attend to the tasks at hand. *The process of determining what kind of behavior is most desirable in the workplace is just as important as the final design outcome.*

A balanced approach is required. At Hewlett Packard Company (HP), open offices long have been an essential element of the corporate culture. Yet despite their employees' familiarity with working in an open office environment, quiet places also are needed sometimes. A major challenge at HP, therefore, has been to provide enough conference rooms and quiet spaces so people can have quiet and privacy when it is needed. At Sun Microsystems, the problem is a mirror image. Engineers must be coaxed out of their private offices into places where they are more likely to interact with each other. Some have to leave their offices to run the code they have written on special servers. Others are lured out by special coffee and food areas. Bump spaces—places where interaction naturally occurs such as corridors, stairways, and common equipment areas—are equipped with easy seating and drawing surfaces.

ENABLES ADAPTABILITY TO COMPETITIVE CHANGE

Because value-based decision making necessitates the discussion of long-term strategy, it encourages companies to constantly keep abreast of the competitive realities of their markets. A value-based approach assumes that change is constant and resists setting policies that rigidly force the organization into only one way of doing things. Since the meaning of the workplace is interpreted and socially constructed by the members of the organization, rather than regimented by externally imposed design standards, the organization may more readily reinterpret the meaning of its setting to fit with new interpretations of the environment. These changes in perception may help the organization to adapt to changes in environmental circumstances more rapidly. For example, early occupants of DEC's Mill related the company's reuse of an old industrial mill to the company's no-nonsense New England roots. Later, the Mill became a symbol of how high technology could exist harmoniously with older infrastructure. When the company needed to promote a radical overhaul of its corporate culture to survive in the dramatically transformed computer hardware industry, the tradition-bound Mill was abandoned in favor of lower cost, modern buildings.[17]

Research has shown that companies operating in moderately certain environments have an easier time adapting to change than companies in highly uncertain environments or very certain environments.[18] Moderate uncertainty inspires both confidence and caution. Discussions of values and the use of symbols help to manage this uncertainty. Too much uncertainty does not allow the organization enough basis to make long-term commitments and real estate decisions are made in a reactive manner. A high degree of certainty encourages standardization and routine. When an organization cannot clearly predict its future needs, but is able to make longer-term commitments, it must establish its image and values so that there is some basis for decision making. These value-based processes aid planning because they extend the vision of the organization beyond what is immediately known. They promote discussion about the direction of the company, provide consistency, and help the company adapt to changing competitive conditions.

Despite the enormous potential strategic benefits to a company, too much use of a value-based approach can be perilous. If the decision makers are out of touch with reality, if the decision-making process is too

Embrace, do not fear, what is new: The ability of high technology to harmonize with older infrastructure was symbolized at DEC by its lobby design and by modern cabling attached to the century-old brick wall.

distracting and demands too much management focus and attention, or if the resulting decisions are so inflexible the company doesn't respond to changing circumstances, value-based processes will fail to enable competitive advantages through Place.

DISADVANTAGES OF A
VALUE-BASED APPROACH
WRONG PEOPLE/WRONG VALUES

Value-based decisions are only as good as the people who make and carry them out. If the person or group making the facility decisions is not in touch with the needs of the organization, resources will be wasted at best, and the organization directed toward decline at the worst.

Like the strategic mindset it serves, value-based decision making can only thrive if there is a clear strategic direction set by senior management. Value-based decision making may require senior management to articulate a direction for the company that may not be well-founded by competitive realities or well-supported by the organization. Strategy also may be set defacto by the real estate decisions that are made. For example, a company may lock itself into a location with limited labor resources because the site selection decision was made for real estate, rather than strategic, reasons.

Engaging employee participation in planning and design minimizes the risk that only one point of view will be represented in the final design outcome. If there is not broad participation, much is left to luck that the people making the decisions will do the right thing. One company I studied set out to incorporate value-based decisions into the design of its new headquarters. The company even developed an elaborate process of involving employees in setting out the requirements for the interior design and workstations. But the senior management team that made the final decisions chose to follow some recommendations and rejected a lot of them. Then they did not report back to the employees why some ideas were used and others weren't. Elaborate designs were concocted for the senior management offices, using a lot of very high-end designer fabrics which were difficult to maintain and replace. Although glass walls and an open plan were used in all other areas, the executives' offices were set apart on a separate floor with an imposing reception area and closed, wood-paneled walls everywhere. In the end, the employees were openly disgruntled with what appeared to outsiders to be a very attractively designed workplace.

On occasion, a large building project will be the final major act of an outgoing CEO. This situation can be dangerous because that CEO may have an outdated picture of the company and may be operating from a very different set of assumptions than the incoming leadership. The CEO may see the building as a lasting monument to his aesthetic values, rather than the place where the future of the company will be shaped. Succeeding management may then share very little sense of ownership in the resulting design. One way new leadership shakes up a company is by changing the work environment. It may be very tempting for these new executives to demonstrate that a change in leadership is indeed occurring by spending even more money to alter the newly constructed facility.

FAILURE TO ADAPT TO CHANGING DEMANDS

Even though the value-based approach encourages the articulation of strategic direction, there remains the chance that these values and strategies may not adapt well to new competitive conditions. The competitive environment may shift in unpredictable ways, so that even the best efforts of value-based decision making must be periodically revisited and, if need be, changed. Change is always difficult, and frequent changes to the work environment may be stressful to the workforce unless a high degree of ongoing change is programmed into the design approach from the beginning.

Value-based decisions later may become embedded as space, design, and operating standards. Then they are subject to the same disadvantages as a standardization strategy. Early value-based statements that get translated into standards are seldom revisited. In an effort to create an egalitarian, open culture early in the company's history, Ken Olsen of Digital Equipment Corporation established that a standard 10' x 10' open workstation would be used by all nonexecutive employees, starting with the Mill facilities. Although over the years design consultants repeatedly demonstrated to DEC senior management that this was not the most efficient or aesthetic module to house the type of work done at Digital, the module persisted even in new construction. DEC standardized the construction of its facilities and applied the 10' x 10' module to window and column spacing, ceilings, and electrical systems distribution, making it even more difficult to consider changing the standard. It wasn't until the company was in a deep financial and strategic crisis that the standard module was finally changed to a more space-efficient 7' x 9' dimension.

CAN BE A COSTLY USE OF TIME AND RESOURCES

The value-based decision-making process of gathering information, synthesizing it, and relating it to the company's unique strategic and cultural demands takes time. In the short term, resorting to standardized solutions to workplace design and management issues often saves time. Incremental decisions also are made more quickly because they are bounded by the limited choices available at the time a decision is forced by external pressures. Timeliness is by necessity.

The multitude of decisions to be made in the design of a major project can be overwhelming, but they also can be a lot of fun, and perhaps preferable to the day-to-day task of running a company. If a clear process for evaluating options and making decisions is not put into place, some value-based approaches can take too much of management's attention and distract them from running the business. We will look further at the benefits and drawbacks of intense senior management involvement in real estate decisions in Chapter Eleven.

Money also can be spent in dumb ways. Precious design details, customized furniture and fabrics, and fine art may appeal to the executives' aesthetic sensibilities, but be lost on the vast majority of the employees, making these items a waste of scarce capital. Lavish details add later costs as well such as higher maintenance and security costs.

Symbolic gestures, which were meaningful to the company at a more intimate size, can become expensive and cumbersome later on. As some organizations grow, they often make efforts to retain some of the physical symbols of the earlier days. As mentioned earlier, Wednesday donut days at Sun started with a few dozen people gathering around some boxes from Winchell's Donut House. It has now turned into a weekly logistics nightmare with thousands of pieces of pastry delivered within a one-hour period every Wednesday morning to dozens of buildings in the Silicon Valley where Sun is headquartered. Similarly, a Christmas turkey was an early entitlement at Digital but it got to the point where refrigerated trucks were pulled up to Digital sites to distribute turkeys to thousands of employees. And like many other ritual preservation efforts, the administrative group in charge of making it happen is facilities. These symbols may still retain a lot of value to the company, which is why they persist, but in hindsight a more flexible and adaptable ritual might have sufficed.

USING VALUE-BASED PROCESSES FOR COMPETITIVE ADVANTAGE

Value-based corporate real estate decision making contributes to competitive advantage by extending the role of facilities beyond merely the functional to also enhance the culture and reinforce the vision of the organization as it moves forward. Along with the advantages discussed earlier, we should recognize that a value-based approach can mediate the pressures for incremental and standardized solutions. Above all, it recognizes that *Place,* the home we create for our organizations, sustains its identity in the hearts of its members.

RELATING A VALUE-BASED STRATEGY TO INCREMENTALISM AND STANDARDIZATION

Value-based decision making is a strategic response to both competitive environments that have become more certain and to those that have become less certain. It ameliorates disadvantages found in both incrementalism and standardization.

The longer-term vision which value-based decision making requires provides a framework around which shorter-term incremental choices can be made. Even though space may have to be occupied piece-by-piece, a value-based strategy sets out the criteria for the type, location, and design of the space that is acquired. Value-based criteria can also be useful when an organization does not have a lot of history or stability upon which to base a standardized approach to decision making. Once basic values are established, a value-based strategy actually can cause decision making to be more efficient. The vast number of practical decisions which even a simple project requires can be overwhelming unless an overall philosophy and method for making decisions is set forth.

Value-based decision making encourages a company to look at its business through fresh eyes, so companies often turn to this approach when they are experiencing increased competitive uncertainty. Highly standardized design and process standards block innovation and adaptation for companies grappling with new uncertainties. Many standards are based upon an assumption that work processes will remain little changed in the future, or that the work to be done can be best accomplished in a very neutral, generic environment. Standards that not only reflect the organization's deeply held values and aspirations but also are flexible enough to change easily when appropriate, attempt to capture the best of both approaches.

To fully employ a value-based approach, however, an appreciation of the qualitative benefits must be understood and shared across the organization. The emotional and behavioral influences of Place must be embraced. This requires the strategic mindset we discussed in Chapter Three, and a new metaphor for how we think about the workplace.

VIEWING PLACE AS HOME TO THE ORGANIZATION

Why should our concept of strategic real estate include its emotional dimension? Aren't we trying to look like hard-nosed business strategists? Won't we lose credibility talking about warm fuzzy things such as symbols, amenities, comfort—the feel of a place?

Think about how you make decisions about your home. For most of us, a home is our major financial investment over the years. And certainly financial considerations play a part when we select a new home, decorate it, renovate it, or choose to move. But money is only one part of the equation. We think about comfort, convenience, providing the right neighborhood for ourselves and our children. Whether we acknowledge it or not, we also think about what our home says about us to our neighbors, friends, and family. We often spend money on it without any calculation of the relative value of our investment compared to other investment options, such as putting that money in the bank, or calculating its future value. When we purchase a new sofa, for example, we buy the best one we can afford—we don't just buy the cheapest one available. We care about comfort, style, and how it fits with the way we live and the other objects in our life. While we are happy to make some money when we sell our home, our memories are mostly about what happened when we lived there, not solely about how it increased our net worth.

So why should we expect, even often encourage, our corporation to think about its home only in purely economic terms? Even if it was desirable to completely quantify all aspects of our real estate decisions, this would require us to place dollar values on employee satisfaction, the ability to attract the right kind of people to apply for employment, our public image, and overall goodwill. Such things are notoriously hard to measure, and there are many intervening variables between Place and organizational success. After over twenty years of effort, white collar productivity is still difficult to measure directly, although helpful indirect indicators, such as time to market or employee satisfaction with the workplace can be gauged. With rapid rates of change in our competitive environments, Place often comes to represent something else besides just efficiency because it can communicate the essence of the organization. As Mark Golen, who directs corporate real estate strategic planning at Sun Microsystems, observed, "In high-technology companies, only the culture and the real estate endure over time—the people and the products can change."[19] Real estate decisions grounded in the core values of the company are more adaptable to change.

Used in concert with incrementalism and standardization as needed for flexibility and scale economies, the value-based approach takes full advantage of the qualitative attributes of *Place* highlighted in the opening chapter. A project initially based upon a value-based assessment opens up for functional analysis in the details.

Even though the three decision-making strategies (incrementalism, standardization, and value-based) have been presented singularly in the last three chapters, over time, all three can be present at various stages of a company's growth and development. The next chapter discusses how corporate real estate strategies are dynamically applied as competitive conditions change over time.

CHAPTER SEVEN

REAL ESTATE STRATEGIES
ARE DYNAMIC

A company's approach to real estate decision making will change over time as its competitive demands change. Factors which influence uncertainty such as growth or contraction of the business, new markets or competitors, mergers or acquisitions, or changes in the use of technology all will trigger a shift in how real estate and facility decisions are made. As we have seen in the past three chapters, greater uncertainty is accompanied by more incremental decision making. Certainty fosters standardization. Value-based decisions enable longer-term commitments when strategic uncertainty makes long-range forecasting difficult.

Although most companies will use all three strategies at various times and in various ways, one approach will dominate during a particular time period or for a particular line of business. Different parts of a company may require different approaches to real estate and facilities decision making depending upon the strategic uncertainty surrounding its product/market segment and the company's approach to achieving competitive advantage.

In this chapter we look at some in-depth case examples of real estate strategies in action. First, two very different companies illustrate how strategies change over time as competitive dynamics change—Sun Microsystems and G-Tech. Second, we examine how one company may employ different strategic approaches to different parts of its business, as in the case of financial services giant Merrill Lynch. Finally, we look at an example of an integrated real estate strategy at Cisco Systems, which attempts to capture the best aspects of all three strategies.

SUN MICROSYSTEMS—EVOLUTION OF STRATEGY: FROM INCREMENTAL TO VALUE BASED

In Chapter Four we saw how Sun utilized an incremental real estate strategy to manage its unprecedented growth. But an incremental strategy, although quite useful for the nascent company or one for which strategic change is endemic, has many cumulative disadvantages. Sun's evolution over the past decade illustrates how an incremental strategy gives way to a more complex, thoughtful, value-based one, as scale and market certainty increase and forecasting horizons lengthen.

By 1988, as Sun reached $1 billion in sales and had over 7,000 employees, it brought in Klaus Kramer, a professional corporate real estate manager. Kramer had experience with high-growth companies. During his eight years at Hewlett-Packard the company had grown from $600 million in sales to $1.8 billion. Kramer then joined Rolm, which he saw expand from $250 million to $1 billion over seven years. Based on these experiences, Kramer believed that companies went through fairly predictable stages in the growth of their facilities management and corporate real estate functions. Careful cost control became more important as scale increased, and there were more opportunities to gain competitive advantages through improved management of the real estate portfolio. One of the first symbolic steps Kramer took when joining Sun was to change the name of the department from facilities management to corporate real estate and facilities.

Sun now was recognized as a major player in the computer industry. Sun had achieved a brand name and a loyal following of powerful customers, mostly engineers and technicians eager to have the latest and greatest at their workstations. These customers were highly knowledgeable as to what technological advances meant and what they were worth. However by 1989, the giant computer companies, notably IBM, Hewlett Packard, and DEC, had all begun to offer competitive workstation products aimed at Sun's customer base.

The period from 1988 to 1990 was still chaotic at Sun, but as the rate of employee growth slowed down in the Bay Area, more attention could be paid to the corporate infrastructure. During these years, Kramer sought to move the company from its reactive, incremental approach to acquiring buildings, to longer-range real estate planning and greater articulation of

Sun's approach to workplace design. By late 1989, he had begun to put into action his desire for a more balanced, longer-term perspective to Sun's approach to facilities planning and its real estate portfolio. He created Sun's first lease database and hired other experienced corporate real estate professionals. While these strategies were being put into place, however, about 2 million square feet was still added to the Sun's space inventory. Despite the continuing pressure for more space, Sun's decisions about major projects began to be framed around value-based decision making.

SUN TAKES A VALUE-BASED APPROACH TO LONGER-TERM COMMITMENTS

Sun applied value-based decision making when it began to shift from a totally leased to a balanced leased/owned portfolio. The company also sought to geographically diversify out of the immediate Mountain View area.

Sun's First Owned Property

Kramer's early goals were for Sun to own more facilities, to gain greater control over long-term costs, and to provide a better-quality work environment. Sun purchased its first property in 1988, a thirty-year-old 200,000 SF building, from Ford Aerospace. This project represents Sun's first foray into value-based corporate real estate decision making. The five-story building was considered a high rise by Palo Alto standards and needed extensive remodeling. A $3 million structural upgrade also was recommended but not required. Sun decided to add the bracing, partially based on the desire to do it right. The upgrade used external steel bracing that added another 50,000 square feet to the building. Three weeks after Sun occupied the facility, the powerful Lomo Prieto earthquake hit the area, rendering many buildings unoccupiable. Due to the prescient upgrading, the old Ford building survived. Sun located the most stable parts of the company, its administrative support functions, in the attractively designed building, nicknamed PAL for Palo Alto. Seven years after its founding, the now $1.7 billion company had an identifiable corporate headquarters. Much more attention was paid to the quality of the interior design than in previous Sun facilities. The walls were washed with soft pastels, an inviting employee cafeteria offered a wide range of menu items, and a spacious comfortable lobby greeted visitors. Still, the corporate art consisted of

attractive photos of Sun products; a gallery of Sun products—including a
replica of the original Sun workstation—was the focal point of the lobby.

Geographic Diversification

Sun also began a more deliberate geographic diversification program. In
the Silicon Valley area of northern California, Sun began to select sites that
were more accessible to the east bay where housing costs were far cheaper
than on the peninsula. The company continued to add support facilities in
Milpitas, optioned a site in Newark, and purchased a 57-acre site in East
Menlo Park. The value-based design process for developing the Menlo
Park site is described in a later section.

Sun also established a few beachhead locations on the East Coast, primarily through acquisition of small companies. The Boston area, more
commonly referred to as Route 128 (the suburban ring highway surrounding the metropolitan area) was second only to the Silicon Valley as a major
progenitor of computer innovation in the 1970's. It is home to DEC, Wang,
Data General, Lotus, and scores of smaller companies, many of which were
beginning to suffer competitive losses from the very product innovations
Sun was advancing—nonproprietary open systems and networked computing.

Despite the setbacks for individual high-tech companies in the Boston
area, the area's greatest strength had not changed—talented computer
hardware and software designers, many of whom had built strong personal
ties in the community. The Northeast's plummeting housing prices (a drop
of 18%–20% from 1989 to 1993)[1] had two effects: First, it was more difficult
for computer industry professionals to relocate out of the area because of

*From sow's ear to silk purse: Sun's conversion of a late 1950's vintage high rise to its
corporate headquarters.*

the potential losses they faced if they sold their homes. And second, it made housing prices much more competitive for entry-level employees than the extremely high-cost housing of the Silicon Valley region.

Hoping to take advantage of both the area's attractive labor pool and to be near the constantly evolving start-ups still emerging from MIT, Harvard, and area entrepreneurs, Sun began to look for sites to house East Coast operations in 1990. Over the years Sun has increased its eastern presence, and began constructing its own East Coast campus in 1997.

Throughout the early 1990's Sun's real estate and facility managers explored a number of options to move Sun out of its costly and inefficiently configured spaces in Mountain View. PAL had given the company some breathing room, and most of the growth in head count was taking place in other locations. Meanwhile, the company's strategic direction was becoming more defined. An understanding of Sun's competitive positioning in the early 1990's puts their real estate activity into context.

SUN MAKES A STRATEGIC COMMITMENT TO DIFFERENTIATE

Although Sun's sales continued their growth trajectory, ($3.2 billion in 1991, $3.6 billion in 1992, and $4.3 billion in 1993) margins were rapidly decreasing because of increased competition, particularly in hardware. Net income decreased as a percent of sales from 5.6% in 1991 to 4.8% in 1992 and down to 3.6% in 1993. Sun's management realized that to sustain superior margins, products needed to be clearly differentiated, otherwise they would be forced to compete on cost alone. Being a strictly low-cost competitor was an unattractive option for Sun, since many manufacturers in the Far East had a clear advantage with lower-cost labor. While Sun's earlier innovations had the added bonus of providing more computing power at lower cost, raw workstation power was no longer the critical selling point. Integration of ever more complex hardware systems into powerful networks, development of proprietary hardware that was still open systems compatible, and the creation of software to support a wider range of applications on those systems were the keys to future success in the industry.

Although Sun's corporate culture was built around being on the cutting edge of technology, the company was still largely located in one of the costliest parts of the world for both labor and real estate. To survive, therefore, Sun would need to protect its product margins by obtaining a price premium in the market, compared to its competitors, and by offering superior, clearly differentiated products. Because it was increasingly difficult to differentiate through hardware alone—and Sun contributed to this through the open systems approach—differentiated software was an increasingly important product. Hardware would need frequent and exciting new enhancements to entice buyers to buy now rather than delay purchases in the hope of further innovations. Retaining customer loyalty was paramount. Along with a much greater effort to create a brand identity for Sun computers and an image of superior quality, Sun put a greater emphasis on customer service.

All of these strategic efforts required greater maturity and sophistication among the Sun workforce. A key challenge was keeping the workforce on the cutting edge of technological development. *Reinvent or die* became a key Sun slogan, appearing on posters, embroidered onto polo shirts, and placed on paperweights throughout Sun's facilities. McNealy declared that the company needed to be intellectually intensive rather than labor intensive.[2] Engineers remained king at Sun. At the same time, Sun needed to carefully understand and track costs.

Lower margins meant a lot less room for product mistakes. Sun could no longer afford to group the cost of administrative overhead across the company—it needed a better picture of which businesses were most attractive to pursue. As part of an overall effort to understand where the greatest profitability in the company was produced, Sun attempted to allocate costs down to the strategic business unit level, including the cost of real estate and facilities.

The new Menlo Park site would give Sun the opportunity to merge competitive strategy with workplace design.

USING WORKPLACE DESIGN TO ENABLE COMPETITIVE ADVANTAGE

The most dramatic representation of Sun's conversion to a value-based real estate strategy is the planning, design, and occupancy of a 1.2 million square-foot campus in Menlo Park. Sun purchased the land from Raychem, a defense contractor that had land-banked the property and was downsizing. The site was strategically located in Menlo Park, only two freeway exits north of the Palo Alto building. More significantly, it sat at the entrance to the Dunbarton Bridge which linked the peninsula with the east bay area. Sun employees could find lower-cost housing in the east bay and not have to commute through the congested peninsula to get to work. Meanwhile Sun senior management could enjoy proximity to all three sites—Palo Alto, Menlo Park, and Mountain View.

The architect Sun hired for the project, Backen, Arrigoni & Ross, did not have much corporate design experience at the time. Their portfolio consisted mostly of wineries, palatial homes, and projects for George Lucas at Skywalker ranch. The architect approached the site planning with the goal of keeping the setting on a human scale, even though a million square feet would be built to hold 3,500 employees. Rather than the anonymous boxes that Sun occupied in leased space, the Menlo Park buildings are a range of warm Tuscan colors, with subtle differences among the buildings, increasing their identity. The massiveness of the build-out is disguised by the scale of the landscaping. Interior courtyards and pedestrian streets connect the buildings, all parking is on the periphery of the site. Each building has several electronically secured entryways allowing employees convenient access. Higher buildings are on the north side of the site where they block the prevailing winds; buildings are lower on the south side to maximize sunlight in the interior courtyards. The courtyards connecting the buildings offer quiet corners with tables and chairs. Employees are encouraged to use these outdoor spaces for meeting in the warm, mild climate. The cafeteria is a pavilion set into a plaza with outdoor as well as indoor seating. Other amenities include a fitness center and a sundry store.

With the usual Sun conservatism, the buildings were laid out on the site in such a manner that other tenants could occupy some of the buildings, in the unlikely case that Sun's space needs would dramatically diminish in the future.

We're not working, we're in Tuscany: Sun's Menlo Park campus is designed for ease of interaction and flexibility. Photos courtesy of Backen, Arrigoni & Ross Architects.

Sun hired an interior design programming consultant to help design a facility that would best support engineering requirements, especially time to market and creativity. Respecting Sun's insistence on single or shared private offices, the design emphasis is on getting engineers out of their offices to bump into and interact with each other. Inside, a variety of different types of conference rooms are easily accessible. A coffee bar takes a prominent place in the center of the floor because that is the best place to get people to run into each other. Elevators between the floors are downplayed, instead, open central stairs with wide landings encourage flow between floors. The stairwells are faced with chalkboard surfaces to encourage impromptu discussions.

By 1998, Sun's operations were spread throughout the Valley in distinct nodes, with some of the original leased buildings in Mountain View still occupied. Sun also opened a campus for light assembly in Newark, across the Dunbarton Bridge from Menlo Park Campus, but also retained assembly and warehousing operations in Milpitas. Figure 7–1 shows the distribution of Sun-occupied buildings throughout the San Francisco Bay area. Sun opened another campus of offices in Broomfield, Colorado, which will eventually hold 4,000 employees in one million square feet of space. Sun also increased its commitment to Massachusetts with a new 140-acre campus in Burlington. The opening of the Colorado campus marked the realization of Sun's three U.S. campuses vision, which enables more location options for employees and diversifies Sun's real estate risk. Additionally, in late 1998 Sun broke ground for another research and development campus in the southern Silicon Valley city of Santa Clara, which will house one million SF of space in two phases.

CHANGES IN CORPORATE REAL ESTATE OPERATIONS

During the time Menlo Park was under development, Sun experienced some internal turbulence in its real estate operations. In early 1991, the corporate resources function, to whom corporate real estate, human resources, and management information systems had reported since the early years of the company, was eliminated and its functions reassigned to different senior executives. At the time, the senior management team at Sun thought it would be a good idea to split corporate real estate and facilities. Real estate, which included design and construction, strategic planning, and international now reported to the chief financial officer, while

Figure 7–1
Sun Microsystems in the Silicon Valley, 1998.

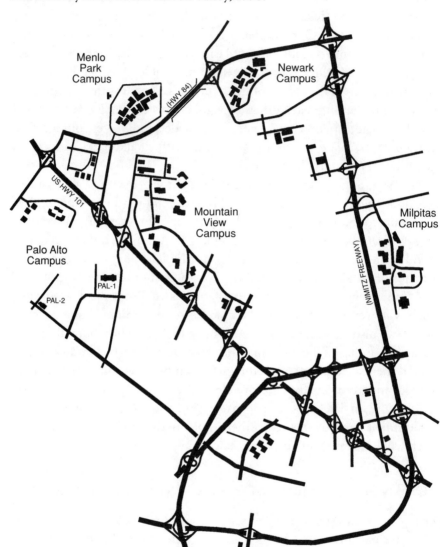

Not To Scale

operations and facility management reported to human resources. Kramer headed up the real estate function, while Dave Streeter, a well-respected corporate real estate manager with a long distinguished career at DEC, took the facilities management helm. Figure 7–2 shows the dual structure from 1991 to 1995. The thinking was that this arrangement would promote debate between real estate expenditures and quality of life issues at the company. Unfortunately, the more frequent outcome was conflict at the project level between those responsible for design and construction and those who would be responsible for operating the space. This conflict, which frequently arises when corporate real estate and facilities management report to different executives, was very visible to Sun's business units whom the functions were supposed to be serving. By January of 1993, Sun management realized the error, and assigned both corporate real estate and facilities management to human resources. But some of the damage from that era left scars, so in spring of 1995 a new executive, Bill Agnello, was brought in to head the reunited corporate real estate and facility management operation.

Agnello, who previously was a real estate service provider at CB/Richard Ellis in Chicago, soon renamed the unit again to reflect his new charter: *real estate and the workplace.* Agnello was determined that real estate at Sun be as innovative as the rest of the company. He initiated two major changes: First, the position of *workplace manager* was created to forge more intimate ties with the businesses. This assigned a senior corporate real estate professional to each of the operating companies at Sun to coordinate all their interactions with real estate and the workplace. Second, Agnello began to emphasize more outsourcing of real estate, facility management, and design and construction tasks. This led to reducing the corporate real estate staff by over half, but those remaining had more responsibility and higher compensation. Those whose positions were eliminated mostly found other jobs within Sun or went to work for the service providers. In recognition of his contribution to Sun, Angello was promoted to officer level with the title Vice President. In the final chapter of this book, we take one last look at Sun Microsystems and how its job function of workplace manager is one harbinger of future trends in corporate real estate management.

Figure 7–3 shows the organizational structure as it evolved under Agnello's leadership.

While Sun is a dramatic example of how a shift in real estate strategy from incremental to value based occurs over time, Sun's lessons seem to be

Figure 7–2
Corporate Real Estate and Facilities Management Organization, 1991–1995

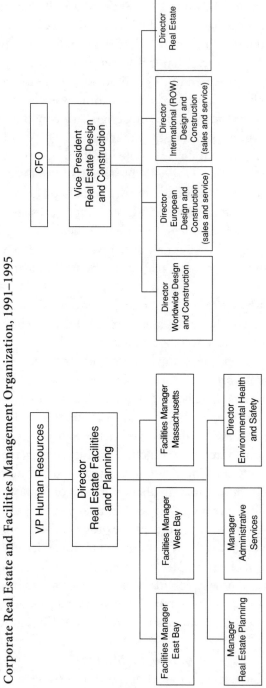

most relevant to high-growth companies in broadly structured industries. What about smaller companies in much smaller industries or focused product niches? Is a shift in real estate strategy as necessary as it was for Sun? The answer is yes. Even at a much smaller scale, shifts in competitive strategy require shifts in real estate strategy.

G-TECH CORPORATION: TWO PARALLEL STRATEGIES ADDRESS DIFFERENT NEEDS

Founded in 1981, G-Tech, like Sun, redefined an industry. G-Tech is the world's leading supplier of computerized on-line lottery products and services. The company pioneered the use of computerized lottery systems

Figure 7–3
Sun Corporate Real Estate and Facilities Management, 1996–1999

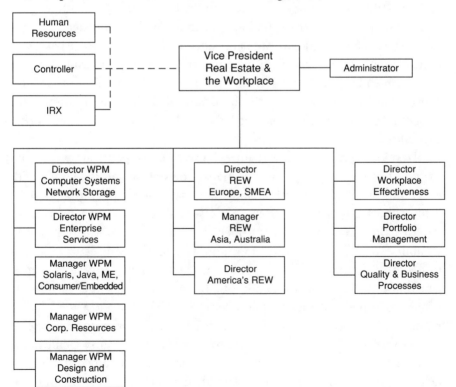

which enabled localities to implement government-sponsored gambling lotteries much more easily. As states found it more difficult to raise funds for social services through raising taxes, lotteries were an appealing way to bring in money with less political opposition. Today, nearly every state in the United States, as well as scores of foreign countries, sponsor sanctioned lotteries. G-Tech, and its competitors in the industry, provide the entire operation from game design to terminals on a bidded-contract basis. Contracts usually were awarded for five to seven years; once won, there was no guarantee G-Tech would be awarded the subsequent contract.

In the early years all real estate and facility planning matters were personally handled by G-Tech's cofounder and CEO, the dynamic Guy Snowden. The company rented space near the rapidly gentrifying downtown core of Providence in an old brick building that had been attractively renovated for use as office space. As we saw in the chapter on incrementalism, the company was able to expand one floor at a time in this location. Rhode Island was a straightforward choice—the founders lived in Rhode Island and the state was one of G-Tech's first lottery customers.

The strategic demands on G-Tech in the late 1980's were both technological and political. The technology to run a state lottery system requires extremely sophisticated hardware and software design. Once the basic system is up and running it then becomes critical to rapidly innovate new games which keep up consumer interest in the lottery. G-Tech insisted on controlling final assembly of the hardware, including the terminals for each retail outlet, and therefore needed to maintain flexible manufacturing capabilities.

Developing new business requires a great deal of political savvy. From the point of view of G-Tech's customers—the state agencies charged with developing and subsequently managing a state lottery operation—establishing the legitimacy of lotteries is essential. Lotteries are referred to strictly as revenue enhancement operations, never as a form of legalized gambling. As states and countries found it increasingly difficult to obtain funds through increasing taxes, they turned to other sources of revenue generation. Since the introduction of a lottery and the firm chosen as the vendor to implement and run the system would be subject to a great deal of media scrutiny, it was essential that G-Tech maintain a squeaky-clean, wholesome image. Snowden's desire to provide high-quality facilities for his employees was consistent with that image. The company's first manufacturing site in Warwick, Rhode Island, had many employee amenities for both the engineers and the manufacturing staff. Snowden even personally helped decorate the employee cafeteria.

By the time G-Tech reached nearly $500 million in revenues, with lottery systems in over 60 states and countries, managers recognized the need to move from their incrementally occupied first home to a facility that would colocate both management and operations into one state-of-the-art facility.

FORGING A COMPETITIVE IDENTITY THROUGH VALUE-BASED PROCESSES

In 1993, G-Tech developed and occupied a new corporate headquarters, modestly titled, World Technology Center. G-Tech purchased the 26-acre site from Digital Equipment Corporation that by 1992 was suffering setbacks in the computer market and needed to dispose of excess property. The site already possessed $18 million in improvements, such as its own exit off of Interstate 95, when DEC backed out and eventually reimbursed the state. Rhode Island was eager to find a new tenant, and home-grown G-Tech was its ideal candidate. G-Tech financed the project off-balance sheet through a limited partnership in which the company is a 50% owner.

G-Tech built a total of 260,000 SF on the site; a three-story headquarters building and the two-story technology center. Company founder and then CEO, Guy Snowden, who had always played a prominent role in G-Tech's real estate activity, was heavily involved in the programming and design of the facility. Snowden and the rest of the senior management team saw the building as a long-awaited opportunity to position G-Tech as a world leader in technology. Although 20 minutes south of Providence, the new facility is relatively isolated, and so many amenities, including fitness facilities, are included. A senior executive at G-Tech explained, "Space is seen as an employee benefit."[3]

G-Tech used its facilities to enhance its outside image in several ways. A major factor influencing the awarding of contracts is the state lottery officials' site visit, which usually lasts for two days. Therefore, Snowden included a state-of-the art conferencing facility where presentations to potential clients are made. The room, equipped with advanced multimedia, overlooks the manufacturing floor. A helicopter pad makes it easy to bring people from Providence or Logan airports. The overall quality of the workplace also is used as a marketing tool. With so many negative undertones to the lottery business due to its early illegal associations with organized crime, the family-oriented, high-technology image of G-Tech's facilities gives great assurance to clients that the entire operation is unassailable.

In contrast to its value-based occupancy of the world technology center, G-Tech approaches its field operations in a highly standardized manner.

COMPETITIVE POWER THROUGH STANDARDIZATION

By 1994, G-Tech's environment had grown a great deal more competitive. New competitors achieved greater market penetration. As with most industries, when strong competition ensues, price competition and lower margins become more prevalent. Since most states and major countries already had instituted lottery programs, the focus now turned to retaining customers through contract extensions, or obtaining contracts from rival's customers when those contracts came up for renewal. Most threatening to G-Tech was the tendency for many of their current customers to feel the political pressure to switch vendors when contracts came up for renewal.

While G-Tech's highly value-based world technology center continued to support the company, standardization in the field was key to both controlling costs and enabling lightening fast roll-outs of new systems. As described in Chapter Five, G-Tech must have the new lottery system up and running in eight weeks once a contract is awarded. A lot of outside service providers are used as needed. Even before the contract is bid, corporate real estate is very involved in all aspects of the contract-pricing process because facilities are an important cost component of lottery operations.[4]

SELECTING THE APPROPRIATE STRATEGY AT THE BUSINESS UNIT LEVEL—THE REAL ESTATE TURNAROUND AT MERRILL LYNCH

Merrill Lynch, the world's largest investment firm, has a long and complex institutional history in which real estate has always played an important role. Merrill Lynch's real estate and facilities strategy prior to 1991 could be largely seen as an incremental, reactive one. A reactive incremental strategy is characterized by *shifts in large commitments,* forecasting that assumes that the present demand will continue unabated into the future, and real estate acquisitions based on concern over real estate values rather than the company's strategic needs. As a major player in world financial markets, it's not surprising that Merrill Lynch was also the two-ton gorilla in terms of space occupation in the world's two prominent financial capitals—New York and London. In New York, Merrill Lynch had accommodated its intermittent but generally relentless growth by occupying a series of office buildings in lower Manhattan. Over time this incrementalism gradually led to occupying numerous buildings scattered throughout lower Manhattan.

Both in terms of personnel and space, Merrill Lynch expanded and contracted in cycles with the financial services industry. By 1985 growth of the financial services industry seemed on a perpetual ride upward. Office rental rates in Manhattan were skyrocketing. Reacting to forecasts for increased space needs in Manhattan, the need for a larger contiguous space, and a desire to avoid future market rate increases by taking longer-term commitments, Merrill Lynch signed on for 4 million square feet in the mammoth World Financial Center, constructed at the southern tip of Manhattan known as Battery Park City. The project, designed by Caesar Pelli, contains a total of 8 million square feet of office, retail, and public space. It is marked by four major office towers of granite and glass that are from 34 to 51 stories high and topped by copper roofs—each a different geometric shape. Occupancy began in 1987.

The stock market crash of 1987 sent the ambitious growth projections of Merrill Lynch, and many others in the financial services industry, into a tailspin. But the firm was locked into a commitment of 4 million square feet that was still at peak 1980's prices. That Manhattan real estate market that once looked so invincible now saw lease rates plummet to well below replacement cost. Meanwhile, corporate real estate and facility costs at Merrill Lynch had been doubling every five years during the 70's and 80's, peaking at $720 million in 1990. Additionally, the facility management staff had been demoralized by a series of scandals arising from bribery charges in the local building trades.

Senior management brought in Alan White to clean up Merrill's real estate act. White began by setting aggressive goals to reduce costs and improve decision making. While facility expenses grew about 15% annually during the 70's and 80's, White aimed to hold expense growth at 4%, with most of this growth attributable to head count increases. Cost savings came from two major sources: First, the amount of space per person was reduced as Merrill Lynch shed underutilized or unneeded space, and instituted new workstation design standards. Second, the company accelerated its migration of jobs out of high-cost locations such as New York and New Jersey, to lower-cost sites in Florida and Colorado. White established a consistent set of metrics in 1991 which helped him track his progress. From 1991 to 1996 the company was able to lower real estate costs as a percent of revenue from double to single digits and decreased space per person by 20%. Even though the head count increased 23% from 1990 to 1996, overall corporate expenses only increased 9% per year. Notably, occupancy expenses declined 3% per year during this period. By lowering headquarters costs, Merrill Lynch was able to free up more capital to invest in global expansion.

White also realized that different parts of the business required different approaches to real estate. Policies appropriate for highly compensated investment bankers and senior management in New York City did not apply to retail brokerage offices around the world, or to large-scale information process functions such as mortgage processing or mutual fund management. The two major lines of business at Merrill Lynch, private client banking and corporate and institutional banking, each have distinct markets, competitors, and cultures.

Private client banking includes such operations as mortgage banking, insurance, and investment brokerage. The scale and highly competitive markets of private client businesses require a standardization strategy to contain costs and streamline operations. Part of this strategy is to relocate as many operations as possible into lower-cost locations, particularly for back-office operations.

Corporate and institutional banking, with its short product life cycles and highly compensated, in demand, and often mercurial investment banking professionals, requires a value-based approach. The need to rapidly act on complex information makes specialty banking spaces, such as trading floors, an extremely important tool in maximizing the effectiveness of the bankers. The demand for complex telecommunications infrastructure is great, far surpassing the cost of the actual real estate occupied. These highly compensated employees can produce substantial profits for the company—so their facility needs are taken very seriously.

Across all parts of the company an incremental approach was taken to reduce occupancy metrics, and thus costs, over time. Whenever space was acquired or remodeled, the more space-conscious standards were employed.

At the corporate level, the company took steps to better integrate its infrastructure. In 1996, Merrill Lynch changed the name of its corporate services group from operations, systems and telecommunications to operations, services, and technology (OS&T) to reflect its broader scope in enabling competitive advantage across the broad spectrum of corporate activities. The function integrates information technology, corporate real estate and facilities, and purchasing; it is further organized into subunits linked to the major lines of business.

In remarks to the global managers of the OS&T group in May of 1996, White related the success of corporate real estate's efforts to the firm's stock price:

> During the period of 1990 to 1996, if occupancy costs had grown at the same rate as head count, which could have easily been defended, instead of coming down, our pretax earnings would have been $200 million less. . . . When you . . . work it through the number of shares and our stock price multiple, [the savings] is worth about $5 per share. Merrill closed at $65 yesterday, without this $5 contribution, it would have been $60. Lest any of you be indifferent, remember we are all shareholders![5]

The many changes implemented over time by Merrill Lynch show that even at very large, complex organizations, a vital link between the company's strategic objectives and its real estate and facilities can be achieved. Each decision-making strategy was used in the appropriate context to solve the business problem at hand, appropriate to the embedded commitments of this venerable firm. Across the country at Cisco Systems, a relative teenager compared with octogenarian Merrill Lynch, the lessons of its elders were taken to heart when developing an integrated corporate real estate strategy.

LEARNING FROM WATCHING: MANAGING FAST GROWTH AT CISCO SYSTEMS

Cisco Systems, a leading provider of hardware and software products for information networks, is one of the great success stories of the Silicon Valley. Because it caught on fire a little later than HP, Apple, or Sun, Cisco senior management learned from watching the experience of these other fast-growth highfliers. Cisco's real estate strategy combines elements of incrementalism, standardization, and value-based decision making to accommodate fast growth, while providing a high-quality work environment for its employees and having space available to accommodate growth.

Cisco Systems' sales experienced a 65% annual growth from 1993 through 1997 to $8.4 billion in 1998. Cisco's growth was largely fueled by the rapid expansion of the Internet and the need for hardware and software to suppport its growth; its stock price multiplied about 80 times from 1990 to 1998.

Founded in 1984, the company saw more than 100% growth per year in its early years, and housed its expanding workforce in leased space in Menlo Park. In 1993, when sales were approaching $1 billion, the company purchased 80 acres of land farther south in San Jose, assuming it would last about four or five years. Instead, the site was built out in two years. Cisco continued to purchase large tracts of land, mostly along Tasman Drive in San Jose. Yet despite these large, forward-looking land acquisitions, Cisco built the buildings incrementally. According to Robert Thurman of Cisco: "The company has always been very conservative in its approach. We try to not get too far ahead and we build flexible, generic buildings that we could dispose of, if needed. We established a basic building design that takes 12 months to get up and running."[6] The standardized approach to buildings helped to streamline not only construction but also corporate real estate decision making about new properties as well.

On the inside, Cisco facilities are also highly standardized, but these standards are based upon a clear articulation of the company's values. Flexibility and function are emphasized, not decor or aesthetics. Most of the company works in systems furniture spaces of 8' x 10' feet. About 15% of offices are closed and all are the same 12' x 12' dimension. All closed offices are located in the building core, while the window walls are left open to allow natural light into the workstations. Even Cisco's CEO occupied a 12' x 12' interior office. The highly egalitarian management offices are a source of pride among Cisco employees. Since all Cisco facilities are essentially the same in terms of space and technology, employees can easily move from place to place, easing the strain of a 150% churn rate. And despite being one of the most heavily networked companies in existence, Cisco still emphasizes colocation of its workforce whenever possible, hence the massive concentration of Cisco employees within a few square miles of

San Jose. This proximity allows the company to easily reorganize to meet new market opportunities, as well as to forge a strong corporate identity among its highly entrepreneurial employees. By the end of 1998, Cisco had acquired over thirty companies in its quest for growth. Whenever possible, the company quickly colocates these new employees within existing Cisco facilities to help them acclimate to Cisco's operations.

The generic approach to buildings, and their clustering on four proximate but separate sites, also give Cisco more flexibility in case of a downturn in the company's fortunes. Cisco senior management has seen its fair share of Silicon Valley crash and burns and wants to avoid being stuck with the burden of excess real estate. The simple nondescript design of Cisco's buildings—described by a *Fortune* magazine reporter as "boxy, standard issue Silicon Valley buildings"—makes them easy to lease or sell to other companies without interfering with other Cisco facilities.[7] Concern about the effects of such large real estate holdings on the company's balance sheet caused Cisco to be an early adopter of off-balance sheet financing. Using synthetic leases gives Cisco the control benefits of owning, while freeing up capital to invest in the core business.[8]

SELECTING THE APPROPRIATE STRATEGY FOR YOUR BUSINESS

As discussed in the preceding chapters, uncertainty from the external environment greatly influences a company's approach to real estate decision making. Which approach is right for your company? The answer to that question will require a great deal of sensitive analysis of your company's competitive position and its operating needs. But to get a quick idea of the relative level of uncertainty your company—or a particular part of your business—faces, use the assessment that follows. It's adapted from my research on corporate real estate decision making.

In Part Three, we will examine in greater detail how design and operating policies are affected by both external and internal forces and how a variety of organizations are using Place to enable competitive advantage.

Sidebar 7–1
HOW DYNAMIC IS YOUR STRATEGIC ENVIRONMENT?

Use it to get a general sense of how uncertainty plays into key elements of your organization's competitive environment. There are no hard or fast quantitative answers, it is a matter of degrees. Companies scoring mostly in the high range are probably dealing with a great deal of uncertainty from external forces. An incremental strategy may allow the flexibility to cope with this uncertainty. Companies scoring mostly low are probably able to make future forecasts with greater confidence and may find operating economies from standardization. Where does your company rate? Has it changed over time? Do different lines of business face different levels of strategic uncertainty?

Financial Uncertainty

	High Uncertainty		Moderate Uncertainty			Low Uncertainty		
Leverage (Debt/equity ratio)	>80	70	60	50	40	30	20	10	0

Market risk Your stock's beta	2.5	2	1.7	1.5	1.3	1.1	1	.75	.5

over 1.5   over 1   under 1

Competitive Uncertainty

	High Uncertainty	Moderate Uncertainty	Low Uncertainty
Market share	0 5 10 15 Low	20.....30.....40 Moderate	50 60 70 Leader
Number of competitors	>50 30 20 Fragmented	15 10 5 Distributed	3 2 1–0 Few
Barriers to entry in your major industry segments	Low, easy entry Many entrants	New entrants possible	High, slow, costly entry
Threat of substitute products	Many near	Few near/ many far	Few far

	High Uncertainty	Moderate Uncertainty	Low Uncertainty
Customer Uncertainty			
Installed base (% market penetration or % of income from service)	None, few	Average for industry	Large, loyal
Switching costs	Low	Moderate	High Captive
Price sensitivity	High Small price increase loses customers	Moderate Buys on product attributes and cost	Low Willing to pay/ cost is small component, or value is very high

	High Uncertainty	Moderate Uncertainty	Low Uncertainty
Supplier Uncertainty			
Raw material/ component availability	Scarce Single/few suppliers	Available Multiple suppliers	Plenty Commodity
Labor	Scarce Highly specialized	Available	Plentiful Low training needs

	High Uncertainty	Moderate Uncertainty	Low Uncertainty
Political Uncertainty			
Degree of regulation	Moderate Uncertainty as to whether will increase or decrease	High High = industry is more visible	Low Not appropriate to regulate
Volatility of legislative/ political environment	High	Moderate	Low

	High Uncertainty	Moderate Uncertainty	Low Uncertainty
Technological Uncertainty			
Rate of change in core technologies	Fast	Predictable	Stable/slow
Life cycle: primary product	<6 mo. short	2–5 years	long >10 years
Life cycle: secondary product	<6 mo. short	2–5 years	long >10 years

Summary

Financial	Debt	H	M	L
	Beta	H	M	L
Competitive	Share	H	M	L
	No. competitors	H	M	L
	Entry barriers	H	M	L
	Substitutes	H	M	L
Customers	Base	H	M	L
	Switching costs	H	M	L
	Price	H	M	L
Suppliers	Materials	H	M	L
	Labor	H	M	L
Political	Regulation	H	M	L
	Volatility	H	M	L
Technological	Change	H	M	L
	Life cycle: primary	H	M	L
	Life cycle: second	H	M	L
Totals				
		H	M	L

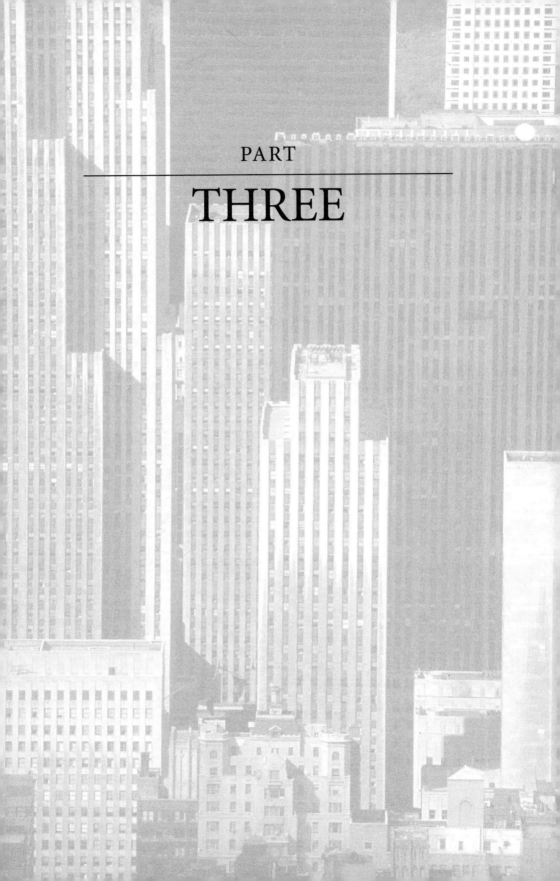

PART

THREE

INTRODUCTION TO PART THREE

Diagnostic Frameworks
for Enabling Competitive Advantage

In the last four chapters, we have seen how several companies have formulated their real estate strategy over time in response to the dynamics of their competitive environments and their internal needs. Now, What should we do at our company? is the big question you must try to answer. Although learning about the struggles other companies have gone through can help you see patterns in your own company's behavior, there is no one set of rules to follow in developing a strategy that will work best for your company. Real estate and facilities are very complex issues which permeate aspects of corporate life from financial performance to employee attitudes. What worked for one company may not suit your organization but there are ways to better think about the businesses you serve and how they are best supported by their physical setting, location, facilities, and workplace.

Recall this statement from the introduction: *While it is true that no real estate or facility strategy, no matter how well delivered, can ever compensate for a lousy product or poor customer service, real estate and facilities can play an important role as enablers of strategic actions.* Enablers are those things which help get the product out the door better, faster, or with less cost. They support the people who do the work and provide an environment where innovation flourishes and common goals are well understood. Part Three provides a framework to help you identify those enablers that are most relevant to your business.

There is no single set of prescribed actions or prepackaged design solutions that can be applied to a facilities' strategy like a recipe in a cookbook. Every company must develop its own unique approach to its real estate and facilities. Even companies which compete in the same industry or marketplace will have different physical configurations and management policies, driven by their need to find a way to develop and exploit any advantage over their rivals.

Yet there are common themes across companies. Each of these specific actions must serve a similar set of organizational criteria. What you *can* do is approach the diagnosis of needs and the creation of solutions in a systematic manner that acknowledges the range of variables which affect the physical setting of the organization. Pressures from outside the organization, as well as the internal demands of the company, must be addressed in a manner which is sensitive to each company's identity. Responding to your company's needs in such a systematic way will position you well to provide a setting for the work which helps the company to be its most competitive.

The factors to be addressed in the design and management of the physical setting exists both outside of and within the organization. As discussed in the Introduction, corporate real estate strategy is a response to two sets of demands: those imposed by the external strategic environment of the company, and those which serve the internal structure and culture of the company. Each of these break down into two components. The external strategic environment is composed of the competitive milieu in which the company operates within its industry and of other environmental pressures which directly relate to the physical setting. Internally generated demands are both structural and cultural: they relate to the processes by which the company and its workforce does business, and they respond to the unique personality and behaviors that have evolved within the organization over time.

As the focus of corporate real estate and facilities evolves from transactions and property portfolios to relationship management and support, the ability to analyze, understand, and implement solutions that enhance competitive advantage is essential. The corporate real estate and facility manager who understands the competitive use of space and time is an important resource to the business. The needs of the business set the criteria by which real estate and facility decisions are made. It is the strategic mindset in action.

Part of managing the relationship between corporate real estate and the business is understanding what the business needs on the business's terms and in the business's language. It is up to corporate real estate and facilities to provide the translation between the business's needs and the physical environment. This requires that today's corporate real estate and facility management professionals be adept at diagnosing organizational demands and be capable of providing optimal solutions which enable the company to compete better.

This section of the book presents these factors in a series of diagnostic frameworks you can use to ask, and then answer, questions about your own company's real estate and facility needs. Each of the next four chapters outlines a series of probing questions to help you relate your business's needs to its choices about *Place*. Answering these questions will help you to set your goals and priorities to determine where your time and money may be best spent. Rather than trying to fit your company into a predetermined package of design approaches that may be fashionable at the moment, you need to consider a range of questions that impact your approach to real estate and facilities and to build your strategy from that analysis.

Note that these diagnostic frameworks are *qualitative.* They describe the relationships between factors and help us to assess relative degrees of strengths or weaknesses of both our company and our competitors, but they do not yield some perfect answer that tells a manager the right decision to make to advance the company's competitive position. Clear judgment, critical thinking, and most of all, an intimate knowledge of your company, including its competitive environment and its internal demands, are needed. The challenge to creative real estate and facility managers is to help their companies see beyond the mere quantification of real estate and

Figure III–1
Diagnostic Framework for Corporate Real Estate Decision Making

Corporate Real Estate Strategy

facility management options, to the more subtle complexities and potentially greater impacts that can result from a broader strategic perspective.

Chapters Eight and Nine examine the factors existing outside the direct control of your company which affect the time horizon, functional requirements, and resources available to plan and occupy space. Chapter Eight adapts frameworks from the strategic planning literature and applies these concepts to corporate real estate strategy and facility planning. The intent is to encourage a dialog between the business strategic planning functions and corporate real estate planning.

Chapter Nine focuses on three other factors which impact the flexibility companies have in competing within their industry, as well as their ability to forecast future competitive conditions. They directly impact a company's ability to make the long-term logistical and financial commitments inherent in real estate and facility management decisions. These *environmental constraints* include technological dynamism—the rate of change and product life cycles for both the technologies that are part of your core product and for the technologies that support its production, the regulatory environment, and financial resources.

Chapters Ten and Eleven help you examine the inner workings of your company. While the external strategic environment drives both the forecasting horizon and strategic goals of a company's real estate and facilities, it is the dynamics within the organization which determine how those facilities are developed, designed, and managed. This combination of demands from the strategic environment and the idiosyncrasies of each company's culture, history, workforce, and leadership are what make a company's real estate and facility strategy unique to any other. Real estate and facilities add value in many different ways, and it takes a thorough understanding of your company to identify where the biggest impact can be made.

In the final chapter, the future role of Place is examined. We look at the wide variety of Place strategies successful companies employ and examine trends ranging from workplace design to location selection. Also examined are ways the corporate real estate function is more closely aligning itself to the core businesses through improved relationship management. Finally, I offer some suggestions about what the design and real estate related professions must do to improve the link between Place and strategy for the companies they serve.

CHAPTER EIGHT

UNDERSTANDING YOUR STRATEGIC ENVIRONMENT

A thorough understanding of your company's competitive strategy is required before determining the best real estate and facility strategies for your company. This understanding starts with a clear diagnosis of the forces of competition within your industry. With a mental model of your industry and the forces that determine profitability and sustained success, you can examine how your company competes with its constraints and opportunities. Once you see the big picture, you can then look at details such as the particular products and market segments which will affect different aspects of the workplace.

Every company competes within one or more industries and each industry has its own dynamics that make it more or less attractive as a battleground for profits. The real estate or facility manager is not responsible for determining which industry or segments of the market their company competes in; that decision is both a matter of history and current actions by senior and line management. However, it is critical that real estate and facility managers have a clear understanding of the competitive challenges faced by their companies, and their relative strengths and weaknesses within its industry, in order to establish the strategic context to be supported by real estate and facilities.[1] Is this an attractive industry for sustaining product margins and profits? What are the biggest threats to profitability in the business? How likely are these forces to change in the future? What do those changing forces imply for our long-range facility requirements? Are these compatible with our short-term needs? Only after these and other more detailed questions are answered can real estate and facilities fulfill its important role as an enabler of competitive advantage.

By using the perspective of competitive strategy to investigate, analyze, and interpret real estate and facility decisions which line managers or corporate executives must make, the corporate real estate and facility manager can help an organization forge a valuable strategic link. The impetus is on the real estate manager to understand competitive strategy, not for the line manager to understand real estate. If both the real estate manager and the line manager understand the potential support that real estate and facilities

Figure 8–1
The Wheel of Strategy. (Where is corporate real estate?)

Source: Michael E. Porter, *Competitive Strategy* (New York: The Free Press, 1980).

can give to the company's competitive strategy, they have achieved the first step toward maximizing the value of these assets for the company.

Curiously, as was pointed out in the Introduction to this book, much of the literature on strategic analysis of industries and competition, including writings on the strategic planning process, overlooks the role played by real estate and facility resources in enhancing a company's ability to compete. For example, the wheel of strategy, a Harvard Business School diagnostic framework (Figure 8–1), was used for many years as a checklist for assessing fit between a strategy and the organizational resources that must be marshaled to implement the strategy. Notice that both real estate and facilities are overlooked. In this chapter we will try to make operational the linkages between competitive strategy and corporate real estate management strategy.

STRATEGIC FORCES IN YOUR INDUSTRY ENVIRONMENT

To begin let's explore some tools for understanding the competitive forces within your industry. Over fifteen years ago, a path-breaking set of concepts regarding how companies compete within industries was put forth neatly by Harvard Business School professor Michael Porter. His first book on the subject, *Competitive Strategy,* was published in 1980, followed by *Competitive Advantage* in 1985.[2] Based on the economic theory of industrial organization, Porter asserted that any industry's structure could be diagnosed, and a strategy for competing could be developed, by examining five factors: power over buyers/customers, power over suppliers, barriers to entry in the industry, the threat of substitute products, and the overall level of rivalry within the industry. Porter's framework, often called a five force analysis, is shown in Figure 8–2. We will use these five forces as a basis for understanding your *strategic environment.*

Figure 8–2
The Five Competitive Forces that Determine Industry Profitability

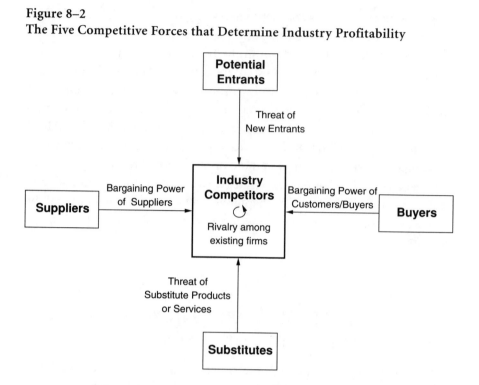

Source: Michael E. Porter, *Competitive Advantage* (New York: The Free Press, 1985).

Sidebar 8–1
HOW DOES A FIVE-FORCE ANALYSIS HELP US TO UNDERSTAND THE COMPETITION FOR PROFITS IN AN INDUSTRY?

To briefly illustrate how the five force framework is used to understand an industry and one's competitive position within it, let's look at two industries: one which sustains high product margins, and the other which has a difficult time being profitable.[3] We will make a simplified and rather uncomplicated analysis of both industries—certainly a more in-depth analysis would reveal greater complexities and contradictions. However, these simple examples do illustrate how the forces within an industry can either function to help firms sustain high profits, or how the same forces can provide imposing barriers to profitability.

Let's first look at the *pharmaceutical* industry, which is populated by several large international companies.

BUYERS: Who buys prescription drugs? There are really two primary buyers: doctors who prescribe the medicine for their patients, and the patients who take the medication to help cure or manage certain heath problems. Most products are differentiated that is, they have certain characteristics that make them unique from other products and are able to achieve a premium price based upon those characteristics. How much do these buyers care about the price of the drug? The doctor's main concern is helping the patient, and avoiding a malpractice suit if his efforts fail. The cost will be passed on to the patient, or to the patient's insurance company. A good test of price sensitivity is to see how readily someone would switch to a lesser known and less-tested product with lower cost. At the extreme, if you or a loved one had a life-threatening illness which only a certain drug could cure, you would probably try to obtain that drug at any cost. In general, an industry in which the buyers are relatively insensitive to price, and which has high barriers to switching, will likely be able to sustain high product margins. This force is favorable to the pharmaceutical industry.

When we think about the incredible power this industry has over its buyers, it is not surprising that the managed care process has evolved as one of the ways in which hospitals and insurance agencies try to reduce medical costs. Volume purchasing by HMOs and other buying cooperatives also has helped to increase buyer power. However, it is difficult to demand change in pharmaceutical pricing, even in the face of strong public opinion, as demonstrated by the controversy over the price of certain life-prolonging drugs for patients suffering from AIDS.

SUPPLIERS: If most components of supply are easily available and those with high costs can have their expense passed on to the consumer, then suppliers do not have much power in the industry. Most pharmaceutical products are proprietary compounds synthesized from chemicals readily available and subject to competitive pricing in the marketplace. These products are the first element of supply. Of course, some drugs are made from costly rare ingredients, but in those cases, the high cost of the ingredients is passed on to the consumer. Labor, the second element, is another critical supply especially the laboratory research scientists who create new drugs. These researchers may be somewhat scarce, and indeed, internal research and development is the highest component for most pharmaceutical companies. A third element of supply is the maintenance of important research relationships with universities and teaching hospitals. Most academic institutions need the financial support provided by these research relationships and are eager to cooperate. In general, there are few sources of supply that can exert much pressure in this industry, meaning that supplier power is relatively weak.

BARRIERS TO ENTRY: How hard is it to enter the pharmaceutical industry? The first major barrier is that start-up costs are enormous. A new company must have a product to sell, but the time from product conception to distribution can be longer than a decade due to the U.S. government's approval processes. Product testing and clinical trials are costly, as is the marketing of the use of the new drug through a specialized sales force to doctors. Even biotechnology companies with breakthrough products need the capital resources of large pharmaceutical companies to make it through the gauntlet of product development. A second major barrier to entry is distribution of any new pharmaceutical product. It takes many years and great expense to develop a highly knowledgeable and well-connected sales force like the kind that most pharmaceuticals employ. The high costs of entry into the pharmaceutical business makes it highly unlikely that new companies will upset the competitive balance. These barriers are favorable to sustaining profits for the existing players in this industry.

SUBSTITUTE PRODUCTS: For most ailments there are few substitutes for prescription drugs. Most patients who pursue alternative forms of therapy such as chiropractic, acupuncture, homeopathy, and other holistic healing techniques use them in addition to conventional drug therapies. Generic drugs can be seen as another form of substitute and these usually carry lower margins than patent-protected drugs. But think about being in an industry where you know years ahead of time exactly when your product will face competition. Pharmaceutical companies know when their patents will expire. They can either make long-range plans to exit this particular market segment at this time or use their years of experience manufacturing the drug to get its production costs low enough to remain competitive even when other companies start producing the drug. Overall, if the threat of substitute products is low, there is less competition to worry about, making it possible to retain high product margins.

RIVALRY: How would you like to compete in an industry where every competitor knows where its rivals stand in the new product development process? The three phases of the new product approval process by the Food and Drug Administration (FDA) are open to public review, so that everyone in the industry can know the status of their competitors' future offerings. The review process can last from six to eight years, long enough for competitors to determine their own response. Further, historically there has been no compelling reason for companies with similar products to compete with each other on price, since buyers are rarely influenced by price. Rivalry was seen only in the marketing efforts used by distributors to convince physicians to try new products—and those rivalries can be substantial. Although more price competition is being seen with the rise of managed-care programs, in general, the rivalry in this industry does not harm margins. Low rivalry in such an industry can result in higher profits for everyone in the business.

Overall, the five forces of the pharmaceutical industry positively assist companies in the industry to sustain high levels of profitability. Therefore it is not surprising that pharmaceuticals typically boast the highest returns on equity of any industry segment in the Standard & Poor's 500, an impressive 26% in 1996. It is also not surprising to find that many pharmaceutical companies have outstanding physical work environments which are designed to support one of their most critical elements of future success: the people who produce their research and development.

Our second example, the U.S. *airline* industry battleground is a startling contrast to the comfortable world of pharmaceuticals.

BUYERS: How different is one airline from another? It is hard to perceive much difference, as long as they fly the route you need. Many buyers of airline services are price sensitive, particularly buyers of leisure travel. They will shop around for the lowest fare and will not take the trip if the cost is too high. The business traveler is less price sensitive, a fact not overlooked by the airlines, as reflected in the stunning differences between midweek fares purchased at the time of the trip, and discounted fares requiring advance purchase and a weekend stay over. One can travel from coast to coast for as little as

$300 on a discounted promotional fare. But buying a ticket for a last-minute midweek flight may hike up the price by four times or more. However, other than the timing of a ticket purchase, most airlines charge the same price for the same service. This lack of differentiation gives a lot of power to the buyer. It's no wonder that airlines make great efforts to increase the loyalty of business customers through frequent flyer programs and special treatment for high-mileage flyers.

SUPPLIERS: Airlines have high fixed costs; the cost of the aircraft and airport fees are the same for an empty plane as a full one, and fuel costs vary only slightly depending upon weight loads. Labor costs in terms of numbers of employees working on the flight also are regulated, so the wage costs of those employees are a critical cost component. Indeed, wage disputes and collective bargaining play a major role in the airline industry as the industry seeks more control over this critical cost component. Little control over supply costs impedes the ability to sustain profits.

BARRIERS TO ENTRY: Despite the inherent disadvantages the industry has overall, it still attracts new entrants who usually choose the busiest and most attractive segments and routes to attack. All a new competitor really needs to enter the airline business is the aircraft and permission from the government to fly the route. However, obtaining gates at airports can be a significant barrier. New entrants often trigger fare wars in the markets they enter, lowering profitability for existing providers.

SUBSTITUTES: For leisure travel there are some notable substitutes to air transportation: auto, train, or any other ground transportation is a more cheaply priced alternative to flying; leisure travelers also have the option of not taking the trip if the airfare is too costly. Business travelers have fewer transportation choices but have a number of other ways to connect such as phone, fax, and videoconferencing. Airlines must be careful not to push their customers into using substitutes by setting prices too high.

RIVALRY: Undifferentiated products often produce intense rivalry. A price decrease or other promotional fare is quickly matched by the airline's competitors on those routes. The airlines know that the game is management of capacity—an empty airplane costs almost as much to fly as a full one, therefore any additional seats that can be sold through price promotions are better than losing the sale entirely. Price competition is a vicious form of rivalry which lowers profitability for everyone in the business.

The intense competition for customers, with many highly price-sensitive customers and a largely undifferentiated product, and high fixed operating costs means that companies in the airline industry are constantly battling to reduce operating costs at every turn. The domestic airline industry has consistently returned some of the poorest profit performances of any industrial sector, frequently posting losses, as the industry's −4% return on equity in 1996 attests.

Once the relative opportunities and constraints within your industry are understood, alternative ways to compete within that industry can be identified and acted upon. Porter argues that there are three fundamental ways a company can achieve a sustainable advantage over its competitors: as *low-cost producer,* as a *differentiator* with enhanced features or services, or by *focusing* on a particular narrow segment within an industry and then pursuing it with either a cost advantage or through differentiation. The way your company pursues its competitive advantage should guide your corporate real estate and facility management policies and practices. Different strategic approaches need different enablers. The next four chapters present examples of how certain real estate and facilities approaches best fit particular competitive strategies.

While the past decade has seen wave after wave of management theories come into fashion and then fade, the five force framework has endured because of its utility and simplicity. I have adapted it for application in corporate real estate decision making because it does not provide normative prescriptions. Instead, its use as a diagnostic framework helps managers to organize their thinking and identify the most critical factors that require their attention. It will help you to ask the right questions about your company's industry, which in turn helps you to look for the answers in the right places.

In brief, the five forces of industry competition are

Power over Buyers: Buyers are the customers for your product. There may be several layers of buyers at the wholesale and retail levels, each with different behaviors, preferences, and sources of power. In general, the more choices a buyer has for a particular product, and the less need the buyer has for your specific product, the more power the buyer retains.

Power over Suppliers: Suppliers are those who supply the inputs into your product. The more you are dependent upon particular sources of supply, the more power is held by the suppliers. Dependency can come from many sources—the input is critical to the success of your product, there are few suppliers to chose from, or the particular brand from your supplier is demanded by your customer.

Barriers to Entry: Barriers to entry are those factors which either make it easy or difficult for outsiders to enter and compete in your industry. Some elements of an industry which may provide barriers to entry are government regulation, scarce raw materials, distribution channels, brand recognition, or high customer-switching costs.

Substitutes: Substitutes are products or services which are fundamentally different than yours, but that can serve the same function for the buyer. Substitutes often appear outside of the traditional boundaries of your industry.

Rivalry between Firms: This refers to the willingness of firms in your industry to aggressively compete with each other. Rivalry can be affected by the number of firms competing, whether their markets are growing or shrinking, the history of the companies, and the relationships between their leaders and executives.

The five force framework is widely used today by both internal corporate strategy groups and by consulting firms which specialize in strategic analysis. By considering whether each force favors or challenges your ability to produce a product profitably, and how much ability your company has to move these forces toward a more favorable direction, you can map out the major competitive challenges and opportunities your industry portends. A five force analysis is used to understand a company's own position, as well as to diagnose the relative strengths and weaknesses of competitors. It also helps companies assess whether certain markets are attractive to enter, and which markets are losing their attractiveness.

GENERIC COMPETITIVE STRATEGIES

The generic competitive strategies of a low-cost producer, differentiator, and focused competitor connect the behavior within the firm to the opportunities and constraints of the external environment. Each approach has very different organizational requirements which strongly influence how real estate and facilities are developed. At this point, a general understanding of these strategies is sufficient. In Chapters Ten and Eleven we will identify the specific real estate and facility implications of these generic strategies in greater depth as we take our diagnosis to the organizational level.

A company holding a *low-cost* producer position within an industry is not merely a company that acts to control costs; rather, it achieves an advantage over its competitors by being able to offer the *same* product at a lower cost. This means that the low-cost producer can either achieve higher margins by charging the same price as its competitors, or it can charge lower prices to the customer and still achieve the same margins as the competition. Either way, the low-cost producer wins.

How does a company secure a low-cost position? There are several basic sources: One, the company may own special assets that lower its raw material costs. For example, one large aluminum producer, ALCAN (Aluminum Company of Canada) has an exclusive agreement that gives it access to a cheap source of hydroelectric power in Quebec. Another aluminum company, Alcoa, owns a low-cost source of alumina in Australia. Two, a company may possess a proprietary technology that helps it to manufacture its product more cheaply than its competititors. Three, scale is a significant source of lowered costs. If a company produces and sells more of a particular product than its competitors, it can spread the fixed costs of production and overhead over a larger number of units, thus lowering the unit cost compared to competitors who must allocate their costs to fewer units. Finally, a company may have entered an industry early enough in the industry's history to have lower land and facilities costs than later rivals, thereby reducing its operating overhead.

A *differentiator* produces a product or service that is in some way superior to the competition and is able to command a premium price from the customer for the benefits of this differentiation. Differentiation can be achieved through offering extra features, higher quality, better service, greater availability, shorter response time, anything as long as the source of differentiation means that the customer buys from you rather than the competition. However, offering additional features is not a reliable method of differentiation if customers are not willing to pay for them.

A *focused* strategy only works if the distinct advantages of serving a particular niche outweigh the benefits of broader participation in a market. Focused companies try to serve their customers' specific needs better and to innovate faster than those companies which try to meet a broader range of customers. Unfortunately, the successful focused player often is tempted to grow its business by expanding into adjacent markets, thus jeopardizing the advantages of their narrow focus. Gerber Foods, for generations a successful manufacturer of baby foods, tried to enter the adult food market in the 1980s and failed.

Companies that cannot compete by either offering the same product at the same or lower cost than their competitors, or who cannot charge any extra money for product differentiation, are doomed to eventual competitive failure. They may not go out of business, but instead just limp along producing mediocre returns to their investors and less than optimal opportunities for their employees. Eventually they may be acquired and restructured. What usually happens to the corporate real estate staff of the acquired company? It's not a pretty picture.

A company which competes as either a low-cost producer or a differentiator or in a focused niche, but has real estate policies and practices that are incompatible with its chosen strategic approach, is also risking its competitive edge. The real estate and facility implications of these competitive positions are discussed in Chapter Ten.

APPLYING INDUSTRY AND COMPETITIVE ANALYSIS TO REAL ESTATE AND FACILITY MANAGEMENT DECISIONS

Real estate and facilities are only rarely the direct source of a firm's competitive advantage. Instead, their role is to help create the conditions which enable competitive advantage to flourish. Real estate and facilities convey value to the company when they support both its strategic goals and its daily operations. They support getting the product out the door better, faster, or with less cost. Facilities also support the people who do the work, by providing an environment where innovation flourishes and common goals are well understood. In the following section we explore the physical implications of the dynamics of each of the five forces of industry by asking probing questions about their relationship to *Place* and drawing upon examples from a variety of industries and companies. Ask these questions of your own company, remembering that the most useful analysis is often at the level of the business unit rather than the corporation.

Sidebar 8–2
THE SPECIAL CASE OF RETAIL BUSINESSES

When businesses have a retailing emphasis, there exists a clear relationship between competitive strategy and real estate and facilities. Both location and facility design are integral to the marketing strategy. The location of your real estate must be relative to your clientele's location, thus retail businesses emphasize differently the variables of cost and accessibility than do corporate businesses. The quality of the facilities must be keyed to the needs and preferences of the customer, and the design of the retail facility must be considered as part of the service delivery strategy. However, as noted in the Introduction, this book emphasizes nonretailing facilities, where the relationships to business strategy and competitive advantage are more subtle, but just as important.

QUESTIONS ABOUT YOUR BUYERS/CUSTOMERS

Companies seek to increase their power over their customers by offering greater value than their competitors. Real estate and facilities impact a company's relationship with its customers both directly and indirectly. If the customer interacts with a company on its premises, there is a direct relationship between facility location and design and the customer's opinion of the company. Under these circumstances, it is possible to measure the facility's contribution to customer satisfaction and service. Do customers give more business to facilities with certain attributes? Can you compare multiple facilities with each other? Can you survey customers about their satisfaction with your facilities?

The indirect role of the facility in properly supporting employees who provide customer service may be less quantifiable, but it is equally as important. How this support is best provided may be open to interpretation, but a powerful argument for quality facilities can be made if links to factors such as employee satisfaction, retention, or other indicators of morale can be established.

QUESTIONS ABOUT YOUR BUYERS/CUSTOMERS

How easily can our customers switch to another supplier of our product or service?

Do we make it easy to do business with us?

Do we support servicing customers?

Does our location make a difference to the customer? If not, is there another location which can either lower our costs or help us to differentiate better?

Does our customer mandate uninterrupted service?

Do our facilities convey the right public image?

RAISING SWITCHING COSTS

Consumers' bargaining power is driven by how easily they can switch to another provider of your product or service. A company gains more power over its customers by finding ways to raise switching costs. If your product has some attributes that are proprietary—that is, no other competitor can offer them—it is hard for your customers to switch suppliers once they have standardized their operations based on your product. For example, computer makers IBM and Digital Equipment Corporation were able to lock in their customers for many years because their computer hardware and software products were not compatible with other computer systems. Once a company settled on a system, their future purchases had to fit with those systems. The customer could not switch suppliers without completely changing their operations.

The key to raising switching costs is to understand who your customer is, how you obtain and retain that customer, and how your product or service conveys value to that customer. If your product is the easiest to purchase and service, your customer may be less willing to switch, and may not mind paying a reasonable price premium for the convenience. Consider the Saturn automobile, a good quality car not that different from any other car in its market, but one which promotes radically different methods of sales and service to the customer. Prices are a fixed rate—there is no haggling between the customer and the dealer. Dealers also are encouraged to follow up with their customers after the sale is made. When Saturn was launched, Saturn limited the number of dealers and concentrated dealer locations on both coasts, where product demand was high and where competing foreign car sales were strong.

Customer power becomes greater when the product or service can be obtained easily, is undifferentiated, or is purchased in high volumes. The less important your product is to the quality and success of their product, the less loyal customers are likely to be.

LOCATION AND CUSTOMERS

What are some examples of how real estate and facilities can help the company to gain strength with its customers? As an aid to differentiation, real estate and facilities can help make the company easier for a consumer to use. If the customer needs to directly interact with the company on its property, the property should be easily accessible. Some professional service firms provide special meeting rooms for clients and make private workspaces available for clients who need to make phone calls or work on other tasks. The company may explore ways to locate itself on the customer's own property. Many of the major accounting firms no longer provide personally assigned offices to their auditors because they expect those auditors to spend most of their work time on the client's premises. Redesigning the auditors' home base and providing the appropriate technology to facilitate working at the client's offices helps to encourage the auditors to be more visible and more responsive to their clients.

Configuring your warehouse and shipping operations so that you can support a customer's just-in-time manufacturing strategy is another example of customer-driven facility location and design criteria.

Colocation relates to outsourcing. Donnelly Enterprise Solutions colocates printing operations with its major law firm and investment banking clients so that financial prospectus documents can be developed, proofread, and produced in the shortest time possible.

In a more indirect manner, support facilities which expedite the work of customer service employees also strengthen the relationship with the customer by enhancing service quality. For example, some companies today are able to offer around-the-clock service to their customers by hiring telephone service personnel in time zones across the globe. Those employees are able to work normal business hours and the company avoids having to manage a graveyard shift. Called a "follow the sun" strategy, the telecommunications system switches from location to location as the day progresses so that an expert is always ready to handle service needs.

The facility that supports the physical needs of the customer service employee helps that employee to concentrate on giving the customer the best-quality attention. In these information-intensive service functions, the design of the workplace must thoughtfully complement and support the information system. The interior workstation layout, including lighting, acoustics, and seating, must support the ergonomic demands of the work. The information and supervisory systems must support the workers' abilities to serve customers effectively and rapidly. For example, a telecommunications company underestimated the importance of having supervisors in visual contact with their customer service employees. Often, supervisors were in a different location and monitored their workers' productivity by computer. However, this electronic monitoring system could not report why a worker was not on the system and could not identify when that person needed help. Since the supervisors could not wander around many problems went undetected and customer service quality suffered.

LOWERING PRODUCT COST

Another tactic to encourage customer loyalty is to offer the lowest prices for a comparable product. A company which is competing as a low-cost producer makes lower facility costs a priority but also balances cost savings with productivity gains. For example, an older building may save on direct real estate costs but have higher operating costs. The overall higher cost of maintaining Digital Equipment Corporation's old headquarters in a turn-of-the-century mill complex led the company to vacate the premises when DEC's products came under severe competitive and cost pressures. Low-cost competitors usually pay close attention to industry benchmarking data and more aggressively pursue the lower end of their industry's space and facility cost standards.

One way to support a low-cost position is to identify whether the location and cost of the occupied real estate really makes a difference to the customer. For example, many information and financial processing functions are invisible to the customer. All interaction is done over the telephone using toll-free 800 numbers, or by mail. No one cares if their check is sent to be processed in New York City or the middle of North Dakota. Not only are land and construction costs often cheaper in exurban locations but lower labor and utility costs also can yield even greater cost advantages over competitors in higher-cost locations. One example is financial giant Merrill Lynch. Over the last decade the company has migrated its back-office operations out of New York City to regions of the country which offer lower costs of living, more affordable real estate, and larger pools of high-quality workers at lower wages.

OFFERING SERVICE REDUNDANCY

Geographic diversity of customer service functions also is used to ensure that service can never be disrupted by a major calamity in one part of the country. Fidelity Investments has operating centers in four locations within the United States. Calls to any of the sites can be rerouted to any of the others. Total daily call volume at Fidelity can exceed one-half million calls per day. In addition, Fidelity provides complete systems backup at each site. This high level of caution is not surprising if you consider that in 1996, 10% of all New York Stock Exchange transactions took place through Fidelity each day—over 70,000 trades per day, servicing a base of 11 million customers and 30 million accounts. Not only does Fidelity want to ensure that it never lets a customer down, many of the transaction functions performed by Fidelity have legally mandated deadlines and other performance criteria.

ENHANCING PUBLIC IMAGE

A distinctive building or workplace often is showcased to enhance a company's public image. A building which matches a customer's expectations of the company constantly reinforces that image in the customer's mind. Banks look safe, all granite and brick, while advertising agencies and architects' offices present a creative, design-conscious face. Facilities design, more fully discussed in Chapters Six and Eleven, plays a direct role in establishing and maintaining customer loyalty by enhancing the customer's experience with the company and an indirect role by reinforcing the company's image. Some buildings are used to establish name recognition, such as the pyramid-shaped Transamerica Tower in San Francisco. Conversely, inexpensive looking facilities imply a no-nonsense attitude that some companies want to convey.

All companies live or die according to how well they satisfy their customers. Whether your customer personally visits your company's facilities, or is affected by them only secondhand through interaction with people housed in your facilities, a clear understanding of how your customer is served is an essential starting point for developing your corporate real estate strategy and for prioritizing your actions.

QUESTIONS ABOUT YOUR SUPPLIERS

Suppliers are powerful within an industry if they can easily raise prices or interrupt the supply of essential components of your product or service. Simply put, the more your company depends upon a certain supplier, the more power that supplier has over your company. Many companies strive to have products which are not dependent upon one single supplier.

QUESTIONS ABOUT YOUR SUPPLIERS

How dependent are we upon our suppliers?

How can we broaden our choice of suppliers?

The most critical supply is often labor: Are we in the right locations? Do our facilities help attract the best employees?

Do we have logistical limits to our location? Do those limits still hold in today's world?

Can we be more competitive by colocating with our suppliers?

REDUCING DEPENDENCY ON YOUR SUPPLIERS

Suppliers try to encourage their customers' dependence on their products by creating switching costs and raising entry barriers. A great example of increased supplier power is the microprocessor produced by Intel. In the past, customers usually were ignorant of the manufacturers of the interior, unseen components of their computers. By promoting a brand identity for their own Pentium microprocessor computer chip and directly advertising its benefits to the computer consumer, Intel created customer demand for their particular chip. Computer manufacturers then were pressured to feature the Intel chip to satisfy their customers; Intel was able to charge a premium for their branded product.

CHOOSING A LOCATION WITH MULTIPLE SUPPLIERS

Easy access to suppliers has long been a basic component of site selection theory, but one which has changed dramatically since the growth of international-scale overnight and fast-freight transportation providers. The hub and spoke system of express delivery pioneered by Federal Express has led to a proliferation of overnight delivery services and a lowering of small package delivery costs. The service map of United Parcel Service greatly improved over the past decade and the United States Postal Service also has made dramatic improvements in performance. Today, many companies are able to eliminate multiple warehouse locations and still ensure rapid delivery of needed supplies to their customers. However, the ability to maintain a choice of suppliers for both goods and services can still be impacted by location. Some goods, such as steel, lumber, or fuel, are too costly to transport great distances. Other companies purposely locate where their suppliers can be accommodated easily. Toyota Motor Company only considered locating in rural Kentucky when the company was assured that its many suppliers could also easily and economically set up operations close to the massive automotive assembly plant.

Other raw materials and supplies are geographically tied to a location for historical reasons. For example, the movie industry originally became based in Southern California because the mild, sunny weather facilitated outdoor filming. Today, most motion pictures are still produced in the Los Angeles area because there is a greater concentration of freelance talent located there than anywhere else in the world. A producer can assemble a local team to develop a movie more easily and maintain a network of contacts that can be brought together quickly if a new project receives financial backing.[4] The volume of production work in the Los Angeles area subsequently attracts more people to locate there, perpetuating that location's advantage. Geographic clusters of professional labor specialties appear to be increasingly important in the site selection process as highly qualified workers seek to maximize their career flexibility and independence by locating in an area with an array of employment options.[5]

OPTIMIZING LABOR SUPPLY

Labor is a critical supply for most businesses. It is most important when labor comprises a large percentage of the cost of producing goods or if specialized skills are required. Labor quality and availability are frequently related to location. The availability of the appropriate labor force is becoming more heavily weighed in the location decision-making process, in part because access to raw material and in-process supplies is less location dependent. For example, companies that are highly dependent on university-based research will have a competitive advantage if they are conveniently located near those universities. Sun Microsystems was created by engineers based at Stanford and the University of California at Berkeley. Indeed, the Silicon Valley owes it growth largely to the presence of Stanford and Berkeley. Today, Sun has a second regional concentration in the Northeast, so it can be close to innovations being pioneered at the Massachusetts Institute of Technology and Harvard University. The presence of many biotechnology start-ups in the Boston area is largely a function of their proximity to Harvard University and Tufts University's teaching hospitals, as well as to other Boston area universities. This is not just an American phenomenon. Recently, many software companies have set up operations in Bangalore, India, where there is a large supply of college-educated software programmers.

Many facility design tactics have been implemented to enhance the labor supply by maximizing productivity and increasing job satisfaction. This book contains many examples of how companies pursue differentiation strategies by attracting and retaining the highest-quality workforce and then supporting them in the most appropriate facilities. Chapter Ten, which diagnoses organizational demands, provides an in-depth discussion of labor supply support.

REEXAMINING LOGISTICS

The term *logistics* has its roots in the words *logic* and *calculation,* and is often used to refer to the entire process of organizing the movement of inputs and outputs. Logistical considerations, such as physical access to suppliers, and the optimum number of suppliers available to choose from, may need to be revisited if the product, market, technology, or transportation systems have changed. For example, some businesses such as veterinary drug suppliers, have been able to reduce their number of warehouses across the county because better service is now provided by overnight delivery services. Other companies have needed to increase their number of warehouses to meet customer demands for rapid delivery and service.

BUILDING CLOSER RELATIONSHIPS WITH SUPPLIERS

Differentiation which is achieved through rapid turnaround from order to delivery or through high product quality may benefit from geographic colocation with certain suppliers or the actual sharing of facilities. For example, in 1988 when Toyota opened its mammoth production facility in Georgetown, Kentucky, dozens of Toyota suppliers also had to build facilities in the area to support its just-in-time production system.

Supplier relationships are the flip side of customer relationships. You are your suppliers' customer, and as you try to become less dependent upon them, they are searching for ways to make you more dependent. By understanding the nature of production demand on your industry, and how it is supported up and down the production value chain, win-win supplier customer relationships can be forged.[6]

QUESTIONS ABOUT ENTRY BARRIERS

Entry barriers are those costs or impediments which make it difficult to enter an industry. If it is easy for another company to enter your business, and the business is yielding attractive margins, over time the industry will become more and more competitive, and hence less profitable and less attractive. Entry barriers you can erect that make it more difficult for competitors to enter your business include early participation in your industry, significant production scale, proprietary technology, or a customer base which has been established either through very high switching costs or great loyalty.

Barriers to entry are not always a direct feature of the product or service. For example, it is still easy to enter into the software design industry—all that is required is a committed group of smart engineers. Many of today's software companies started with no real estate or facilities, just a garage furnished with some tables and chairs and enough computer hardware. However, to compete within the software industry today, strong distribution channels are required to get the product out to the customer.

This ability to distribute the product is not necessarily related to the quality of the software, but it often determines who will succeed in the marketplace.

QUESTIONS ABOUT ENTRY BARRIERS

Real estate related entry barriers:

Can we make it more difficult for competitors to enter our business?

Are we in the optimal location? Does it either lower our costs or help us to differentiate?

Can we share resources across our company better than our competitors?

Do we have regional advantages?

REAL ESTATE RELATED ENTRY BARRIERS

Real estate and facilities are an important part of what are called first mover advantages. These are the competitive strengths that are the result of entering and serving a particular market ahead of the competition. Having your facility up and running while a potential competitor is still trying to set up its operations can be a difficult advantage for a competitor to overcome. Most first mover advantages come from establishing scale and a brand name. Scale lowers your cost of manufacturing, as fixed costs can be allocated across more units of production, while an established brand name can lower your marketing and sales costs.

Entry barriers derived from lower real estate and facilities costs can provide long-term advantages. For example, a company which locates in a geographic area ahead of its competitors can expect greater cost advantages over time as inflation raises the costs of comparable land and buildings for new entrants. It is much more expensive for new companies to establish operations in the Silicon Valley today than it was for early arrivals such as Hewlett-Packard (HP). Back in 1956, start-up HP leased land in the newly developed 579-acre Stanford Industrial Park adjacent to the campus in Palo Alto. HP is now the largest tenant with over 1 million square feet of space. Companies which now want to locate in the Silicon Valley face some of the highest rents in the country for R&D space.

LOCATION AS AN ENTRY BARRIER

Location can be a barrier to entry if it offers a company advantages that its competitors cannot easily achieve in other locations. Along with better physical access to lower-cost supplies, a company may dominate the local labor supply for industry-related skills. Even if a competitor could move to your location, you may have already tapped out the local labor supply. It also may be difficult for your competitor to move to a new location which has the same benefits as yours due to its physical infrastructure and its workforce.

SOLIDARITY THROUGH SHARING OF RESOURCES

Another important entry barrier is the ability to share resources and their costs with other parts of the business. One example is the snack food industry. Truck delivery to small storefront retail locations incurs very high fixed costs. Therefore manufacturers either try to extend their product offerings to increase their share of shelf space at each store, or they enter into distribution agreements with other companies. Either way, one delivery truck can make larger deliveries to each storefront location, thus lowering delivery cost per unit.

QUESTIONS ABOUT THE THREAT
OF SUBSTITUTE PRODUCTS

Substitute products are those which perform a similar function or convey a similar benefit as your product but are different in a fundamental way. They are not simply a more technologically advanced product. For example, silicon chips were a substitute for vacuum tubes, but subsequent generations of chips with improved performance are not considered substitutes. The history of product innovation is also a history of product substitution. Cars were a substitute for horses, planes a substitute for trains. The telephone obliterated the telegraph. Substitutes can entirely change the rules of competition in an industry.

**QUESTIONS ABOUT THE THREAT
OF SUBSTITUTE PRODUCTS**

Meeting the threat of substitute products:

Does technology support new ways of delivering our product to the customer?

How are substitute products changing our real estate requirements?

Do our facilities support innovation and the rapid development of new products?

TECHNOLOGY AND SUBSTITUTION

Technological advances in other industries can play a powerful role in product substitution. As the performance of computers has increased and the cost of that performance fallen dramatically, we have witnessed product and service substitution at an unprecedented rate. Consider this retailing example: Efficient computerized inventory management systems, improved and lower-cost delivery services, and cheaper telecommunications systems with toll-free calling for customers have allowed catalog shopping to become an increasingly attractive alternative to shopping at a retail store. This has changed the nature of real estate for many retailers. Only the highest-traffic retail locations survive. If the retailer decides to also provide catalog shopping, a new set of real estate decisions surface: where to put the phone sales and distribution centers, what to own, and what to outsource. Automated teller machines (ATMs) have greatly reduced the need for retail banking locations and have radically changed how commercial banks configure their remaining network of retail locations. We will further address the relationship between technology and changing real estate and facility requirements in Chapter Nine.

Substitutes are particularly threatening if they convey greater benefit to the customer for the same cost or offer the same benefits at a lower cost and are themselves profitable for the companies that produce them. Consider the development of mutual funds; these pools of investment funds with diversified risk can be bought and sold easily. They have eroded the demand for traditional savings accounts by offering higher long-term returns to investors with acceptable risk. Not only was a whole new industry spawned, banks and savings and loans institutions have had their traditional base of capital support undermined.

SUBSTITUTION AND REAL ESTATE AND FACILITIES

The role of real estate and facilities in fighting substitute products is often indirect. The work environment should enhance the company's ability to differentiate through constant improvement and innovation, and it should be able to respond rapidly to changing competitive conditions. For example, facilities which encourage interaction and creativity certainly play a role in enabling the development of differentiated products. In Chapter Seven we looked at how Sun Microsystems' Menlo Park campus is devoted to developing new and differentiated products faster and better than any of their current or potential competitors. Flexible facilities also help a company to change its work systems and services easily in response to competitive threats. A company also must avoid overinvesting in the support of a product with a limited life span.

FACILITIES AND PRODUCT DEVELOPMENT

Understanding the role substitution plays in your industry will help you to better think about the forecasting horizons for your major facility commitments. For example, some sophisticated manufacturing plants, such as those for computer chip production, have extremely short lives because the processing technology changes so rapidly. Payback calculations on investments are over a few years, rather than decades.

QUESTIONS ABOUT RIVALRY
WITHIN YOUR INDUSTRY

Rivalry among existing competitors is a fact of life, but some industries elicit more head-to-head combat than others. Rivals attempt to improve their market position at the expense of their competitors. Examples of rivalry in action include price competition, aggressive advertising—especially promoting a competitor's weaknesses—or the addition of a service or product enhancement. Rivalry reaches the harmful stage when it lowers profitability for all the players in an industry to the extent that no single competitor benefits. It can be especially bitter when the overall growth of the market is small, or when there are high fixed costs or high barriers to exiting the business, or when competitors are not able to offer much differentiation. Shifts in rivalry occur as a product matures; over time a successful product will invite imitators, resulting in greater price performance pressures. Rivalry also may increase as a result of acquisitions or mergers as fewer competitors vie for industry dominance. Finally, more than any other industry force, rivalry can be driven by the personalities of senior management.

An example of a long-standing competitive rivalry is that between MCI, AT&T, and Sprint for long-distance service in the United States. At stake is a multibillion-dollar market where usage is growing, but the number of potential customers is stable according to population growth. In the customer's eye, long-distance telephone service is largely undifferentiated—one carrier's service seems pretty much the same as another. Those in the industry also know that consumers are reluctant to switch carriers once they are happy with one. Companies offer incentives to customers who switch carriers, but they do not obtain customer loyalty because switching costs are so low. Some consumers switch all the time to get the best deal. The resulting tug-of-war between providers has reduced prices to the consumer, but lowered profitability greatly for all. For a long time, AT&T tried to market its image rather than low prices, but has since started competing aggressively on price as well, as the company has lost market share to its tenacious rivals. The contest has become more fractious now that local telephone companies can enter the long-distance business.

Rivalry also has reached dangerous extremes in the airline industry. A competitor may drastically cut airfares on a particular route to build volume and customer loyalty, but such fare cuts are quickly met by the other airlines serving the route. Some volume of travel on the route may increase, but in general, all competitors lose in a price war since the benefits of lower prices are conveyed to all customers, regardless of their willingness to pay higher prices.

QUESTIONS ABOUT RIVALRY WITHIN YOUR INDUSTRY

How much interfirm rivalry exists in your industry?

Are real estate and facilities used to send signals to rivals?

Do better-quality facilities give you an advantage over your competitors?

RIVALRY'S INFLUENCE ON CORPORATE REAL ESTATE DECISIONS

The desire to outshine rivals may lead senior management to build a grand building as a statement of power. Chrysler, once on the brink of financial disaster in the 1980's, celebrated its recovered strength in the automobile industry by constructing a 3.3 million SF technology center to house new product development on a greenfield site in a suburb distant from Detroit. In 1996, Chrysler also moved its headquarters from Detroit to the Auburn Hills site and built an additional 1.1 million SF for a corporate headquarters with a tower shaped at the top like the pentagram of the company's logo. Chrysler has often featured the technology center in its advertisements and openly discusses how the new buildings help the company accelerate innovative product development. In all, the $1.1 billion dollar complex is the largest facilities investment in the history of Chrysler, now known as Daimler Chrysler.

In contrast, crosstown rival General Motors (GM), which has suffered the most at the hands of its competitors over the past twenty years, deliberately chose a very different strategy for its new corporate headquarters. When GM sought to consolidate its Detroit area operations into a modern facility, it chose to participate in the rebirth of downtown Detroit by purchasing the once glorious Renaissance Center and committing to bring the 1970's development into the twenty-first century. In doing so, GM not only made a vital contribution to the very survival of Detroit as a city, but garnered a great deal of favorable press about GM's own renaissance. On a practical basis, the facility allows GM to bring together offices from about

40 locations into one completely redesigned 2.1-million-square-foot building that will help it to centralize functions long balkanized within GM's many different automotive product lines. The price was also in line with GM's diminished product margins in that GM paid about $72 million for a building that originally cost $340 million and that would cost about $750 million if built today.[7] For both Chrysler and GM, form not only followed function, it followed the marketing message: Chrysler as an innovator, GM as a stalwart presence with a heritage.

THE SYMBOLIC EXPRESSION OF RIVALRY

Real estate and facilities are sometimes used to signal a shift in rivalry and strategic intent. For many decades, RR Donnelley & Sons, the largest printer in North America, occupied modest corporate offices near an old printing plant on the south side of Chicago. When Donnelley changed its competitive strategy to emphasize information services companies, it deliberately signaled its change in strategy by moving its corporate headquarters to a stunning high-rise building overlooking the Chicago River, designed by the renowned architect Ricardo Bofill.

Real estate and facilities can be used to send signals about strategic capabilities, even when the company may not intend to exercise those capabilities. A company may put everything in place to build a plant which will add additional capacity, without really intending to finalize plans and construct the plant. Instead, the company may just want to let its rivals know it can add capacity faster than they can, if need be.

RIVALRY IN RECRUITING
AND RETENTION OF EMPLOYEES

Rivalry between NationsBank (now Bank of America) and Citizen's Bank in Charlotte, North Carolina, has had a positive impact on the city. Both banks try to attract the best labor in the area, especially from among a relatively small pool of banking professionals. Both banks offer many amenities to their employees, such as high-quality offices, day care facilities, and other human resources support programs. More attractive facilities may be used as an amenity to lure away employees from rival firms. During its high-growth years, Sun Microsystems offered closed offices as a workplace amenity to help lure engineers in the Silicon Valley away from other employers, most notably Hewlett-Packard and DEC, which both use open office planning extensively.

FINDING THE FIT BETWEEN STRATEGY AND STRUCTURES

Understanding the five forces of competition within your industry will not magically point your company toward the right competitive strategy. This analysis helps identify opportunities to build competitive advantages, but there may be several ways to approach exploiting those opportunities. And you may work for a company which is not even clear about the strategy it wants to pursue. What these tools give the corporate real estate manager is the ability to reflect upon the business. They will not only help you ask the right questions of the line businesses which you support but also help you frame the discussion around strategic issues, not real estate issues. There is no static way to test how well your real estate strategy fits your competitive strategy at a certain point in time; it is a continually evolving process of maintaining fit as competitive conditions change. This strategic mindset, as discussed in Chapter Three, lets the needs of the business drive the real estate and facility decisions, rather than fitting the business into predetermined real estate solutions based upon the real estate market or the lowest direct cost solution.

Corporate real estate also faces other external pressures which affect a company's ability to plan, build, and alter facility solutions as the needs of its business change. Technological change impacts both the business and the workplace, and regulatory and financial constraints may be deliberately directed on real estate and facility issues. The following chapter discusses these environmental constraints.

CHAPTER NINE

NAVIGATING ENVIRONMENTAL CONSTRAINTS AND OPPORTUNITIES

Understanding the five forces of your industry's environment and the role of generic competitive strategies is not sufficient to completely diagnose the pressures imposed on real estate and facilities by your company's external environment. Three environmental constraints also impact both a company's flexibility in competing within an industry, as well as its ability to forecast future competitive conditions. These factors include technological dynamism—the rate of change and product life cycles for the technologies that are part of your core product, as well as for the technologies that support its production; the regulatory environment; and your firm's financial resources. They directly impact a company's ability to make the long-term logistical and financial commitments inherent in real estate and facility management decisions. In addition, environmental constraints may have a direct impact on the location, design, or use of your facilities, or they may control aspects of your product or operations, which in turn relate to the planning and management of real estate and facilities.

HOW DYNAMIC ARE YOUR TECHNOLOGIES?

Technology, defined as "the application of science, especially to industrial and commercial objectives," plays an increasingly important role in understanding the competitive dynamics of an industry.[1] Technology is either integral to your product itself, or else it serves to improve the production and distribution of your product. Here we term the former "driving technologies," and the latter "enabling technologies." Technology often plays a role in the product substitution process. It can be used to differentiate a product or it can help to lower costs. While we have already looked at the role technology plays in developing substitute products, we need to take a closer look at how technology impacts our current product and processes and then assess its impact on both the physical and organizational infrastructure supported by corporate real estate and facilities.

QUESTIONS ABOUT DRIVING TECHNOLOGY

Driving technology is an integral part of your product or service. The first question you must ask is what specific roles technology plays in the development, manufacturing, and distribution of your product. Only then can you begin to assess how the physical setting supporting your products is affected by technological change. Does your product have a fairly stable technology? Or do technological innovations dramatically shorten your product life-cycle? Semiconductor chips are an example of a rapidly changing product. Many years ago, Gordon Moore, Intel's founder and chairman, coined "Moore's law," which predicted that semiconductor chips would double in power every year while declining in price. His prescient understanding of this phenomenon helped him to build Intel into the world's largest maker of computer processors, holding 75% of the world's market by 1996. Since the design and manufacturing of semiconductors is subject to very short product life spans, manufacturing processes have to be adjusted each time a new generation of product is introduced, often requiring major facility modifications.

While you are not expected to master detailed knowledge of your company's most complex technologies, the effective corporate real estate manager must comprehend enough in order to understand its impact on the company's forecasting horizon. Sufficient knowledge to ask the right questions and to formulate a real estate strategy in response is essential. Do your products follow a predictable evolution from introduction to maturity, or will they encounter radical change in the near future? As these technologies evolve or more radically change, what impact does this have on facility requirements?

QUESTIONS ABOUT DRIVING TECHNOLOGY

In what ways are technologies an integral part of your product or service?

Do short life cycles require scenario planning and inventorying of options?

Can you enhance speed and creativity through workplace design or management?

Can you demonstrate the use of your own product technology?

Assuming that Products and Markets Will Change Rapidly

Research and development (R&D) activities are essential to staying on the cutting edge for those industries in which advanced technology is an integral part of the product or service, such as computer hardware, software, or pharmaceuticals. Having the right space available at the right time can be critical to competitive success. However, since R&D space may be very expensive to build, many companies are reluctant to make the capital investment required unless there is a good chance of payback in new products. Some companies have found innovative solutions to this dilemma while others have floundered, as the following examples illustrate.

A fast growing computer manufacturer in New England in the 1980's routinely kept several projects "in inventory" by optioning land and designing a base building for the site. By investing a relatively small amount of time in the planning and design process up front, they gained several months' advantage when a facility was needed to prepare a new product for market. Their head of corporate real estate realized that the majority of project costs are not incurred until earth starts to get moved. This manager was able to convince senior management of the need to spend some money up front on site planning by comparing those costs with the time that could be saved. Figure 9–1 graphically illustrates this relationship. If it turned out that the land and building were not needed, the company could still sell its option, or the land itself, most likely at a higher price than they originally paid, since having the permits in place increased the land's value. Of course, a land banking strategy must be done in coordination with an overall financial strategy because if the carrying costs of the land ownership are capitalized, a loss of book value might result if the land is sold without being developed.

In contrast, a major pharmaceutical company was unable to get a new product line to market in a timely manner because it did not have a real estate planning process in place that anticipated changes in facility requirements based on changes in manufacturing processes.[2]

Corning Bio, a subsidiary of Corning Life Sciences, only manufactures the experimental products developed by other biotechnology companies.

Figure 9–1
Up-front planning for potential projects accelerates time to occupancy with minimal cost exposure.

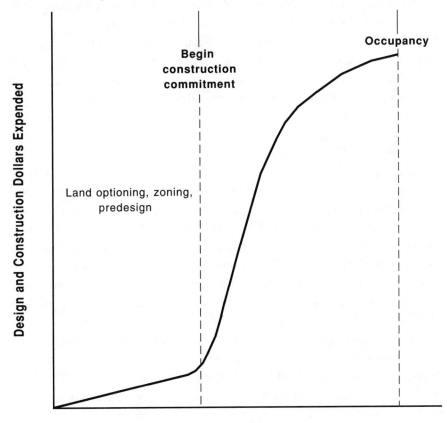

By manufacturing early stage products under contract in their state-of-the-art facility, Corning Bio lets its customers delay an investment in manufacturing capacity until their product has been tested in the marketplace and approved by the necessary government agencies. This way they are able to reduce both time-to-market, and the inherent risk of developing new biotechnology products.

As product life cycles shorten, the useful life of the facilities that are constructed to support them may also be limited. The life of a building can be extended if an ability to upgrade equipment is planned initially. Raised floors that can easily accommodate multiple changes in office technology are one common approach to flexibility.

Supporting Innovation Through Workplace Design

The workplace design of R&D facilities has also been shown to play an important role in competitiveness. Professor Tom Allen at Massachusetts Institute of Technology has conducted considerable research which shows that the physical layout of R&D facilities can greatly impact the interaction patterns of research engineers. Designs which encourage informal "bumping" into each other increased their ability to innovate and to get products to market faster than their competitors.[3] Ideas for supporting the work process and culture are further discussed in Chapters Ten and Eleven.

Loving Your Own Product

Some companies also use their workplace to demonstrate the use of their own products. This requires that they be willing to invest in the installation, and be prepared to make adjustments to the product as they gain more first-hand experience with its use. Office furniture companies often test their own products first. Steelcase's innovative "Corporate Development Center" located near Grand Rapids, Michigan, is filled with prototype designs for office furnishings. They are used by Steelcase's employees to both fulfill their practical needs in the office as well as to test the product for future customer installations. Since it is more costly to use a new, untested technology, using the corporate offices as a testing ground requires a clear commitment from senior management. Back in the late 1980's, the decision to install ISDN cabling throughout New England Telephone's (NET) new headquarters was stymied by an argument over who would pay for the more costly technology, the developer or NET—the tenant. The disagreement was even more complicated since NET also held an equity position in the building. NET could not get its corporate parent NYNEX to make a decision to approve the expenditure until well after the interior spaces of the new building were planned and framed into place. By the time the corporate blessing to put ISDN throughout the building was secured, the utility closets and other support space in the new building were too small for the new equipment and had to then be reconfigured at significant extra cost to the project.

QUESTIONS ABOUT ENABLING TECHNOLOGY

Increasingly, technology is a critical tool for businesses who do not have technologically based products per se. These technologies help deliver products to the customer better, faster, and more cost-effectively. For example, financial services such as banking and insurance are highly dependent upon information technology to remain competitive. Consider how enabling technology has changed this industry over the past ten years. High-speed computer networks have allowed many retail bank locations to be closed in favor of automated teller stations, while telecommunications technology permits many more transactions to be done over the telephone. Similarly, the use of phone service centers which can be located far away from the customer has grown rapidly. Electronic imaging is changing the paper-handling requirements of the back office. Most recently, on-line services are allowing customers to make banking transactions from their home computers.

QUESTIONS ABOUT ENABLING TECHNOLOGY

How does technology support your business operations?

Does your use of technology make alternative officing an option?

Will they make you more productive and lower your *overall* costs?

Can you accommodate advances in enabling technology in your present or future facilities?

Support of Enabling Technologies

The interaction between people and technology happens in a particular space and time, making Place a key part of that interface. As work becomes more information technology intensive, the physical requirements of the workspace change radically. Utilities, HVAC, lighting and furnishings must all be reevaluated when office equipment changes.

Alternative officing arrangements which are enabled by technological advances in distributed, networked computing, and wireless telecommunications, appear to lower a company's cost position by reducing space per employee and overall occupancy costs. These advances also offer potential productivity gains by helping workers to avoid commuting and have greater flexibly in work hours. It is critical to remember, however, that you cannot consider technological changes in the way work is done without examining the human resource, operational, and real estate and facility implications of the change. Any assessment of costs and benefits must include a full cost and benefit assessment and comparison of each point.

Accommodating Future Advances in Enabling Technologies

Planning for inevitable changes in office technology can enhance the ability to differentiate and can lead to cost advantages. A simple example of this is the St. Paul Companies' decision to construct raised floors throughout its headquarters addition: 450,000 SF of office space which the company occupied in 1991. The St. Paul realized that as a response to new market opportunities in the casualty insurance business, not only would its departmental organization structures change, thereby increasing churn rates, office technology would change substantially in the future as well. Although construction of raised floors was initially more expensive than conventional floor slabs, the payback period was short. Soon after construction, new networking technology was installed. Raised floors made it much easier and cheaper to install the new system. Churn at the St. Paul was also even higher than anticipated because of new products the company introduced. Interestingly, the only floor without a raised flooring system was the senior executive floor. Here, the raised floor would not provide a rapid payback due to the high ratio of square feet per occupant, and less intensive use of technology.

The planning and design of laboratory facilities are greatly affected by the rate of technological change and the relative costs of different building and mechanical systems technologies. It is often difficult to predict how long the asset will be useful. In such cases, simple payback period calculations can be more helpful than more complex discounted cash flow analyses. The cost of a short asset life must be balanced with product-market demands and opportunities for high margins. Any additional profits which result from accelerating the time needed to bring a product to market must also be factored into the real estate decision.

INFLUENCES OUTSIDE THE DIRECT CONTROL OF YOUR COMPANY

Firms have less ability to influence their outside environment than they have to direct their own internal actions. Much of the political lobbying efforts undertaken by corporations are attempts to have some influence on the regulations that impact their business. Firms also have little direct influence on the overall behavior of the capital markets. A firm can influence the quality of its balance sheet, but usually cannot exercise much control over the price and availability of investment capital which must be obtained from sources outside of the company. In order to mitigate the impacts of unfavorable environmental conditions, or to maximize the benefits of positive environmental changes, the effective corporate real estate manager must remain well informed about the company's external operating environment.

QUESTIONS ABOUT THE REGULATORY ENVIRONMENT

Despite political rhetoric advocating a reduction in government regulation, many industries still have some degree of regulation influencing their competitive behavior. Regulatory change reconfigures the power structure within industries by changing the rules of the game. They may place constraints on competition, or make it easier for new competitors to enter. Consider what deregulation of the telecommunications industry has done to increase competition in telecommunications services. It has both lowered prices and expanded telecommunication services to the consumer.

Changes in interstate banking laws have led to massive consolidations in retail banking, as larger banks acquire smaller local banks in an effort to build a national presence.

Regulation may concern company operations overall, or may be specifically targeted to control the use of physical assets and the workplace. This regulation may be overt. For example, airlines are often required to serve certain less traveled markets in exchange for access to more attractive locations. Price competition is still somewhat regulated in the telecommunications industry. Mandates concerning hiring, safety or environmental conditions may have secondary effects on either the operations of the company or on its physical setting. Other government regulations direct the use of physical assets. Although regulations are intended to have the same impact on every competitor within an industry, some companies are better able to respond to regulatory pressures and to changing regulatory demands through better planning and greater flexibility.

QUESTIONS ABOUT THE REGULATORY ENVIRONMENT

Assess the real estate and facility impacts of government regulation of your operations:

> Market and competitive regulations

> Service delivery mandates

> Labor and local hiring agreements

What regulations directly govern your physical assets and the workplace? e.g.:

> OSHA

> Americans with Disabilities Act

> Clean Air Act and other pollution legislation

> Brownfield liabilities

> SEC regulations

Can you anticipate the impact of regulatory change?

> Will it allow new competition to enter?

> Is regulation increasing your business's risk profile?

Regulations Concerning Company Operations

Regulations which control or monitor the company's operations can have an indirect impact on a range of corporate real estate and facility decisions from site selection to workplace design and management. There are many diverse examples.

Overhead costs, such as real estate and facilities, are often monitored in regulated businesses. Until recently, regional telephone operating companies had regulatory supervision over their facility expenditures because they impacted the costs of providing telephone service. Rates for services to the consumer were set by the public utilities commission based upon these costs. For example, the relatively high cost of Pacific Telesis's operating headquarters, a two-million-square-foot mega-structure built in San Ramon, California in 1985, resulted in pressure to maintain high occupancy rates in order to lower the facility cost per person. As reductions in the workforce took place after deregulation of the phone companies in 1984, it was difficult to keep the floors uniformly full of workers since most reduction took place with a few people per department at one time, leaving empty places scattered all over. Yet multiplied over the vast floors of the building, these vacancies increased the average square footage per person. At the time, Telesis managers reported being nervous about how looking "wasteful" might weaken their bargaining position with the regulators.

Today deregulation of the telecommunications industry affects the design and management of facilities in other ways. Now established telecommunications companies, such as the regional Bells, must allow their competitors to colocate their equipment on the local telephone company's own premises.

In the financial services sector, government regulations set time requirements for when financial statements must be mailed, and when payments (such as workers' compensation benefits) must be made. To assure compliance, companies must build operating redundancies, such as utility supply backups, redundant computer and telecommunications systems, and sometimes must maintain multiple sites. Otherwise, if a building or system is put out of commission by a natural disaster or other calamity, the company could anger customers, lose contracts, or even face legal action.

The 1990 Clean Air Act tied federal funding of transportation projects to state and local compliance with air pollution reduction efforts. In turn, states and municipalities have forced many companies to take responsibility for the number of automobiles traveling to and from their facilities.

Along with encouraging car pooling and subsidizing alternative forms of public and private transportation, companies have been forced to aggressively pursue alternative office approaches such as telecommuting and satellite offices. The pressure has been greatest in the state of California, where commuting distances are some of the nation's longest and air quality is known to be the worst. Not surprisingly, companies in California have been the leaders in implementing telecommuting programs.

Government tax codes often are based on regulatory intent and can affect decisions such as whether a facility is purchased or leased, the timing of acquisitions and dispositions, and the flexibility to invest in new equipment or property.

Local regulations can govern companies that accepted local and regional economic incentives for locating in a specific area. They may oblige a company to hire its new employees from that area and provide them job training. This in turn affects the company's employee demographics and may inhibit future flexibility in deploying and managing its workforce.

Regulations Directly Governing Physical Assets and the Workplace

The most obvious set of regulations governing the workplace come from the Occupational Safety and Health Administration (OSHA) which was established in 1970 and is an agency of the Department of Labor. Although largely concerned with factory work and other tasks which can place workers in mortal danger, OSHA's standards cover nearly every aspect of the workplace. OSHA not only inspects workplaces to assure compliance but also works with states, companies, and labor organizations to develop safety and health programs. Since OSHA's inception the workplace mortality rate has been cut in half. Compliance with OSHA requirements has become standard operating procedure at most companies today as a result of nearly three decades of awareness building and enforcement by this government agency.

The Americans with Disabilities Act (ADA) was signed by former President George Bush in 1990; when it took effect in 1992, this act had both operational and physical implications for companies. It prohibited discrimination in hiring disabled persons. Further, it mandated that all public buildings (including places of employment owned by private companies) be accessible to people with a wide range of physical impairments. This meant that many companies were required to extensively retrofit their existing facilities to accommodate workers using wheelchairs or with vision or other impairments. Ultimately, many companies found complying with the ADA cost them less than they had anticipated. A 1995 survey by Louis Harris and Associates of 404 corporate executives found that for the 81% who made changes to their offices in accordance with the legislation, the median cost was only $233 per disabled person.[4] Newly designed workplaces now frequently utilize universal design standards that make all spaces accessible to those with disabilities, rather than setting apart the adapted facilities.

Regulatory constraints in the operation of brokerage offices affect the extent to which alternative officing arrangements can be used in the commercial securities business. Although the sort of work that investment brokers perform, such as intense computer and telecommunications use, appears easily transferable to a telecommuting-based approach, federal regulations require that each work location be separately licensed. Therefore each location a broker worked from would need a license, even the home. Furthermore, many securities firms are comfortable with the regulatory status quo on work location. Since firms are very concerned about retaining their brokers, they worry that it will be difficult to reinforce loyalty to the firm if the brokers are given the opportunity to perform their work outside of the offices which the firm provides.

Fear of government regulation regarding liability over on-site pollution in the past has kept many companies from occupying older industrial sites in or on the outskirts of cities. Over the years, in an effort to make the polluter pay, government regulation has encouraged companies to abandon these brownfield industrial and commercial sites. Consequently, companies have preferred to locate on greenfield land, such as former farmland or undeveloped land which they were confident was pollution free, but which often was located farther from the urban core. Recently, federal and state government policy has focused positive attention on the development of brownfield sites, in an effort to bring more industrial and commercial activity back to cities. At the state level, action has been taken to ease the cleanup requirements at moderately contaminated sites, and as a result, more sites are being redeveloped. Further, pollution levels may not be as onerous at many of these sites as once was thought. Major legislative protection from liability, along with a variety of tax credits or other development incentives, are encouraging companies to reuse these abandoned sites closer to the city and are likely to have a major impact on site selection criteria in the future.

Anticipating the Impact of Regulatory Change

Since most legislation takes several years to be approved and enacted, regulatory change is the easiest of the environmental factors to anticipate and prepare for. Companies which anticipate changes in the regulatory environment can save themselves costly retrofits later. Although many of the ADA regulations just discussed had not been passed into law yet, the St. Paul Companies headquarters project also made sure that alterations in the project's second phase (which was being designed during the period ADA was under discussion in Congress) intentionally exceeded the standards then under discussion. The company hired an advocate for the disabled to consult with them on the design. Not only did the accessibility contribute to the positive image the company wanted the facility to portray to the public, the St. Paul Companies also avoided the need to upgrade the building later at a potentially higher cost.

Scenario planning techniques can be used effectively to anticipate the possible consequences of major regulatory changes in your industry. By modeling the consequences of new customers or new competitors on the sales and profitability of your company, you can estimate the range of demand for additional, different, or even less space. These analytics are best done in cooperation with your business's strategic planners, who are probably developing such models as part of their agenda.[5]

Understanding the specific impacts regulation of your industry has on your company is an important form of intimate knowledge. The effective corporate real estate executive will maintain close contact with the company's point person for regulatory compliance.

QUESTIONS ABOUT FINANCIAL RESOURCES

Financial resources determine the ability a company has to invest in new facilities and to upgrade existing facilities. Financial resources can be clearly quantified, such as the available cash a company has, but they also are perceptual. Financial strategy and whether a company's financial strategy holds risk or not is largely a product of the industry it competes within. Also, different senior managers have different attitudes toward debt.

Real estate and facilities are significant consumers of both operating and investment capital. According to NACORE, real estate and facility

---

QUESTIONS ABOUT FINANCIAL RESOURCES

What sources of investment capital are available for real estate and facilities?

How intense is internal competition for capital?

Should you lease or own your properties?

    Project characteristics

    Real estate market conditions

    Corporate context

    Financial considerations

    Hybrid financing approaches

What impact will a major real estate commitment have on your capital market position?

---

costs constitute about 25% of the average corporation's total annual assets for Fortune 500-type companies. Total value of U.S. corporate real estate assets may exceed $3 trillion. Facility operating expenses, which are deducted from operating income annually, include lease payments, property maintenance, utilities, the corporate real estate and facility management payroll, and other direct costs of running the facilities. Capital expenses, which include the purchase and development or ownership of facilities, and the purchase of long-lived items such as furniture and fixtures which can be depreciated over time, are accounted for as a depreciation expense and also contribute to the interest expense from financing these investments.

Sources of Investment Capital

The availability of investment capital, the cost of that money, and internal competition for its use affects how far a company is willing to extend its real estate commitments. Where does the money to invest come from in the first place? Understanding the various sources helps us to understand the pressures that arise from allocating and spending that money. Simply put, companies obtain money to invest through either operating or capital expenditures in three ways.[6] First, they earn the money every year by selling products. After all of the costs of producing that product have been paid, a profit is left over. That money can be invested that year, retained as earnings to spend in future years, or distributed to shareholders of the company in the form of dividends. Second, the company can borrow money to invest. The company hopes that the money produced from the investment will be able to cover operating costs, pay back the debt, and also be enough to pay back the interest on that debt. Any profit left over can then be used as previously described. A third option for obtaining money is to sell investors shares of the company. Those investors become part owners of the company and are entitled to shares of the company's profits and proceeds from the sale of the company, if and when it is ever sold. These investors also may hope to make money by selling their shares to other investors if the value of the company increases. Over a lifetime, most companies only have a few opportunities to sell to outside investors to obtain investment capital. Most subsequent exchanges of shares occur between outside investors who are trading on the value placed on the company by other investors in the stock market, not on the intrinsic value of the company's assets alone.

While external financial resources will tend to be similar across a particular industry, competitors within that industry have different internal financial profiles depending upon their credit history, their financial performance over time, and their own distinct financial strategy. These differences will affect how they approach investing in real estate and facilities.

Sources of capital vary among companies depending upon their life stage, the maturity of their product markets, and the attractiveness of their industry to outside investors. Start-up companies are usually very short on capital. They often initially obtain financial resources from their founders, often relying on their own personal debt capacity. In order to grow the company more rapidly, the founders may need to access venture capital, but in exchange, they must give up part of the company's ownership. When the company offers its shares to the public, most of the initial proceeds are used by the company to invest in growing the core business. Later secondary stock offerings may be more aimed at returning profits to the investors and founders.

High-growth companies may have high profit margins, but their need for capital outstrips their ability to internally generate funds. To seize opportunities in the market, they must invest in long-term assets. High levels of debt are particularly frightening not only because of the interest costs but also because the stock market may think the company's debt level is too high and therefore too risky, and the price of the company's stock will drop. Some mature companies have an excess of capital to invest. They believe that they are in long-lived markets. Often, there is strong price competition in their markets; therefore, cost control and financial stability become more important issues.

Most companies want more money to invest than is available to them from any of these sources. Managers always are coming up with ideas on how to grow the business or finding new businesses to enter. This brings about competition for financial resources within the company.

Internal Competition for Investment Capital

Companies constantly face dilemmas in capital allocation. There is usually less money available to invest than there are opportunities for investment. What is the best use of the company's investment capital? Real estate often is caught in the middle of this dilemma. On the one hand, companies can find many other uses for the money used for real estate and facilities. On the other hand, some level of facility investment is required so that there are adequate production and management facilities to get the product out the door in a high-quality and timely manner.

Too little attention to facility investment can have adverse competitive consequences. A major international consumer products company has long been hampered by inadequate facilities: old buildings which cannot support the newest office technology, and departments which should be located together to accelerate new product development, rather than being spread out over several locations many miles apart. Numerous studies have been made of the savings that would result from consolidation, modernization, and colocation; the suggested changes also meet the investment hurdle rate set by the company. However, its board of directors still prefers to invest only in new product acquisitions as a way of growing market share. Their philosophy is that any available cash or additional debt burden must yield an immediate increase in sales volume. Meanwhile the company's new product introductions are consistently beat to market by a company with state-of-the-art offices designed to foster product development and teamwork.

The ways in which both operating and capital expenses are accounted for and charged back to business units or product lines varies from company to company. Some companies try to track costs directly and apply them to the part of the business that benefits from them. Other companies pool all of their real estate costs together annually, and then allocate those costs evenly across the company, based upon the amount of space each business unit occupies. In general, the more closely a business allocates its real estate and facility costs to the business units and products that they serve, the more closely middle managers pay attention to their use of these assets.

THE LEASE VERSUS OWN DEBATE

The most critical real estate investment decision a company faces is whether to own or to lease the facilities it occupies.[7] The ownership decision extends far beyond its balance sheet impact. Where and how the debt shows up is more an issue of financial strategy. The strategic real estate question is how much control the company retains over the property. Companies tend to own their facilities when the activity housed is either highly specialized, such as manufacturing; requires extensive technological infrastructure, such as a data processing center or research and development labs; or has a long forecasting horizon for its use, such as a corporate headquarters. Companies tend to lease their facilities when they are needed only short term, when they merely require generically designed space, or when they require less space than an entire building. Owned properties usually can be customized more to the particular needs of the organization than a property which is leased from another owner; in that way, owned property may provide more of a competitive advantage. On the other hand, unwieldy real estate commitments can hamper a company's ability to invest in growing its main line of business. The decision to purchase or lease a particular facility is based upon several business considerations, both quantitative and qualitative.

Ownership versus tenancy is not a black and white debate. Many shades of gray are produced through hybrid legal and financial ownership structures. These may provide flexibility to vacate the premises when it is no longer needed, or may lessen the financial impact of building on the company's balance sheet. For example, a capital lease which has distinct characteristics is carried on the balance sheet as a fixed asset, and the present value of the lease commitments is included as long-term debt.[8] It has nearly the same effect on financial performance ratios as ownership. In contrast, the costs of operating leases are expensed against income every year and are not counted into the asset base or the debt burden of the company. Synthetic leases are gaining in popularity because they combine the best of both worlds. A synthetic lease is considered a purchase on a company's federal tax return so it can expense its depreciation like an asset. At the same time, a synthetic lease is accounted for as an operating lease, and the lease cost is deducted as an operating expense yearly. The asset and corresponding liability do not appear on the balance sheet although the obligation is footnoted in the financial statements. Because they are considered low risk, synthetic leases are charged at the corporate borrowing rate, which is typically lower than the rate real estate developers can obtain in conventional real estate financing. However, when evaluating the overall performance of the company, most lending agencies, Wall Street stock analysts, and investors take into account the long-term obligations of the operating leases reported in the footnotes of the company's financial statements.[9]

Four considerations dominate the lease-buy decision: the characteristics of the facility required, the dynamics of the local real estate market, the overall context of the company, and its financial position.

Project Characteristics: The most critical question is one which addresses the planned use for the facility. Generally, the more specific the facility's use is to the needs of the company, the more appropriate it is for ownership. It is less likely that a highly specialized facility will already be available for lease in the location that it is needed. If nothing suitable is available on the market, the company has little choice but to build the facility, although the specific property ownership structure can be flexible, as discussed below. The length of anticipated use is also a factor. Short-term occupancy (ten years or less) usually favors leasing. If a building is going to be occupied for a long period with a fairly stable use, such as a corporate headquarters, the more favorable long-term economics of ownership should be considered.

A facility that will be entirely occupied by your company is a better candidate for ownership than one in which you are one of several tenants. Basic office space, particularly in increments of smaller square footages, is better leased than purchased. Of course, planning lead time is also critical. If your need for space is acute, you may not have the time to develop your own project; in that event you will have to either lease or purchase an existing facility. Your choices will be limited by whatever happens to be available in the local market. To help avoid this dilemma, it is important to have an ongoing inventory of options for both expansion and contraction.

Real Estate Market Dynamics: The most important factor in the real estate market is whether a building which suits your needs is actually available for lease in the location you prefer. If such a property is found, then the costs of leasing the property can be compared easily to ownership. If nothing exists on the market, and the type of facility you need is fairly generic, such as general office space, you can choose whether to develop your own building, or to work with a developer, depending on your time frame. In the economic environment of the late 1990s, very little speculative office development receives project financing. A major tenant commitment, preferably with a highly creditworthy company, is needed before a lending institution will provide long-term financing. This gives the corporate real estate client substantial power in the lease negotiation process, but remember that the deal must make economic sense for the developer and the lender, with a healthy profit margin for both, before the dirt starts getting moved around on the site. A company's willingness to allow that profit depends largely on its need to retain the greater flexibility and shorter commitment horizon that leasing can offer.

If your project is being built in a greenfield location, and your company's presence in the area is going to attract a great deal of subsequent development, you are potentially adding a great deal of real estate value to the location. Under these circumstances, it may make sense to own the property so your company can benefit from this potential appreciation. Some companies even use such a greenfield development as a real estate profit-making venture, by buying land and even developing additional buildings in the surrounding area. Electronic Data Systems's (EDS) development of the Legacy office park, discussed in Chapter 12, is an extreme example of such an effort. Companies must be careful, however, not to get seduced into making real estate decisions which may be profitable in the short term but lead to poor logistics or impaired operations for the business in the long term.

Corporate Context: Companies differ on their general philosophy about property ownership. The company's recent rate of growth, length of product life, comparative operating margins, and use of financial measurements to evaluate and reward executive performance all influence its attitude toward ownership of real estate.

Companies in a high-growth mode, such as Sun Microsystems was in the 1980s, prefer to lease in short-term increments, keeping their long-term debt burden as low as possible while investing as much as possible in growing the core business. Their high operating margins cover up the higher-cost effects of leasing.

Companies with stable strategic environments, long-lived products, and predictable market demand tend to prefer the lower long-term cost benefits and greater control of ownership. However, industries with these predictable characteristics are becoming increasingly rare.

When competing as a low-cost producer of a long-lived, undifferentiated product with strong price pressure from competitors, lowering operating costs is imperative to success. Under these conditions, ownership of most real estate assets, where the total cost impact is usually lower than leasing, makes sense.

Ownership is also attractive to companies that like to retain a great deal of control over their physical surroundings. They purchase large tracts of land around their buildings and retain them either as open space or as a site for future facility expansion. This motive often leads companies to a green-acres location strategy, as discussed in Chapter 12.

Financial Considerations: The amount of debt and equity capital available and its relative cost will influence whether a company prefers to own or lease most of its properties. Most corporations can obtain debt at a lower cost than a developer. Through ownership, a company can access lower-cost debt, and avoid paying a profit to the landlord. Corporate debt, secured by a range of stable corporate assets is generally seen as less risky than debt taken on by speculative real estate developers, so the interest rate charged is correspondingly lower. However, if a company's debt rating or stock market valuation is adversely affected by its real estate holdings, ownership of many real estate assets will be unattractive.

The ways real estate costs and the uses of investment capital are accounted for within the company, and in particular how the company uses financial measures in executive performance evaluation, also affects ownership preferences. If a company frequently transfers executives from one part of the business to another, corporate real estate deals yielding lower short-term costs usually are favored if they translate into a higher bonus for the executive decision maker. This may occur even if the deal is more expensive or riskier to the company in the long run. The desire to minimize the impact of real estate costs is another reason why off-balance sheet financing schemes are often favored by senior management.[10]

Ultimately, if the company only views its real estate commitments as directly competing against other capital commitments, the company may avoid any sort of facility investment, including ownership, whenever possible. If real estate is seen only as a costly burden, rather than as a mechanism for enabling competitive advantage, no amount of clever financing is going to change the company's attitude, as we discussed in Chapter 3.

Hybrid Development and Financing Solutions: Many hybrid approaches to real estate development and ownership are evolving in response to corporate needs. In a build-to-suit arrangement, the developer encourages the corporate occupant to keep the eventual disposition of the property in mind and to design the facility parts so that they can be subleased or easily converted to meet another company's needs. Synthetic leases, discussed above, offer some of the off-balance sheet attractions of leasing, with other benefits of ownership.

A summary of the broader pros and cons of leasing versus ownership is shown in the sidebar. Notice that the pros of one position, say, leasing, often are not the mirror opposite of the cons of another position, say, owning.

Sidebar 9–1
THE LEASE VERSUS OWN DEBATE—A SUMMARY

	PRO	CON
Lease	• Can keep much of facility costs off the balance sheet. • Leaves real estate development, market risk to professionals.	• Restrictive clauses in leases limit flexibility. • Inability to expand space at will.

- Leaves property management to professionals.
- Can lease additional space for short or long term, or sublease unneeded space.

- Less control over abutting occupants.
- Lease is still considered a capital commitment by rating agencies and investors.

Own

- Real estate market may not have or may not be willing to provide the type of leased space you need in the location you desire. Over time, the overall cost of occupying a facility usually costs less.
- Fixes annual mortgage expense at a point in time; not subject to inflation or market-driven rent increases.
- May be a good place to hide excess capital. Can refinance via sale/leaseback if funds are needed later.
- Capture benefits of asset appreciation.
- Better control of surroundings, especially with campus design.
- Can design facility to meet specific corporate needs and to promote corporate culture and values.

- Can exaggerate balance sheet liabilities and adversely affect financial performance metrics.
- Over time, appreciating assets carried at book value may attract corporate raiders.
- Developing and owning property may distract senior management from running the business.
- If project includes tenants, you are in the real estate business by default.
- Property disposition can be inconvenient and potentially costly.

Sidebar 9–2
ANTICIPATING THE IMPACT OF A MAJOR REAL ESTATE COMMITMENT ON YOUR CAPITAL MARKET POSITION

Investments in corporate real estate are often seen as indicators of a company's general well being. There is some evidence that facility-related announcements do affect share price, at least in the short term. However the studies also indicate that investors pay close attention to the nature of the investment, not just the expenditure. One study found that share prices rise when a headquarters relocation is announced (1.29% during two-day period after announcement) with relocations to areas with high labor supply, low cost of living, and where firms are laying off workers eliciting the highest stock price increases. In another study stock market reactions could be attributed to what investors inferred about the firm's future prospects based upon the reasons given for the move. Four sets of reasons for the move using information were gleaned from company press releases. Two reasons conveyed positive prospects for the company: (1) either an expansion of the business to gain cost savings or (2) operating efficiencies. Move announcements claiming these reasons resulted in an immediate increase in the price of the firm's stock. In contrast, reasons which conveyed negative prospects prompted negative stock market reactions: either closing a facility or moving production to another existing site, or the consolidation of facilites which implied capacity reduction.[11]

Certainly no major project should be undertaken without consideration of the financial impact on short-term corporate earnings; not only to assess the balance sheet effects, but to anticipate the potential stock market reaction. However, short-term financial impact—the minimize cost mindset—should not outweigh the long-term strategic purpose. Ultimately, the link to a clear corporate strategy is the most important consideration.

CHAPTER TEN

DIAGNOSING STRUCTURAL DEMANDS WITHIN THE ORGANIZATION

While the external strategic environment drives both the forecasting horizon and strategic goals of a company's real estate and facilities, the internal dynamics of an organization determine how those facilities are developed, designed, and managed. This combination of demands from the strategic environment and the idiosyncrasies of each company's culture, history, workforce, and leadership are what make a company's real estate and facility strategy unique to any other. Real estate and facilities add value in many different ways, and it takes a thorough understanding of your company to identify where the biggest impact can be made.

It is within the context of the organization that the duality of an organization's physical setting, its logistical support role, and its symbolic role, are most apparent. There is no one set of guidelines a company can follow for developing the optimum physical configuration and environment. Instead, it is a constantly evolving effort to find the best fit that meets current and future demands. And while fit can be felt by the occupants and often seen by outsiders, it is hard to quantify and can even be difficult to articulate clearly.

Structural demands come from the way the company is organized, the work it performs, and the people who do the work. The physical requirements are very real, yet they can be interpreted and realized in many ways.

Like your analysis of the strategic environment, a diagnosis of structural demands may be most appropriately done at the business unit level, depending upon how different those businesses are in terms of their workforce, work processes, history, and culture.

QUESTIONS ABOUT STRUCTURE

A clear understanding of your company's organizational structure, and its implications for real estate and facilities, is an important first step in analyzing your internal requirements. The way your company is structured will affect its physical design approaches as well as the processes by which real estate and facility management decisions are made. How your company chooses to compete, either through low cost or differentiation, broad or focused, sets the context by which all structural decisions should be made. That structure then prescribes the management level at which decisions are made, and the autonomy which exists for idiosyncratic solutions. Structure also affects the way the costs of real estate and facilities are charged back within the company.

QUESTIONS ABOUT STRUCTURE

Overall context for structure: How does our company achieve competitive advantage? Are different strategies pursued according to the business unit?

- What formal organizational structure predominates? How centralized or decentralized are major decisions within the company?
- Which function does corporate real estate and facility management report to? Which other parts of the company report to that function?
- How autonomous are the business units or lines of business within the company? Does that level of autonomy affect real estate decisions made for the business units?
- How are businesses charged for their use of real estate and facilities?

Setting the Context: How Do You Achieve Competitive Advantage?

The first set of questions that must be asked relate to the way in which your business chooses to compete within the limits imposed by your strategic environment. In Chapters Eight and Nine we examined the external environmental forces which influence how a company sets and carries out its real estate strategy. Depending upon the competitive dynamics of your industry, the historical capabilities of your company, and the current resources you command, your company will find success either by being the low-cost provider of a product or service that is similar to one offered by your competition, or by differentiating your product or service in such a way that your customers will pay a price premium for it. A company which competes as the low-cost producer in its industry will need to approach its real estate and facilities differently than a company which competes through differentiation.

Clearly, a low-cost strategy means that the costs of real estate and facilities will be carefully scrutinized. But cheap properties and buildings do not help if the work environment impedes low-cost production. The total cost picture must be examined; such factors include direct labor costs, labor productivity, supply costs, product distribution costs, and ease of operations.

Companies which differentiate also must carefully weigh the costs and benefits of real estate and facility investments. Qualitative considerations will play a larger role in a differentiated strategy as the company places a premium on creativity, flexibility, and timeliness.

Whether as a low-cost, differentiated, or focused competitor, every company must develop its own set of solutions to the work environment to optimize the company's resources, workforce, and future goals.

OVERALL ORGANIZATIONAL STRUCTURE

The overall structure of the organization will affect real estate decision making. Although many hybrid organizational forms exist, there is one structural element at the core of the issue: centralization or decentralization. Which decisions about real estate and facilities are made at the corporate level and which are made by the business unit, by the work group, or by geographic region? The desire for central control over expenditures and long-term commitments is always balanced by the need for timely decision making and local knowledge of the specific situation.

There is no one best way to organize an economic enterprise. No wonder companies reorganize so frequently. Reorganization is one of the most common causes of churn—moving employees from one work location to another. While reorganizations can be annoying, changing the balance between centralization and decentralization in the corporate structure is one important way to adapt the organization to changing competitive conditions. Because real estate decisions are often highly visible and tangibly affect the workforce, the level at which they are made in the organization is often a source of controversy. Since space—where and how much—is one of the ways in which growth can be controlled in a highly decentralized company, the chain of command for real estate decisions may not match the overall organizational structure of the company.

CORPORATE REAL ESTATE AND FACILITY MANAGEMENT WITHIN THE ORGANIZATIONAL STRUCTURE

Where real estate and facility management reports in the organization varies among companies. At some companies the functions report to a senior administrative executive, who also oversees other support functions such as information technology, purchasing, or human resources. As with overall issues of organizational structure, there is no one best place in the organization in which to place corporate real estate and facilities. It depends upon what tasks are most linked to competitive advantage. For example, a company which needs to have the highest-quality workforce within a tight labor market, will want a close link with human resources. A company which requires a heavy investment in technology and has a lot of active projects will want to make sure that there is a great deal of interaction between information technology and real estate.

Although the two functions are becoming increasingly integrated, at some companies they still may formally report to different executives.[1] In particular, real estate may report directly to the chief financial officer while facilities may report to operations. In a stable organization, where few changes are being made to the work environment, this approach may work, but companies with a lot of active projects and high rates of growth or change will likely benefit from having corporate real estate and facilities reporting to the same executive, who then in turn reports either to the chief executive or some other very senior corporate officer.

CHARGING BACK FOR COSTS

As above, there is no one best way to allocate real estate and facility costs within a company. I find that asking about chargebacks is one of the best ways to truly understand an organization's attitude toward corporate real estate and facilities.

Like any other transfer pricing issue, the appropriate question is What behavior do you want from the business units? Do you want them to move to lower-cost locations? Then pass along the cost advantages of those locations in the way they are charged for space. Or do you want to avoid churn and space wars with business units jockeying for lower-cost buildings? Then blend the costs for all buildings in the area. Do you want them to adhere to a consistent set of standards? Then use uniform pricing. Want to discourage building the Taj Mahal? Charge them directly for all nonstandard construction. And like all other structural considerations, changing the methods to fine-tune attitudes and behaviors is a useful tool for adapting to changing demands upon the organization.

QUESTIONS ABOUT WORK PROCESS

Work process refers to the way tasks are physically accomplished in your organization. We typically think of work process being applied to the layout and function of a manufacturing facility. Equipment and personnel are placed along the factory floor in a sequence which maximizes productivity, quality, and safety. But information processing, professional service, research and development, marketing and sales, and all sorts of other office intensive work also has a process, although it may be less immediately obvious to an outsider's eyes. Information also moves through space and time, and although it may not need a physical road on which to travel, it still needs an electronic road. Examining the physical and information processing steps your product or service goes through from creation to the customer will help you highlight the role of the physical environment and the decisions needed to be made about how an activity is housed and supported.

As discussed earlier, many of our traditional beliefs about how work is performed have been radically changed by information and communications technology. For most of this century, work was typically organized by the division of tasks into the smallest parts possible and then placing these tasks within a hierarchy of decision-making power. The scientific management advocated by Frederick Taylor at the turn of the century—a precursor to today's industrial engineering processes—was well suited for mass production and low-skilled labor. Taylorism sought to decrease the amount of skill needed by workers, thereby minimizing management's dependence on them. By designing the work process to function with minimal input from workers, their capacity to do the job relied less on their judgment and decision making, and more on their ability to complete tasks. Taylorism was most effective in mass production environments where the goals were increasing output and decreasing costs.

In contrast to the scientific management approach of dividing up tasks into their smallest elements, the complex tasks of today's information work are better suited to high-performance approaches to work design. High-performance work processes bring people together from a variety of specialties to work collaboratively to solve problems. The power to make decisions about the work process is held by the people who perform the tasks.

One method which holds promise as a way to clearly and simply establish work process requirements as they relate to building function has been developed by the International Centre for Facilities of Ontario, Canada. Known as the *Serviceability Tools and Methods,* the assessment system is based upon building performance standards from both the American Society for Testing and Materials (ASTM) and the International Standards Organization (ISO). Different functional attributes of the workspace are rated as to their use and importance to a particular work group, building spaces are then rated according to the same measures, and fit is assessed.[2]

A work process can be analyzed at several levels. At first analysis, we want to examine the entire process from the point where the product is created to the point at which the customer receives and uses the product. In a second analysis, we examine each step in the process in greater detail to identify the real estate and facility components that support those steps. A variety of methods are used for depicting work processes—flow charts, physical work flow diagrams, and maps.[3] At the strategic level, one frequently used approach to visualizing the entire production and delivery process is a value chain analysis.

QUESTIONS ABOUT WORK PROCESS

- What elements of our value chain are affected by the physical setting? What is its impact?
- Which modes of transaction best fit the requirements of the various tasks we must perform?
- When is face-to-face contact critical—between whom? How often? Where?
- Have we reexamined our work processes and physical settings in light of organizational changes?

  Reengineering

  Greater use of teams

  High-performance work systems

  Flatter organizational hierarchy

  Use of physical supervision

- Is our changing use of technology impacting our physical work process?
- What kinds of office automation are in use?
- How paper intensive is our work?
- Can we foresee increased use of electronic media for document creation, transmission, or storage?

THE VALUE CHAIN OF ECONOMIC ACTIVITY

The value chain is the entire sequence of activities that design, produce, distribute, market, sell, and support your product.[4] If we think of *value* as the total revenue produced by a product, a firm is profitable when value exceeds the cost of producing the product. Therefore, your strategic goal is to create value beyond your costs.

The value chain is divided into primary activities and support activities. Primary activities physically create the product and get it into the customer's hands, while support activities provide the infrastructure to enable production. Support activities may reach across the entire company and may be purchased from the outside. A generic value chain is depicted in Figure 10–1.

The business unit or product level is the best point at which to examine the value chain. A company which supports many different businesses may have multiple value chains, but will often share common resources across those sets of activities. Competitors in the same industry may have value chains that look quite different, depending upon how the firm chooses to compete.

The first task in a value chain analysis is to visualize all the steps your product goes through from beginning to end. From that point, you can identify the relevant places where real estate and facilities infrastructure and policies support the value chain. For example, ask what must move physically through the value chain? At what points in the chain is access to physical artifacts (records, files, materials) required? Where is there face-to-face contact? Between whom—company employees, customers, or suppliers? How is this work accomplished today? Are there ways of doing it better? Faster? More cheaply?

A company does not need to directly own each piece of its value chain. Activities that are upstream in the value chain may be performed by suppliers and not take place on premises controlled by your company. Activities downstream also may be carried out by suppliers, distributors, or

Figure 10–1
The Generic Value Chain

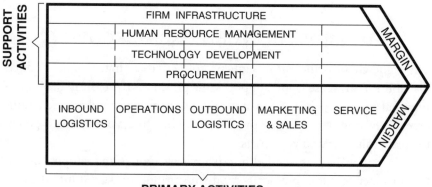

Source: Michael E. Porter, *Competitive Advantage* (New York: The Free Press, 1985).

contractors. Where are your physical boundaries on the value chain? Are there ways in which you can make better physical contact with your suppliers?

A second and critical task in a value chain analysis is to identify and better understand the links connecting the steps in the value chain. How does one activity affect the subsequent costs of another activity? Can improving performance at one point in the value chain also have a positive impact on other parts? One physical example of this impact is the improvement of product quality during manufacturing so it requires less after-sales service. Another example is an informational linkage: Better customer input into the product's initial design can result in easier sales and marketing. Corporate real estate and facilities affect both physical and information linkages by providing the right kind of space in the right location to accomplish the necessary tasks. However, while physical logistics may be straightforward to diagnose, the information linkages may be subtle and more difficult to identify. Information is not only content but also context.

With so many options for communicating information to choose from today and with the cost of these options varying widely, it is helpful to focus on what each information link within the value chain requires in terms of interpersonal context and immediate response, so that we may create the greatest value for our customers at the least cost to our company.

A "MODES OF TRANSACTION" FRAMEWORK FOR ANALYZING THE SPATIAL IMPLICATIONS OF ACTIVITIES WITHIN THE VALUE CHAIN

The way in which production throughout the value chain is best carried out in space and time determines how it should be supported by facilities and technology. One way to approach this analysis is to consider all economic and organizational activity as being composed of transactions between two or more individuals. *Mode of transaction* refers to the physical way information in a transaction is conveyed in space and time. At each point in the value chain, we need to ask which mode of transaction provides the best information in the most timely manner at the most effective cost. The number of possible modes of transaction have grown dramatically in the past twenty years due to advances in communications technology thus increasing our choices of where and how we conduct these transactions.

We can compare modes of transaction along two dimensions. The spatial dimension recognizes the degree of personal contact allowed by the mode of transaction. The time dimension represents the immediacy to which content can elicit a reaction and response. Figures 10–2 and 10–3 compare the typical modes of transaction available two decades ago to the much wider range of choices available by the late 1990's. Over the past decade this more complex and wider range of choices has helped to increase the strategic importance of corporate real estate and facilities.

Along the spatial dimension, face-to-face contact, as further discussed in the next section, is the most personal and immediate. It is the richest way to exchange information. We can not only react to the content of the factual information but also pick up interpersonal cues that place that content in context. As we have all experienced, many nonverbal cues enhance

Figure 10–2
Modes of Transaction, Circa 1970's

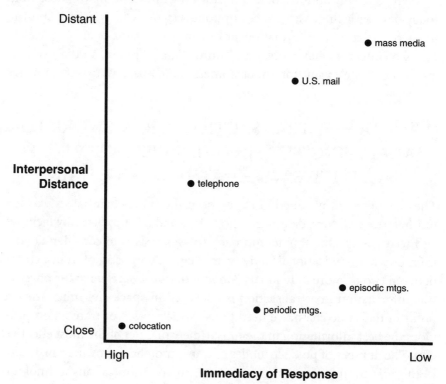

Figure 10–3
Modes of Transaction, Circa 1990's

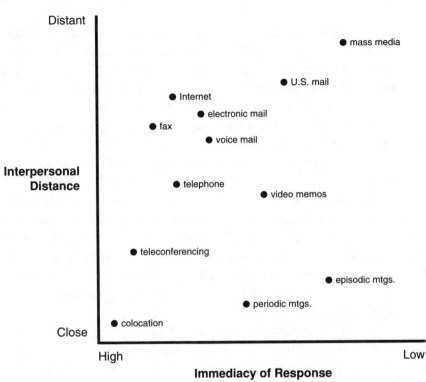

verbal communication. Quickened breath, reddened skin, and perspiration can all be readily detected in a personal exchange. Eye contact, posture, and vocal tone also convey sentiments. We can give and receive subtle cues without directly confronting the other person.

As we move along the spatial dimension, we lose some of the subtleties of personal contact. For example, while videoconferencing allows individuals in separate locations to view each other on television and to share visual material, the visual and spatial range are limited. Body language can be seen but more intimate perceptions are difficult to sense. There is a feeling that we are on stage for the camera rather than having a casual encounter. A telephone call transmits only auditory clues, such as the tone of voice and the pace of the conversation. A letter is even less personal because the visual and auditory context is lost and the author may be reluctant to commit her true feelings in writing. A newsletter, newspaper, or a magazine is less personal than a letter because it is aimed at a broader audience.

The dimension of time is represented by immediacy: How much time does it take to respond to the information in the transaction? Information which is immediately exchanged can permit quicker reactions to changing conditions, and the organization may benefit from obtaining and processing information faster than its competitors. Modes of transaction vary in how immediately they permit a response. Face-to-face contact is the most immediate mode. Information can be exchanged and reacted to without delay. This face-to-face interaction can be constant, as when two people are located where they can see each other, or it may be periodic, and take place through scheduled or accidental meetings. A telephone call permits immediate verbal response, although only after connecting with the person to whom the call is directed. It may take several days for a letter to be drafted, typed, delivered, read, and responded to, making it a less immediate mode of transaction. It can be sent immediately by facsimile, as can an electronic mail message, but both must still wait until the receiver chooses to review her mail and respond.

The qualitative dimensions of time are more subtle than those of space. Rapid response time does not automatically convey advantages. Some complex information must be absorbed and compared to previous experience, so immediacy of response may not always be preferred. The time needed to absorb the information and make decisions must be considered. Some modes of transaction give more control over reaction time to the sender or to the receiver, and the speed of a reply may depend upon the perceived importance of the transaction. The ability to make someone wait for a reply can indicate that one possesses resources which are in demand—a source of power. Therefore response time is not only functional, it may have symbolic value, too. Time is also physically and sequentially bounded. Certain activities naturally must take place before others. Although not as physically apparent as distances and walls, social conventions regarding how time is allocated and the natural sequences in which action must take place can be highly fixed, regardless of the mode of transaction chosen.

Even though information can flow immediately from place to place electronically, direct personal contact between people is constrained by distance and physical barriers. By its very nature, the place of work—its geographic location, buildings, and walls—are highly static. People can move from one place to another but that movement incurs transportation costs and travel time. Our choice of mode of transaction at any point in time is limited by physical barriers and by the communications technologies available. Physical proximity and time are both finite resources. Face-to-face interaction—the mode of transaction that brings people together most closely and immediately—should be allocated to serve those transactions which provide the greatest value to the organization. It requires special consideration when analyzing work processes.

SPECIAL CONSIDERATION OF FACE-TO-FACE CONTACT IN THE WORK PROCESS

Face-to-face contact is the most personal and immediate way of transacting business. However, as not everyone can be in the same place at the same time, it can be more costly than other modes because of costs associated with travel and space needs. An analysis of face-to-face contact requirements is essential before any consideration of alternative officing approaches is implemented. At the strategic level of workplace diagnosis with which we are working here, we simply need to establish a general sense of how much personal contact is typically required by the work process.

One of the first questions to ask when beginning to consider any sort of alternative approaches to the workplace is What will happen to face-to-face contact? The need for direct personal contact, whether it be between co-workers, managers and subordinates, or company personnel and customers or suppliers, varies according to the work they perform and where they are located. Face-to-face contact varies by frequency, duration, and the type of setting most suited to the interaction. Different kinds of settings may be needed to best support interactions between co-workers and those between company personnel and customers, suppliers, or other outsiders. The emphasis on face-to-face contact will also vary according to the individual culture or work style of the company or different groups within the company.

Work which is inherently face-to-face requires instantaneous feedback and real-time decisions; it depends upon the interpersonal cues that only face-to-face contacts truly allow. One example of this kind of work is trading on a trading floor, such as a stock market or commodities exchange, although much international trading activity is now being done in virtual space through computers. Another kind of intense face-to-face work is counseling, whether it is in the context of a therapeutic relationship or as part of employee development.

It is also critical to understand the need for both formal face-to-face contact, such as meetings and conferences, and informal contact which occurs spontaneously. Informal contact is often the lifeblood of a company. Consider the benefits attributed to MWA, managing by wandering around. This works best in a setting which facilitates a manager's movement around the office, allowing visibility to and among co-workers.

Research has shown that the product development process can benefit greatly from informal, serendipitous contact. As discussed in the previous chapter, Tom Allen of the Massachusetts Institute of Technology found that frequent, informal face-to-face contact between colleagues in the research and development process increases productivity and improves technical performance.[5] Contact between engineers working on different projects was especially valuable. Allen recommends that the R&D work environment be designed to encourage chance encounters and frequent contact.

We cannot limit our thinking about settings supporting face-to-face contact to those places which are part of the company's own premises. Many tasks requiring high personal contact actually take place outside this formal setting. Sales and service often are conducted best on the customer's premises. Indeed, much of the early work on alternative office design was based upon the recognition that sales and service people who are doing their jobs are rarely in their offices and are most often with their customers. Customers and suppliers are often sources of early, important information on your product's performance and on the actions of your competitors, so maintaining high contact is essential. Employee education and training also requires high personal contact, but often is delivered best outside of the company's facilities, free from the distractions of the workplace.

Moderate levels of face-to-face contact are needed when the work is primarily done by individuals working autonomously but who still require easy access to each other for questions, feedback, and collaboration. It is important to ask how much of this collaboration can be accomplished over the telephone or though electronic mail or groupware, and how much requires the special qualities provided by face-to-face contact.

Jobs requiring low face-to-face contact with fellow employees are often those with a great deal of information technology interaction or those relying upon the efforts of only one person. However, an examination of how remote workers were supervised in a telecommunications firm revealed that a great deal of informal personal contact was still needed to deal with unanticipated problems.[6] People whose jobs require low contact to accomplish their tasks may still crave the informal human interaction of the workplace and be less productive without that personal touch.

CHANGES IN ORGANIZATIONAL STRUCTURE AND WORK PROCESS

Although your company may have updated and redesigned its work processes recently to better reflect advanced uses of technology and communications, it is likely that your real estate and facilities have not changed much to accommodate these new work systems. Since most companies only make a major facilities move every ten years, offices are seldom completely redesigned in the interim. Don't confuse everyday churn that relocates employees from one workstation to another, or departmental moves from one part of the building to another, with the major rethinking of office space use that is advocated here.

Recent innovations in organizational structure and work process have had a significant impact on facility planning and design. Among the structural changes most commonly experienced by companies in the past several years are

- Reengineering
- Greater use of teams
- Flatter organizational hierarchy
- Use of physical supervision

Reengineering: The term *reengineering* has been highly overused and often misapplied over the past decade.[7] Essentially, reengineering is the examination and redesign of a work process from the ground up. One major driver of reengineering is information technology. As information technology grows in sophistication and performance, many companies apply technological solutions incrementally, without fundamentally reexamining the impact of the technology on the work. When companies examine their work as if they'd never done the task before, they often are able to eliminate many unnecessary steps in the process and focus resources on those tasks which add the most value to the product. Reengineering often identifies the need for major alterations to the physical way a product is developed and delivered.

Greater Use of Teams: Teams of people, often from different departments, are now being assigned responsibility for accomplishing a broader range of tasks in organizations. When assigned responsibility sequentially throughout a process, teams tend to solve many problems better and more quickly than individual managers. Even portfolio investment management has been found to be more effective when research and decisions are made by a team rather than by an individual in the lead position.[8] Teams not only require different types of work space and support space but also tend to change their membership over time and can result in high levels of churn.

Flatter Organizational Hierarchies: Often as a by-product of reengineering, many companies are reducing the levels in their management hierarchy to help speed decision making. The quality of decision making also can be improved by giving the power to make decisions to the people closest to the work. This empowerment approach requires many changes to both the systems and the culture of the company. Companies which have long based their office design standards on a rigid hierarchy will find them woefully out-of-date. And unlike the traditional pyramidal approach where more space was allocated per worker as one moved up the hierarchy, the frontline lower-level employee may need more space and equipment than a worker higher up in the organization's formal structure.

Changes in Physical Supervision: The ability to electronically monitor a worker's productivity has, in some circumstances, reduced the need for physical supervision. People can work from home or other remote locations and still be monitored. This monitoring requires the assignment of tasks which have clear output measures: amount of data processed, customers served, or sales completed. The ability to remotely monitor work has led companies to explore alternative officing approaches such as telecommuting. However, as noted earlier, it is still not clear whether physical contact provides important but subtle benefits which are lost when supervision is virtual rather than physical.

In general, these structural changes lead to the need for more group space, more use of different types of space for different types of activities, rather than the one-person, one-place approach. In particular, high-performance work systems, based on teams and oriented toward speed and creativity, require supportive work settings.

HIGH-PERFORMANCE WORK SYSTEMS

High-performance work systems do not have a precise definition, but generally refer to management practices that emphasize the involvement of frontline workers, continuous improvement, product quality, flexibility, employee training, and incentive structures that are tied to the company's success. Teams are usually at the core of any high-performance approach. As more companies attempt to use teams to achieve competitive advantage, they are discovering that offices designed for people working individually with clear departmental boundaries and rigid hierarchies are ill suited for use by high-performance teams. Change is needed if the work setting is to facilitate the work of teams, not reinforce barriers to communication and responsiveness. High-performance work systems need to be supported by facility designs and management policies that best support the way people work together and which are flexible enough to allow for rapid change and continuous improvement. Examining the major characteristics of high-performance teams illustrates the ways the work setting must be adapted for the team to work at its greatest effectiveness.

Facilities should enable high-performance work teams to exhibit the following features:

Interdisciplinary

One of the most important features of high-performance teams is that they usually cut across departmental boundaries of the organization. A useful analogy is that of a rugby team where all the members of the team are in the field and involved in continuous play. This contrasts to the more traditional relay race mode of operation, where different departments or functions work on sequential stages of the project and then hand off the results of their work to the next group. This serial process often leads to problems in later stages which can be solved only by going back to the beginning. The relay race model too often leads to redundant effort and wasted time. Delays and costly reworks result. On the other hand, the rugby model enables the total team to work together throughout the life of the project, with different members providing leadership during the different phases. Rather than traveling up and down the chain of command in each department to either obtain information or get authorization, high-performance teams incorporate members from all involved departments. The team is empowered to get information and make decisions.

Traditionally, office space has been organized by grouping all members of a department together physically, allowing managers to directly supervise the people who report to them. In today's new work environments this is no longer necessary or relevant. Employees are more self-directed in their daily activities. If they are on cross-functional teams, they often spend more time with people outside their department than they do with those in it. Further, as levels in the hierarchy are reduced, spans of control for managers become much wider, making it impossible to monitor individual activities through proximity, even if that were desirable.

Work Across Managerial Levels in the Company

High-performance teams are most productive when freed from formal hierarchies designed to maintain internal control and predictability within a relatively stable competitive environment. Symbols of hierarchy in the organization, such as office size based upon rank rather than function, send outdated messages and can waste valuable space. They also build in rigid rules about how space can be used (e.g., by someone who deserves it), as well as slowing down the speed with which groups can be rearranged as needs change. Many companies have moved away from multiple levels of office design based upon rank in the company by replacing six or eight different office sizes with two or three basic standards, or even a single universal footprint workspace which can be customized by the user.

Self-Managing

Today's high-performance teams tend to take responsibility for their own resources and tools, including their work settings. If something is missing or outdated, they note it and set about changing it, rather than waiting for those at higher levels to tell them what to do or grant permission. If it is difficult for teams to get the resources they need, their performance suffers.

Both the design of the work environment and the policies which guide its use must allow sufficient autonomy for teams to manage their own activities.

Information Rich

Today's changing environments require that companies constantly scan for problems or changing patterns of action. The chief rationale organizations use when changing to a team approach is that it promotes a freer and more rapid exchange of information. The team model contrasts with departmental structures where each function keeps its own piece of the puzzle to itself and then cannot see the whole picture. Michael Brill of the Buffalo Organization for Social and Technological Innovation (BOSTI) estimates that engineers still receive up to 80% of their information face-to-face.[9] Personal contact helps individuals to filter and interpret information, and the workplace has a strong effect on whom one talks to and when. It also can influence what information is received through the use of signs and symbols.

Flexibility

Adaptability to change is one of the key attributes of high-performance teams. They need flexibility in terms of who is on the team, patterns of how and when they interact, how quickly information is shared, roles that members play, and how they relate to internal and external groups. They need to be able to regroup quickly as the task changes. The work setting needs to allow flexibility as the task, the work requirements, and even the makeup of the team change over time.

Varied Personal Work Styles

While they share a common purpose and overall goals, high-performance team members should bring different backgrounds, points of view, and styles of work to the effort. Heterogeneity broadens the team's ability to function in different situations and modes. Not surprisingly this diversity will be reflected in the uses they make of their workplaces. For example, some people prefer quiet, private space for specialized tasks, while others thrive on activity and contact. Preferences for seating, lighting, and acoustics differ. The workplace should accommodate different work styles naturally.

Colocation

While the virtual office—the ability to work anywhere with a modem and a fax—has received a great deal of attention, the effectiveness of most group work is enhanced through face-to-face contact. Personal contact is especially important when communicating across disciplines or across cultures where differences in context play a critical role in understanding. Face-to-face contact is also critical to creativity in teams. For example, Quantum Corporation, a major manufacturer of computer disk drives, found that colocation was an important factor in the success of new product development teams. In the following section, we present examples of companies who, despite the use of sophisticated electronic communication systems, still place high value on face-to-face contact.

Connections to Networks Across the Organization

Effective teams turn outward and cultivate resources and information across the organization. This process can be facilitated by bump space, where people from different parts of the company informally meet each other and learn about each other's roles and functions. Cafeterias, common service areas (coffee, copy, fax, amenities such as fitness facilities), and entry places and hallways can all serve the added function of bringing people together across the organization when they are designed for that purpose. Companies are now planning office buildings in ways that enhance social interactions between employees to facilitate greater creativity and exchange of ideas.[10] These organizations recognize that often serendipitous interactions foster the most innovative results.

Supported by Senior Management

For high-performance teams to be effective they must perceive that they are supported from the top and actually receive that support. It is not surprising that companies undergoing major strategic change often change their physical environments as well. This change is driven not only by the type of functional argument we are advancing here, but by a symbolic purpose as well. "When you create a new culture, you need to provide quick and visible evidence of change," according to the CEO of AT&T Global Information Solutions.[11] A new physical environment sends strong messages about an organization's willingness to change. It can help break down obsolete behaviors and expose people to new parts of the organization.

Sidebar 10–1
PHYSICAL CHARACTERISTICS OF FACILITIES DESIGNED FOR TEAMWORK

DEDICATED SPACES FOR GROUP WORK

Researchers at Steelcase estimate that many people now typically spend from 50% to 80% of their time outside of their individual workstations, typically in group meetings, using other resources or traveling out of the building. Although the look of team work areas may be quite different depending on the industry, they share certain commonalties:

Conference Rooms: Places to meet that provide good visibility and acoustics, and an appropriate scale of setting. According to *Facilities Design and Management,* the most commonly needed size of conference room accommodates six to ten persons, a typical team size.[12] An interior designer profiled in the article noticed that conference rooms for groups of eight to twelve people are now more frequently requested. Most offices designed more than a few years ago lack sufficient conference space.

Formal Team Spaces: Teams may need some sort of center which is identified with them, such as a dedicated project room or war room that they can use spontaneously and fill with current information which doesn't have to be removed after each meeting.

Informal Social Spaces: They also have spots for relaxing together, often with comfortable seating and food and drink (a great bonding element). These social settings are a key mechanism for creative sharing of ideas and insights.

Other Work Spots: The rich team setting includes good places for a variety of activities such as writing, reading, or testing products.

Accidental or Bump Spaces: Teams interact among themselves and with other parts of the company in all of the circulation points— stairs, hallways, cafeterias. Providing informal seating and tackboards or wall writing space can increase the usefulness of these areas.

WELL-DESIGNED TECHNOLOGICAL SUPPORT FOR COMPUTERS AND TELECOMMUNICATIONS

Today's teams need to communicate in multiple media and have access to global linkages; therefore, they need effective technology for computing, electronic communication, videoconferencing, and the like. Some companies are using single address phone switching that allows an individual's phone number to follow her from place to place. Others are using wireless telecommunications both in the office and on the road. The wiring for local area networks and sophisticated telecommunications and multimedia systems can place a strain on buildings designed prior to these technological innovations. Upgrading systems in existing buildings can be costly.

LARGE FLOOR PLATES
If a team is relatively large (about thirty or more) or needs to work closely with other groups, it helps to have a single floor large enough to have all the members colocated. In Tom Allen's studies, traveling horizontal distances across a floor has been found to be a much less significant barrier to interaction than traveling between floors.

USE OF OFFICE AUTOMATION EQUIPMENT

Nothing else has had as great an impact on office design over the last twenty years as office automation equipment—word processors, personal computers, networked computers, printers, copiers, and facsimile machines. As its price has fallen and its performance increased, this equipment has proliferated throughout the office. While in the past printers were often shared among a large group of users, many employees now have their own individual printers. Some people now have more than one computer terminal on their desks—one for local work and one connected to the broader company network. Other companies are utilizing large-screen computer workstations capable of running multiple tasks at the same time.

The ergonomics of supporting intensive office automation is now well researched and documented. There is a large body of literature established to guide the design of air-conditioning systems, lighting, sound masking, and the interior layout of workstation components. An important strategic consideration is to determine which office equipment is shared and which is assigned to a single user. The issue is not necessarily to get the most productivity out of an expensive piece of office equipment, as most equipment is relatively inexpensive compared to the cost of the worker who uses it. Rather, the issue is to consider whether commonly shared equipment helps to promote the sort of informal contact and interaction which leads to better information sharing within the organization.

HOW PAPER INTENSIVE IS YOUR WORK?

A widely shared myth surrounding the increased use of office technology, particularly networked computing, is that it will naturally decrease our use of paper. Declarations of the paperless office as embodying the office of the future have been with us for nearly two decades, but the fact remains that, as of the late 1990's, our use of paper is at an all-time high. The paper industry projects an 11% growth in the use of printer paper and 25% growth in fax paper through the end of the decade. Even filing cabinet sales are up with a 29% annual increase from 1991 to 1994.[13] Even though many workers now have computer terminals on their desks that offer both local and remote electronic storage options, 90% of documents created electronically are still printed out as hard copy and 90% of the information at a worker's desk is still in the form of paper.[14] Laser printers, fax machines, and photocopiers distributed liberally throughout the office and low-cost desktop publishing software make it even more tempting to proliferate the use of paper.

The management of office documents is a professional office planning specialty in its own right and only can be touched upon in this book. Electronic media document management systems are predicted to grow rapidly over the next several years. Any new facilities planning effort today needs to examine thoroughly how paper is used, stored, and retrieved and what alternative media (magnetic tape, compact or optical disk, microfilm, etc.) can be substituted. Paper takes up space and space is costly. Isn't it preferable to lessen the space used for paper and increase the space for people? It often takes more time for personnel to physically retrieve a document than it does to call one up from a system electronically. A review of paper usage should examine what is used and stored at an individual's workstation (remembering that what is stored may not necessarily be what is used), and what is kept available in the immediate work area within the building complex or archived at a remote location in less costly or more secure surroundings.

Despite the ubiquity of paper, keep in mind that new developments on the horizon may at long last reduce our organizational and cultural reliance on paper. The cost of electronic storage and retrieval technology is dropping rapidly. Optical scanners are now part of office equipment packages and priced under $100. High-capacity Zip and Jaz drives and recordable compact discs, coupled with document management software, can handle desktop or small business storage needs, while larger optical systems are one-tenth the price they were just a few years ago. Advances in the quality and security of climate-controlled storage spaces, and the proliferation of service businesses specializing in document storage have increased the choices available for remote storage. For example, the market for data backup services was forecast to grow twentyfold between 1995 and 2000.

A major stumbling block to the transition from paper to electronic media storage has been the legal admissibility of electronically stored documents. But more courts are accepting optically stored records if the record is created and used in the regular course of business; the Internal Revenue Service and state tax agencies also now accept electronic documents as legal records.

A final barrier which may not be overcome for several more years is the look and feel of electronically stored documents. The eye favors the smooth, matte finish of paper. Paper documents are easy to read for long periods of time, are readily portable, and can be flipped through easily. How many of us print out what we find on the Internet, rather than reading it on-line? While this author can hardly write without using a computer to compose her thoughts, she still prints out her drafts on paper for editing. Until computer screens are as easy to read as paper, which will require screen displays that do not rely on constant refreshing, paper will be preferred.

The next generation of information workers, our computer-literate teenagers and children who are growing up using electronic information daily, will be far more at ease with the use of these technological aids. Perhaps only at that time will the paperless office of the future actually become reality.

QUESTIONS ABOUT DEMOGRAPHICS

Demographics refers to the profile of the people who work at your company—their age, education, and lifestyle. Different kinds of people at various stages of their lives have different preferences about location, the type of environment they work in, and the amenities it features. If your human resources are a source of competitive advantage to you (and it is the rare company where the quality of the workforce doesn't matter), facilities play an important role in increasing employee satisfaction and can greatly impact morale and productivity. Demographics play a role in setting a company's real estate strategy at two different levels, facility location and workplace amenities.

QUESTIONS ABOUT DEMOGRAPHICS

- *What kinds of people work in your company?*

  What are their ages? What kinds of education do they possess? How diverse is your workforce? How many are male or female? Are most of your employees married with children? Do they tend to be in one- or two-income families? How are these demographics distributed throughout the management hierarchy of the company? Are there different kinds of people in different parts of the company?

- *Given this population: What are their locational preferences?*

  What are their lifestyle preferences, residential preferences, recreational preferences? Are these best met in an urban or suburban setting?

- *What on-site amenities best serve this population?*

  What pressures do they face in their daily living that might affect their work? How can the company provide help to lessen these pressures? Should you provide day care on-site or nearby? Is day care at or near your facilities desired?

- *Can you attract better workers with better facilities?*

- *Will your future workforce needs be met in your current locations?*

DEMOGRAPHICS AND LOCATIONAL FACTORS

Location preferences may differ by age and education. A company which hires a lot of young, well-educated people may find its best prospects in cities with large college student populations. The same sorts of public amenities that serve college students, such as entertainment, bars, libraries, and museums, also appeal to young urban professionals. These younger workers usually have not started their families and like living in or near the city to take advantage of nighttime activities. Access to health clubs and other recreational and sports venues also may be a factor.

A company which hires mostly older workers with families may be under a lot of pressure to locate in the suburbs where housing is less expensive and more plentiful and there are better-quality schools. Those workers may value a short commute from their homes to the workplace and have very little interest in, or time for, the activities of city life.

An example of how employee demographics can shape locational preferences can be seen in Fidelity Investments' move from Boston to Covington, Kentucky. The company found that employees' reactions to the relocation varied strongly according to their lifestyle. Young unmarried professionals sorely missed the urban attractions of Boston, while those employees with young families appreciated the rural setting and large, affordable homes nearby. One senior manager who helped implement the project admitted: "It's great here while my kids are in school but as soon as they move out to go to college, I'm transferring back to Boston. I miss the city life."

Location also influences the cost of your labor. If you have relatively highly paid employees, they may be able to afford living in a more costly urban location and be willing to pay the premium for an urban lifestyle. If you rely on lower-cost labor, you should be located where the cost of living is less. Lower-price homes allow employees to accept lower wages, while an excellent school system helps employees to avoid paying for costly private schools. Location is a two-way street. A company's initial location gives it access to a certain quality of labor force, and its continued presence in a location helps determine the kind of new employees it can attract.

DEMOGRAPHICS AND ON-SITE AMENITIES

The design of your facilities, and the range of amenities you wish to provide for your employees, also will be influenced by the demographics of your workforce. High-technology companies, populated by recent college graduates who are totally absorbed in their work, have learned to provide a wide range of support services to their workers. Their buildings need to operate on a 24-hour basis since all-night programming sessions are not uncommon. Recreation areas, such as health club facilities and game rooms, help people to blow off steam. Tour a high-tech company in the Silicon Valley and you are as likely to find Ping-Pong tables, video games, basketball hoops, and stereo systems as you are to find conference rooms. Some companies, such as Netscape Communications Corporation, have even experimented with providing on-site futon rooms for employees who want to work through the night, and have found that providing these accommodations further encourages such behavior. Other companies provide rooms at nearby hotels so that their employees do not have to drive home, sleep deprived, in the middle of the night.[15] Additional food service, including breakfast and dinner, is often required, as well as microwaves and vending machines close to employee offices. Companies with a young workforce also may encourage their employee's social lives by holding frequent beer busts and parties.

On-site fitness and recreational facilities serve several purposes: They are more convenient for employees to use than facilities off-site, they may encourage employees to stay fit and therefore help the company to lower its health care costs, and they provide another forum for informal interaction among employees. Younger employees may enjoy more social recreation activities such as basketball or volleyball, while older employees fighting middle-age spread may prefer a quick intense workout on a treadmill or stair climber. A government contractor based in Cambridge, Massachusetts, even provided a swimming pool for its employees at its headquarters. During the summer, which coincides with the heavy proposal writing season, the poolside activity on a Saturday was as busy as the office is on a weekday. Family and friends also were invited to use the facility, making it possible for them to swim and sun while employees put in some weekend hours at the office.

Companies which employ a lot of parents from two-income families stress conveniences such as dry cleaning pick up and delivery. Some companies have caterers that sell prepared meals to employees to take home for dinner. Eli Lilly & Company surveyed employees at its corporate offices in Indianapolis and found that only 20% of the employees have a spouse at home during the day. In response, the company now offers a plethora of on-site amenities to support its employees, including on-site child care and fitness centers, a dry cleaner, shoe repair, and convenience store. College courses also are conducted on-site. Across the board, day care, usually for children but sometimes for elderly family members, is now a critical employee amenity for many companies, whether it be provided on-site or available nearby.

Sidebar 10–2
IS ON-SITE CHILD CARE DESIRED?

Companies with many employees from two-career families, or with a high percentage of female employees, often face demands from their employees for child-care assistance. For some companies, providing child-care facilities on-site or adjacent to their facilities has become an important employee benefit and a symbol of corporate values as well. A survey conducted by the Conference Board of New York in 1996 found that parents are happier and more productive when their children are in a safe, quality environment that is easily accessible. It is estimated that parents who miss work because of child-care problems cost American companies about $3 billion per year in lost productivity and absence-related expenses. Reduced absenteeism and turnover as well as increased employee morale are the major drivers behind corporate-sponsored child care. Over half the companies surveyed in the Conference Board study confirmed these benefits.[16]

Although 85% of the 1,050 U.S. companies surveyed by Hewett Associates in 1995 provided some sort of child-care benefits to their employees, only 10% of these companies offered on-site day care. Companies are more likely to consider on-site day care if they have a large proportion of female employees or employees from two-career families. Suburban locations tend to include child-care centers more than downtown locations do, because the workplace is closer to home than a downtown location and the suburbs often do not have other day-care resources. A company needs to be large enough to be able to operate a center of sufficient scale, although several smaller adjacent companies may join together to develop a communally supported facility. It is easier for companies today to provide on-site day care now that they can choose from several successful nationwide chains which specialize in running corporate-sponsored centers. Day-care centers are of greatest interest to parents of preschool-age children and babies, although some centers now offer after-school care to older children and full-time summer activities. Parents enjoy the reliability of a nearby center, the opportunity to spend more time with their children by having lunch with them or even just sharing the daily commute, and the reassurance of being physically close by in case their child needs them. Although at some companies only 5% of the employees actually use the day-care facility, the family friendly atmosphere they project improves the company's overall image with its employees. Some companies just provide part-time care: Deloitte & Touche provide child care on Saturdays during tax season, some law firms provide regular Saturday care, and other companies run special summer day camp programs. On-site day care appears to be a growing trend: In 1985 *Working Mother* magazine found only four private companies with on-site child care; a decade later they identified seventy-six. The federal government operates more than twenty-five on-site centers in the Washington, D.C., area alone.[17]

Providing a facility on-site is a major investment. A 1993 study by Catalyst, a New York City research firm which specializes in workplace issues, found that the companies it studied spent an average of $500,000 in start-up costs, with an annual operating cost of $280,000, which can be offset by the fees parents pay for the service. The study also found that having a champion at the senior management level was required to get the center established, and that many senior executives did not really understand the need because they were still living in a traditional family structure with a spouse at home.

There are several approaches companies can take to provide a day-care facility on or near their work site. Some companies provide the both the land and the building, others supply the land with an outside contractor building and managing the space, while others lease space to an outside provider. Types and levels of subsidy vary: Some offset the cost indirectly by providing a low- or no-cost facility, or directly through paying part of employee's fees. Calculating the relative costs and benefits of on-site day care requires input from both corporate real estate and human resources, since the benefits will be found largely in human resources cost savings. For example, at one Los Angeles area bank, users of its day-care center were absent from work 1.7 days a year less than average and turnover among this group was 2.2% compared with 9.5% turnover among a similar profile of employees and 18% turnover of bank employees overall. The study estimated that the day-care center saved the bank from $138,000 to $232,000 per year in human resources costs.[18]

Companies that are physically isolated on campuses or in suburban office parks are often pressured to provide more amenities on-site than companies in urban settings where the physical density of workers is great enough to support a variety of local businesses. Food service, with variety and quality, is essential and its cost is often subsidized by the company. Sun Microsystems' corporate headquarters and its million square foot Menlo Park campus both feature "Sunstores" where employees can rent videos, buy fresh flowers and greeting cards, and even get film developed.

DEMOGRAPHICS CHANGE OVER TIME

A major real estate commitment has a long time horizon. A company needs to consider more than its future operational requirements, it must also envision what personal resources its employees will need in the future, both in the general location and on-site. Some companies which have expanded rapidly from start-up stage have seen their population age over time. While Sun Microsystems still hires significant numbers of recent college graduates, its middle and upper management ranks have grown up with the company and are now in their middle years. These managers find themselves facing work and family issues that were rarely addressed during the company's start-up days, when the average age of the workforce was under thirty, and sixty-hour workweeks were the norm. Affordable housing, child care, and the balance between work and family time are now significant human resource issues for Sun as the middle-management population ages. Companies which saw their population of female managers grow during the 1980's, when more women were obtaining graduate business degrees than at any other time, now have to pay more attention to their family policies as these women begin to have children and seek greater flexibility in the workplace.

Other companies continually turn over their workforce in such a way that their basic demographic profile does not change much over time. Firms with strict up-or-out policies, such as law, accounting, and consulting firms, tend to retain the same proportions of eager young graduates and seasoned managers over time. Recruitment of hot young talent is a greater priority than retention.

Understanding the demographic composition of your workforce, how it has changed over time and how it may change in the future, will help you to make long-range decisions, such as new facility locations or major site relocations, that will best position your company for its future needs.

Clearly, the corporate real estate and facilities manager cannot begin to answer these important questions about demographics without a lot of help and involvement from the human resources department. As discussed in Chapter One, companies that depend more and more upon their people as their source of competitive advantage need to think broadly about what it means to provide a supportive workplace. Employee surveys and focus groups can help you get a better idea of preferences and what services or amenities would be most valued by your employees. Benchmark against other companies in your industry across the country, as well as other businesses in your location. These companies may be competing with you for the best employees. Can you meet or exceed their challenge? Surveying what other companies are doing also can help you to generate new ideas, and perhaps to learn from other's mistakes. Look around your own community for resources, such as local companies that might provide additional services to your site without any direct cost to your company. A service-oriented facilities management mentality benefits the company by helping to create a better work environment. It also helps to demonstrate facility management's strategic value to the company.

BEYOND SEATS FOR BUTTS—RESPONSIVENESS TO STRUCTURAL DEMANDS

Truly understanding the structural demands of your company goes far beyond merely providing some sort of spatial accounting for each person on the payroll. While anticipating the demand for space generated by head count is in itself a challenge, especially in dynamic industries, strategically oriented corporate real estate and facility managers go well beyond simple forecasting to anticipate their company's broader spatial needs into the future. Even diagnosing and tracking structural demands is still not enough, because each company also has unique requirements grounded in its culture, history, and senior management's personalities. We address the special contribution Place can make to the development and enhancement of culture in the next chapter.

CHAPTER ELEVEN

DIAGNOSING CULTURAL DEMANDS WITHIN THE ORGANIZATION

While structural demands drive many functional requirements of the workplace, cultural demands on the physical setting arise more from the feelings and personal experience of the organization's members. Every organization is a product of its history; the people who founded it, helped it to grow, and those who manage it today. Cultural demands sometimes appear to be myopic and capricious. But responding to cultural demands through the design of the workplace also can be a source of competitive advantage. Much of the work of modern organizations is based upon interpreting and communicating information. Many tasks cannot be pre-programmed into an operating manual. Instead they must rely upon the personal discretion of the worker to do the right thing when faced with a unique situation. Strong, clearly articulated cultures help companies guide their employees' behavior to assure that products and services are presented to the customer in a consistent and appropriate manner. A company's culture is strengthened by channeling behavior within the work setting through the way it is designed and managed, and by reinforcing the company's culture through physical symbols and symbolic behaviors. Senior management can use actions and symbols as well as words to communicate their vision of the company's future.

QUESTIONS ABOUT HISTORY

Every company possesses a history. Where the company was founded, by whom, and for what personal reasons as well as market opportunities profoundly affect the way future decisions are made, especially those which are highly visible and symbolic. A company's history contributes to its identity and culture. It is important to understand how your company has evolved over the years to what it is today, for past successes often pave the way for competitive advantages in the future. Some companies become stuck repeating their own histories and have a hard time changing to meet new demands.

QUESTIONS ABOUT HISTORY

What parts of your corporate history should be preserved and nourished?

How do you use your facilities to depict your history?

What impact do local hero ties have on your operations?

What corporate rituals must be preserved?

WHAT SHOULD BE PRESERVED AND NOURISHED?

Throughout American history, commerce and industry have profoundly shaped our society. The innovative development of new products within a free market system has focused on creating and satisfying consumer demand, and those products often change how we live. Companies that have participated in these landmark innovations are proud of their accomplishments, whether they are as visible as laundry soap or as unrecognized as water filtration systems. Many companies strongly identify with their earlier history, and consciously seek to inculcate in their current employees the meaning and culture surrounding that history. This is especially true of companies whose products have changed how we live our lives today.

Even young companies are not spared the ghosts of companies past because the founders of the new company will probably react to past experiences when setting policies. Like the childhood experiences which shape us and influence how we want to raise our own children, some founders want to replicate what they liked about their past workplaces, while others defiantly try to do things very differently now that they are in charge. The ways senior managers present their preferences during times of organizational restructuring is explored later in this chapter.

The physical setting of a company becomes an important symbol to both employees and customers. Any major change in the physical setting should be viewed in the context of how it relates to the company's history. What does the company want to preserve and nourish? What needs to be changed to grow and meet new challenges? These are important questions to be posed to senior management.

The location of a company's headquarters often has a relationship to the early history of the company, even though the logistical reasons for selecting that location may no longer apply. Companies which played an important role in the development of their local communities will often have important sentimental ties to that area, particularly if senior management also grew up in the area.

History also sets important precedents about the relationship between the company and its workforce. Companies founded and managed by one family may have a very paternalistic attitude toward employees, which often translates into greater employee amenities and generous benefits. Those companies with a high level of sustained success over many years may have many policies in place that will prove too costly when competition in their markets intensifies and margins are eroded. IBM realized it needed to modify its no-layoff policy and generous benefits package when computer hardware became more of a competitive commodity and the company could no longer count on high product margins to support their corporate generosity.

Even relatively young companies try to place their development in a larger historical context. Sun Microsystems displays a historical diorama in its headquarters lobby, featuring the company's past and current products, and including a replica of the first Sun computer ever assembled. This is not exactly an artifact of ancient history since that computer was first built in 1982, only seven years earlier than the new headquarters.

Sometimes a clean break with history is needed. When Digital Equipment Corporation suffered devastating losses in the early 1990's due to major competitive shifts in its business, they needed to do more than simply reengineer the company. They needed to make a gesture that would symbolize to employees a break with tradition. At the time, their corporate headquarters were housed in an old mill complex; as they had been located there for many years, the place was rife with symbolism of the company's founding and past successes, and closely associated with its strong-willed founder and longtime chairman, Ken Olsen. By moving out of the Mill and into a modern company-owned suburban office building, DEC sent a powerful message that it was no longer business as usual, but that the company was entering a leaner, faster moving world than the one to which it was accustomed.

History sets the context for all change in organizations. Memories are strong, and people use past experiences to help them anticipate future demands. To boost competitive advantage, a company must balance respect for its history with a willingness to embrace change.

HOW DO YOU DEPICT YOUR HISTORY THROUGH YOUR FACILITIES?

Although some companies decorate their office spaces with art, others prefer decor that has personal meaning to the company and that tells a story. Companies often choose to depict their company history through their facility design. This is a common design theme in lobbies. The lobby of Procter & Gamble's elegant headquarters in Cincinnati, Ohio, is a museum of the company's history which parallels the evolution of commerce in the United States: The development of the first mass-manufactured bar soap (Ivory), their early sponsorship of soap operas targeted to an audience of housewives, and the company's subsequent leadership in the innovative delivery of numerous consumer products.

Materials and forms also echo the company's history. The top of Chrysler's new headquarters in a Detroit suburb recreates the pentagram shape of the company logo. The history of a facility itself may be depicted. Visitors stepping off the elevator at Pacific Bell Directory's headquarters in Rincon Center, San Francisco, were greeted by a wall-sized gold painted plaster cast of the hand prints of the employees who worked on the design and development of the facility. These symbolic uses may be directed toward communicating with employees, or they may be used to represent the company to the community.

LOCAL HERO TIES

The historical ties of a company to its local community may be strong. These local hero ties often drive the commitment to remain in a particular location, even after the original reasons for being in that location no longer serve a function. Such ties influence the level of visibility desired by the company within the local community and the extent of its involvement in local politics and economic development activities.

Local hero ties also increase participation in civic and charitable activities. When Pacific Telesis developed its 2-million-square-foot operating headquarters in San Ramon, California in the early 1980's, the local municipality was barely incorporated. Pacific Telesis allowed community groups to use its meeting spaces in the complex after hours; even the local city council meetings were held there until a city hall was built.

IBM considered making a break with its historical home in Armonk, New York, but after much lobbying by state legislators and the granting of significant financial incentives—$27.4 million—IBM decided to remain on the site and build a new $70 million headquarters building. The new building better supports office technologies such as teleconferencing, while being smaller than the old headquarters. Even without the development incentives however, it would have been extremely surprising if IBM would have moved, given their other corporate real estate holdings in the area, and above all the large number of IBM employees who own homes there. Although the company planned to sell their old 420,000 SF headquarters building, dating from 1964, IBM was never able to find a suitable buyer. As it turns out, the reinvigorated company actually needed the space after it had sold off many other real estate assets in its portfolio.[1]

Some companies take on a strong leadership role in local development far beyond that of their own properties. These corporate Medici look beyond their own corporate facility needs to the needs of their surrounding community, to the benefit of both company and locale. NationsBank (now Bank of America), which through a series of acquisitions had become one of the largest retail banks in the United States, has been extremely proactive in the community development of Charlotte, North Carolina, where its headquarters are based. Led by its dynamic chairman, Hugh McColl, who has a deep personal commitment to the city, NationsBank not only built a landmark corporate headquarters designed by the renowned architect Caesar Pelli but also acted as financier or developer for a variety of projects designed to improve downtown Charlotte. McColl wants to see Charlotte's downtown area remade into a 24-hour full-service city with places to work, live, shop, and be entertained. Local development projects with NationsBank support include a major sports stadium, a 700,000 SF office tower, and 20-story high-rise condominium project codeveloped with Trammel Crow, as well as several high-density housing projects for the downtown. The company also spent $9 million to build a new downtown bus transit depot on city land. McColl even brought the Neighborhood Assistance Corporation of America to the city to spearhead efforts to provide mortgages to low-income residents, and pledged $500 million in mortgage loans for the program. Along with First Union Bank, another aggressively growing bank, senior management in NationsBank corporate real estate organization have become involved in the development of these projects, expanding the scope of the traditional corporate real estate role. Charlotte has now become the third most dynamic commercial banking city in the country, after New York City and San Francisco. McColl's dedication to Charlotte was recently tested, and his allegiance to the city won out, albeit with some sacrifice. When NationsBank announced its merger with San Francisco giant Bank of America in 1998, McColl gave up the name NationsBank and allowed the new combined financial powerhouse to be called Bank of America. In return, at McColl's insistence, the new Bank of America is headquartered in Charlotte, not San Francisco.

CORPORATE RITUALS

History also plays a role in the rituals that companies sustain—those regular events which employees count on to mark the passage of time or to highlight key events. Since many of these rituals have a physical component, it often falls to real estate and facilities management to carry the torch. As we have seen, Sun Microsystems' Wednesday morning ritual of delivering doughnuts, bagels, and muffins to every Sun facility is the responsibility of the facilities management department. This ritual is now particularly tricky, as all deliveries must take place within a 30-minute timeframe. At G-Tech, a new flag is raised outside the corporate headquarters every time a new country or state is added to their roster of customers—and the facility manager makes it happen. The coordination of company-sponsored facilities' tours, along with any food and entertainment required, is also usually assigned to facility management.

While at first consideration, the responsibility of managing such activities seems rather trivial compared to the other important tasks facility managers must accomplish, such rituals are an important way to increase the visibility of the facilities management function. This personal touch can increase employees' awareness and appreciation of the company's facilities, and of those who manage them. Additionally, many of the excellent facility managers studied during the development of this book actually welcomed the opportunity to help keep the flame of their company's history burning, seeing it as an occasion to fulfill an important service to their fellow employees, while increasing their own exposure in the company. This increased visibility builds the informal networks of contacts that facility managers need to get earlier and better information about potential changes in the company's plans. If rituals are important to your company, you need to have both the attitude and the staffing to support these rituals in an effective and meaningful way.

QUESTIONS ABOUT CULTURE

A company's culture evolves over time and is a product of many influences, both deliberate and accidental. The corporate culture transmits the rules of behavior within an organization. These rules, often unspoken, have a powerful effect on the way people treat each other and how they relate to the organization. Both the functional and symbolic aspects of the physical setting contribute to the evolution of a corporate culture. The setting can either support or hinder certain behaviors, leading to the development over time of behavioral norms. Further, aspects of *place* can be interpreted as symbols of the organization and read as an indicator of a company's attitude toward its employees and the community, whether those symbols are deliberately set forth or not.

QUESTIONS ABOUT CULTURE

Which aspects of your present culture do you want to emphasize and which do you want to change?

What symbols of your culture are represented by your facilities or your facility policies—do they send the right message for today's environment?

What level of participation in the facility planning process is appropriate, given the culture of the company? Do employees feel empowered to change their work environment if change is needed?

EMPHASIZING CORPORATE CULTURE THROUGH FACILITY DESIGN

As the CEO and cofounder of G-Tech explained during the planning of G-Tech's corporate headquarters, "Style is the most important strategic resource to manage; style is the manner in which a company states its culture."[2] An open discussion about style is useful for the communication it encourages within the company about the company's goals, values, and image; it also helps develop the actual design solutions. When a company changes its physical setting, it has the opportunity to design the new space to suit new objectives. It can encourage certain behaviors by the way the space is designed and use the design to make symbolic statements. This is a time when it is useful for the company to examine whether its current corporate culture is compatible with its future strategic demands. It would be appropriate to ask whether some changes in the culture might help the company to better compete. An examination of corporate culture, and a discussion of how it relates to the company's physical arrangements, is highly characteristic of companies using a value-based mode of real estate decision making, but culture influences nearly all real estate and facility management decisions to some extent.

Do the function and feel of the place support the culture? Imagine, for example, a company whose senior management occupies closed offices along the outside wall, with secretaries lined up outside their bosses' offices. These offices are furnished with dark wood historical reproductions. You are likely to interpret this as a conservative environment; it might lead you to assume that the company valued tradition and hierarchy. The closed offices would prevent a lot of informal interaction, and the clear status distinction between managerial and support staff would probably inhibit casual conversation. An outsider could not enter this space unobtrusively. In contrast, imagine a floor plan featuring lots of low panels and few closed offices, with managers mixed in with support staff. Lots of open access to the windows, light, bright colors, and plenty of areas for informal conversation suggests a different set of behaviors. We would expect that such a setting would encourage interaction among employees and place less value on traditional hierarchical management and more value on impromptu conversations. We could probably wander through the office easily.

The question is not which design is good or bad, but whether the design approach supports the kind of behaviors that will help the company meet its strategic objectives. Does the setting fit the culture by sending the right kind of messages to both employees and visitors? To answer this question, try to understand the culture of the company and how it is represented and reinforced by the physical work environment. Consider the freewheeling environment of an advertising agency, with a young workforce accustomed to the shared spaces and camaraderie of a college campus. This company may thrive in an office where much of the space is not assigned directly to individuals (such as in a non-territorial office). Yet members of a law firm, who frequently work alone and with great concentration, and who labor steadfastly for years to achieve a large partner's office with custom interior decoration, would be aghast at trying to function in that type of space.

Also recognize that many subcultures exist within some companies. These subcultures may evolve because the work done in that part of the company is different, or because it employs different kinds of people than in other parts of the company. When designing space for these subgroups, a company must make a clear strategic decision whether to emphasize their subculture which is occupying the space, or instead to reinforce the overall culture of the company.

USING THE WORK ENVIRONMENT TO PROMOTE CULTURAL CHANGE

The work environment can be used to influence cultural change by facilitating some behaviors and impeding others. Sun Microsystems wanted to promote more collaboration between its software developers so it put certain equipment needed for testing code in shared laboratories adjacent to the developers' private offices, forcing the engineers out of their private lairs. Sun also provided lots of space for easy interaction—coffee bars, open stairwells, and recreation areas.

A frequently used strategy to reduce the emphasis on hierarchy is to reduce the number of space standards and put more managers in open offices. The important questions to be asked are: What behaviors do you want to encourage and what do you want to change? What new policies or practices may be difficult for your people to adapt to without other cultural changes? Are the changes in the office design consistent with other behavioral changes you are championing throughout the company?

Remember that just changing the space will not automatically change behavior. For example, a company that has long emphasized the importance of the hierarchy and has made visible status distinctions between management levels through office size and furnishings, can expect a great deal of resistance to any new space plan which eliminates many of these distinctions. Other ways of making distinctions may arise. One company designed a floor plan to feature open workstations of the same size. However, employees found that the type of chair a person was given correlated to their status. For instance, clerical staff were given chairs without arms. During a tour of the company it was also pointed out that one could tell the secretaries apart because their cubicles had one wall that was lower than the others. It seemed that hierarchical distinctions were still important at that company and that employees figured out subtle ways to continue interpreting status through office design.

THE APPROPRIATE USE OF CULTURAL SYMBOLS

While the power of symbols can be put to very good use by a company through the design and management of its facilities, the insensitive use of symbols can highlight hypocrisy and a reluctance on the part of senior management to "walk the talk." For example, management is deceiving itself when it claims to want to reduce an emphasis on hierarchy but still has special reserved parking for senior management. Similarly, companies that reduce the amount of space allocated to each employee, put more managers in open offices, and then proceed to lavish space and amenities in senior management's offices should not be surprised to have the new design met with skepticism. Although their office interiors have since been altered, the same Pacific Telesis Operating Headquarters that put nearly all employees in three standard-size, open-plan cubicles through most of its 2 million square feet, also had lavish private offices for senior management located at the center of the complex behind imposing, ceiling-high wooden doors. One felt a bit like she was going to see the Wizard of Oz when entering that sanctuary. It sent a clear message that senior management was considered far more important to the company than the rank-and-file workers.

A thorough discussion of the anticipated effects of office design alterations, and an effort to check out these projections with employees, is not a trivial exercise in corporate navel gazing. Rather it is an effort to use a valuable resource to its best advantage. People inevitably interpret their physical environment symbolically. What does yours say about your company? Is it the message you want to convey?

EMPLOYEE PARTICIPATION IN THE FACILITY PLANNING PROCESS

There are a wide variety of ways to involve employees in the facility planning process. As discussed in the last chapter, employee involvement in designing facilities to enhance the work process is critical. Employees need to feel as involved in facility related decisions as they are in other corporate issues. Therefore, there is no right level of involvement, but it should be consistent with the culture of the company. Curiously, if you ask people for their opinion, they expect you to listen, and to either act on their ideas or to tell them why you didn't. The biggest pitfall when employees participate in the office planning and design process is a lack of feedback on their ideas. Any effort to involve employees, whether through surveys, interviews, pilot programs, or other approaches, should have a clear feedback mechanism included in the plan.

QUESTIONS ABOUT SENIOR MANAGEMENT PREFERENCES

The preferences of senior management, especially the CEO and president, play an important role in the design and management of the work environment. This role is not voluntary. As the recognized leaders of the company, everything these executives do is examined by all the stakeholders for symbolic meaning. Employees look for clues to appropriate behavior within the organization. Investors look for signs of management's future intentions. Others watch to see what benefits the company will bring to the community. Indeed, many organizational theorists argue that one of the primary tasks of a leader is to manage the physical symbols that guide and reinforce the organization's culture. Management professor Henry

Mintzberg has observed that virtually everything a manager does is examined by subordinates for clues as to preferences and future intentions.[3] In this way, senior management's attention to the relative importance of particular aspects of corporate real estate and facilities sends powerful messages throughout the organization.

Many executives consciously manage through the use of symbols and by demonstrating symbolic behavior. They realize that their actions are closely examined by people within and outside of the organization for insight into their attitudes or future direction.

Why should corporate real estate managers consider the preferences of senior management? The most important reason is that the more senior management appreciates how real estate and facility managers help the company to better sustain its competitiveness, the more recognition they give to their contributions. By defining your role as one that helps senior management use the workplace as a tool to increase productivity, employee satisfaction, and customer responsiveness, rather than just as a capital asset, you can help advance the strategic paradigm. Working with an enlightened senior management, one that operates under the strategic paradigm rather than under the cost or market paradigms, can make your job easier and cause your contributions to be acknowledged.

If you are a member of senior management, this part of the chapter will help you to realize that your involvement in corporate real estate and facility management decisions has great importance, even if you have not placed much emphasis on that role in the past.

QUESTIONS ABOUT SENIOR MANAGEMENT PREFERENCES

What aspects of corporate real estate get the most attention from senior management?

- Assets
- Amenities
- Aesthetics

The involvement of senior management in all aspects of real estate and facilities focuses on three key issues: asset management, amenities, and aesthetics. Asset management refers to how the organization allocates scarce financial resources, and the extent to which real estate assets are equated with other capital assets. Amenities are the features of the workplace which convey status, promote comfort, or serve employees' personal needs. Aesthetics refers to a concern with visual pleasure and design quality. My research has found that senior management's relative attention to these three issues, and their use of the work environment to symbolize the organization's mission, culture, and values, is most influenced by two major factors: strategic uncertainty in the competitive environment—as also exemplified in the corporate real estate strategy—and the individual personal preferences of the senior manager.

In general, asset management tends to be of high or at least moderate interest to all senior managers. The more visible the use of the company's financial resources, the more attention senior management will likely pay to the financial aspects of the project. This is one reason why financial measurement of corporate real estate effectiveness is so highly emphasized at many companies. In the absence of a clear strategic imperative for a particular design or management approach to a facility, the cost represented by that facility usually dominates discussions of the project with senior management.

The intensity of interest and involvement in amenities and aesthetics is more influenced by the personality and preferences of individual senior

Figure 11–1
Senior Management Attention to CRE Is Related to Strategic Uncertainty

Level of Strategic Uncertainty	Corp. Real Estate/FM Strategy	Typical Use of Symbols	Senior Management Emphasis		
			Asset Management	Amenities	Aesthetics
High Uncertainty	Incremental Chapter 4	Precedent setting	Minimize risk	Support technical needs	No frills
Moderate Uncertainty	Value-Based Chapter 5	Institution building	Serve organizational needs/agenda	Share the wealth	Symbolic statement of values
Low Uncertainty	Standardized Chapter 6	Institution maintaining	Financial strategy	Maintain power relationships	Symbolize permanency, status quo

managers, although the focus of their concern also appears to vary according to the company's strategic uncertainty. Figure 11–1 summarizes the predominate priorities given to assets, amenities, and aesthetics at various levels of strategic uncertainty. Let's look at some examples of how the senior management of companies approached asset management, amenities and aesthetics under varying conditions of strategic uncertainty.

SENIOR MANAGEMENT PREFERENCES UNDER CONDITIONS OF HIGH STRATEGIC UNCERTAINTY: INCREMENTAL STRATEGY

When a company is in its early years, which is usually a time of high strategic uncertainty, senior management has a great deal of opportunity to set precedents regarding the work environment. At the same time, however, the company may be constrained in the resources it can commit to the workplace. In a highly uncertain strategic environment, the CEO tries to balance the need for constant concern about future survival, with sensitivity toward the precedents that will be set as the company becomes more mature. Since resources are scarce, they must be carefully allocated to the most critical parts of the company's operations. A highly uncertain strategic environment compounds the problem by absorbing most of senior management's attention. To reduce risk, facilities are added in small increments, as discussed in the chapter on Incrementalism. To encourage careful management of resources and to project a public image of a company serious about making a profit, the CEO will often discourage the presence of nonessential amenities or expensive-looking design aesthetics. The examples cited in Chapter Four, from Molecular Devices' CEO's reluctance to take an office that was larger than other managers, to Sun Microsystems' CEO's abhorrence of fine art prints as lobby decor, communicate their priorities more than a frugal ideology.

Asset management is most critical to these companies. Their forecasting horizon is very short and they are reluctant to make large, visible commitments without the business volume in place to support the costs. If they are venture capital supported, every expenditure they make is closely monitored. If they have recently issued stock and gone public, their behavior is scrutinized by the investment community. No wonder, when the database software company, Informix, was forced to sell off the 27 acres of land it had acquired for future expansion in the Silicon Valley, the senior management team was highly criticized by the financial community. The Informix dilemma shows how quickly a company's fortunes can change in a highly uncertain competitive environment: In the eleven months between buying the property and then putting it back on the market, the company's stock price had fallen from about $27 a share to less than $7.[4]

Faced with a short forecasting horizon and capital constraints, senior management looks for short-term, flexible commitments. Their preference for short-term leases, however, must be balanced with the ability to accommodate rapid growth without unnecessary disruption to their organization. Leasing of office furniture and equipment, and purchase of second-hand furnishings are other short-term tactics. The difficult question for senior management is when to move from these highly incremental solutions to longer-term solutions which better help to communicate the culture and strategic direction of the company, and help to extract the greatest benefits from the workplace design.

Amenities play less of a role in a start-up firm because most of the firm's senior management is focused on making the business a success and on the future personal wealth they may achieve through their efforts. Any available money is earmarked for product development, marketing, or sales. Employees at smaller companies are often very vocal about their needs and preferences and get highly involved in the planning and design of the workplace. At one start-up I observed, the engineering staff would gather after-hours to pore over the space plans for their new offices, making many changes and often having heated arguments about how the space would best be used. While these employees may not have been interested in fancy design details, they cared a great deal about food service, recreation, and the ability to take a nap during an all-night work session. If they want something in their workplace, they are likely to just go out and buy it or bring it in from home. While these ad hoc approaches may work in a very small company, they often can lead to clutter at best and hazardous work conditions at their worst as the office becomes more populated. Some unresolvable differences of opinion about the design of the workplace are inevitable. This is often when senior management steps in to set some rules and establish some workplace standards. Even when senior management prefers to ignore the work setting, certain patterns of behavior in the organization will establish themselves and corporate values will still be developed and inculcated.

Like amenities, aesthetics are a low priority for the incremental company—indeed there may even be an anti-aesthetic bias, as though a concern for surroundings might detract from fierce, hungry entrepreneurialism. Employees at start-ups are often highly involved in the aesthetic decisions that are made, especially if they are used to sharing power in a small group of co-workers. The actual quality of the aesthetic outcomes in any such project are far less important than the meaning that the occupants derive from the resulting design.

SENIOR MANAGEMENT PREFERENCES UNDER CONDITIONS OF MODERATE STRATEGIC UNCERTAINTY: VALUE-BASED STRATEGY

A company under conditions of moderate strategic uncertainty has greater financial strength to allow more longer-term commitments to capital investments. The company is becoming established as an institution, as discussed in Chapter Six. A clear articulation of the company's values, and its reinforcement through the design and management of the workplace helps the company to position itself for the future. Companies which are making the transition from incremental to value-based decision making are often at the point where a major real estate commitment is imminent. The founder of the company may still be in power and may perceive this time as an opportunity to influence the company's long-term direction. At this time a CEO's management style and personal taste have the greatest impact as the institutional characteristics of the organization are developed and refined.

There is a shift in the way the workplace is perceived by management when it uses a value-based strategy for real estate and facility management decisions. The workplace is seen as an investment in establishing and maintaining competitive advantages, not just as a cost item.

Amenities are tied to the demographics of the company. Often a company will want to share the wealth with the employees by improving everyday working conditions. More secure in its markets and in its future, senior management is less concerned with appearing extravagant to the outside world and more concerned with supporting the workforce and cultivating the appropriate work style.

Aesthetics are used to emphasize the culture and values of the company. This may be through the use of symbols, the depiction of company history, or an effort to portray the company's relationship with the community. Those outside the company may have difficulty understanding why certain aesthetic selections have been made, but those outcomes may be very meaningful to the organization's members. The assortment of frog figurines in the corporate offices of Fidelity Investments might strike the outside visitor as a bit odd, but Fidelity employees fondly see them as a charming symbol of the paternal idiosyncrasies of their firm's majority owner and CEO, Ned Johnson, who has collected, or been given the frogs over the years.

Corporate art collections also reflect the aesthetic tastes of company senior management, and can either serve as an unnecessary distraction or an important symbolic tool, depending upon how they are curated and managed.

Sidebar 11–1
CORPORATE ART COLLECTIONS

Even in this age of lean and mean management, corporate art collections continue to thrive. It is estimated that over half of the Fortune 500 companies have corporate art collections, and that many professional service firms and private institutions such as hospitals, also collect. While in the 1970's and 1980's the emphasis was on collecting well-known artists and on big ticket acquisitions, many companies now focus on the use of artwork in a particular facility setting. Collecting dropped off in the early 1990's as corporate downsizing and shareholder value were the order of the day, but by the late 1990's companies have begun building their collections again. Today's collections often focus on less expensive pieces from local and regional artists; they are likely to include prints, photography, textiles, and ceramics, as well as original paintings. While the focus on corporate art as an investment has waned, interest in decorative art to warm and humanize the workplace, has not. Some companies limit the value of their purchase to $1,000 and under, while others directly commission pieces for specific areas in their buildings.

Corporate art collections often receive a great deal of senior management involvement. The CEO may be a collector in his personal life and considers it a personal mission to bring quality art to the employees. At other companies an employee-based art commit-tee oversees purchases. Some art consultants recommend that com-panies establish a theme around which to build their collection, or develop a vision statement to guide their acquisitions. This also helps to reduce the chance that the collection will be based too closely on one person's individual taste, even if that person is the current CEO. For example, Pacific Telesis collects only art from Cal-ifornia artists, and prefers artwork that depicts a California theme.

Whether or not these collections appreciate in value at the same rate that investment in the company's core business might return is a matter of speculation. Art markets rise and fall with the general economy, and most purchases or sales of art involve a 15% commission. Sometimes the corporate art collection serves as a sort of corporate piggy bank to tap when times get rough. In 1996, IBM grossed $31 million through the auction of 300 works of art, many of which had been in storage rather than on display. Other benefits cited by companies with art collections include aesthetic enhance-ment of the workplace that increases employee morale, and good public relations resulting from supporting the local arts community and from loaning out artwork for exhibitions.

Management of the corporate art collection often falls to facility management. Companies need to keep their inventory and appraisals up-to-date. All documents pertaining to both the artwork and the artist should be retained for future reference. Sometimes lesser known artists are hard to track down when future appraisals are needed. Art that is no longer needed can be disposed of by donating it to a museum (that will want only the very high-quality pieces) or through auction—sometimes giving employees first shot at the pur-chase.

Increased use of open plan offices has reduced the need for cor-porate art in office interiors. The Sears Corporation jettisoned 1,300 pieces of art in 1992 when it moved out of the Sears Tower to smaller, more open planned offices in a Chicago suburb. In 1995 the Aluminum Company of America (Alcoa) made the transition to a new headquarters building with a very open office plan, few private offices, and lots of glass walls. The Pittsburgh building had very few walls suitable for display of Alcoa's renowned collection, so Alcoa donated four pieces to the Carnegie Mellon Museum of Art and put sixty-five works of art up for auction with Sotheby's. Art not suitable for Sotheby's was sold to local Alcoa employees and retirees, with the remainder auctioned off in the community.

Art collections can make a positive contribution to the company. They can symbolize the values of the company, promote excitement and dialogue among employees, and can help encourage the local arts community. But they also can be seen as a reminder of corporate largess and misplaced priorities, depending upon how the art is selected, displayed, and managed. Those collections which best serve their owners in the long term reinforce the culture and values of the organization, increase the positive image of the corporation in the community, and do not distract senior management from the far more important issues of managing the business on a day-to-day basis.

SENIOR MANAGEMENT PREFERENCES UNDER CONDITIONS OF LOWER STRATEGIC UNCERTAINTY: STANDARDIZATION STRATEGY

By the time a company has established itself in a fairly stable strategic environment, it has routinized much of its facility planning, design, and management. A variety of stakeholders—employees, investors, and the public—rely on the organization's predictability. Perhaps the senior management has had a generation or two of predecessors, and much of senior management may have risen up through the ranks of the company. They are highly socialized into the organization's existing culture. CEOs and other senior managers in a low uncertainty strategic environment usually see the workplace as reinforcing the existing status quo of the company. However, a major project, such as a new corporate headquarters, may give senior management the opportunity to redefine the company, if that is on their agenda.

When GTE, the second largest telecommunications company in North America at the time, developed its operating headquarters in Los Colinas, Texas, the then president of telephone operations, Kent Foster, was highly involved in the project's design. Even after his long work hours, he would review design details in the evening—it was reported that he even approved the selection of interior door handles. A facility manager at GTE observed, "It doesn't take them [the senior managers] a long time to make these design choices. I think it is kind of fun for them—it's relaxing and easy compared to what they usually spend their time doing. They have good personal taste and enjoy making these kinds of decisions."

Asset management is less of an issue for companies in stable strategic environments. They tend to own their corporate headquarters and other key dedicated facilities because the long-term cost of owning is less than the cost of leasing. Such an inventory of real estate assets also can be an important source of organizational slack if times get tight later on. The assets can be sold and then leased back, or surplus property can be sold or developed.

While senior management involvement in corporate real estate and facility management issues varies according to both personality and business, any position that is taken is seen as a communication of values and priorities. The opportunity to positively impact the organization, both strategically and culturally is great, and in my opinion, should not be overlooked.

THE PROACTIVE USE OF PLACE

By using Place proactively to communicate and reinforce core values, organizations strengthen their cultures, reflect pride in their history, and open up an important vehicle of communication between management and the workforce. Place becomes an important tool in strengthening the organization's ability to meet the challenges of competition and change.

CHAPTER TWELVE

THE FUTURE OF PLACE
FOR ORGANIZATIONS

As we anticipate how organizations will use Place for competitive advantage in the future, consider the corporate real estate strategies of two highly successful, profitable, and well-regarded global companies. Both embrace technology and are aggressively preparing their companies to compete in the twenty-first century. Yet their approaches to Place couldn't be more different.

Microsoft, with many of its employees holding engineering or related degrees, may well be the world's most technologically sophisticated major company. Beginning with founders Bill Gates and Paul Allen's development of an operating system for personal computers that now is the de facto standard worldwide, to Microsoft's latest efforts to lead the expansion of the Internet to all facets of commercial and personal use, Microsoft is an organization with both eyes on the future. Microsoft's product development requires envisioning how we will work and live. Microsoft promotes a vision of the future where at any time everyone is electronically linked to everyone else. Its slogan emphasizes virtuality: "Where do you want to go today?"

Given the company's constant orientation toward the future, how does Microsoft house its own employees? Shouldn't this also be the ultimate networked organization, living contentedly in cyberspace. Hardly.

At the world's largest software company, nearly all of Microsoft's software development takes place in a 260-acre campus of forty-plus buildings 17 miles northeast of Seattle, in Redmond, Washington with another 36-acre campus nearby. In total, Microsoft occupies over 5 million square feet of space in Redmond, with facilities ranging from the earliest cluster of 60,000 SF buildings to its latest developments of 500,000 SF buildings. Over 18,000 Microsoft employees work within a short walk or shuttle ride to each other. Most employees are given private, 9-foot by 12-foot offices. Fifteen cafeterias serve their daily needs.

Microsoft provides more than just plain vanilla office space to its employees. Windows are everywhere, even in the stairwells. The buildings and the surrounding landscaping are beautiful. The original 1987 complex, "complete with a tree-filled park in hopes that the relaxed setting would be (more) conducive to the exacting task of writing software codes than a traditional office complex," looked more like home to a college, not a corporation.[1] Employees have even held their weddings in the park.

It is acknowledged throughout the company that for some important tasks, everyone must come to Redmond, despite being one of the most electronically networked companies anywhere. Microsoft, and some of its executives, have endowed educational and cultural venues throughout the greater Seattle area. The firm's presence has encouraged many other technology and related companies to locate in the area, creating a major boom in housing and other industries. Place matters at Microsoft.

Asea Brown Boveri (ABB) is another leading global competitor, embracing technology as one of the world's largest electrotechnical engineering enterprises. ABB is a highly decentralized group of some 1,000 companies, producing a wide range of high technology products for heavy industry. With sales in excess of $30 billion and operations in over 140 countries, ABB builds not only power plants but also the equipment to run them.

ABB has no traditional headquarters. Of the company's nearly 220,000 employees, fewer than 200 work in Zurich, the official headquarters in Switzerland. Instead, the executive management committee meets every three weeks in a different location around the world. The meeting destination often coincides with an important company event in that location. The company relies on a Lotus Notes–based corporate intranet to maintain an extensive web of communication around the globe. According to one senior ABB executive "The computer is a sophisticated telephone for me."[2]

Corporate real estate is as decentralized as the rest of ABB. Only two corporate real estate professionals are based in Zurich, instead there are local real estate managers in 78 countries. They meet in annual workshops, although the senior real estate executive travels nearly constantly. In most businesses ABB competes as a low cost producer, however, it is efficiency first, and cost second, when real estate performance is measured. The firm's worldwide design approach is guided by a belief that attractive facilities encourage employee's workplace identification and productivity.

Which of these global titans has it right? Both companies do. The very different approaches taken by these two companies underscore that there is no one single solution to designing Place in a virtual world. Place depends on your strategy.

Microsoft frequently reorganizes—minor shuffles are constant and a major realignment occurs about every eighteen months. Colocation of all developers eases the task and speeds up transitions. While many of Microsoft's daily activities do rely on virtual communication, colocation makes the concomitant necessity of face-to-face interaction as easy and fast as possible. The quality of the physical work enviroment is also emphasized in Microsoft's employee recruitment efforts. Further, Microsoft relies on a strong culture to sustain it in a turbulent competitive environment. Deep ties to Place give employees more reasons to stay with Microsoft rather than spinning off as start-ups. Its centrality of Place helps reinforce Microsoft's identity and internal cohesiveness.

As a truly global competitor, ABB highly empowers its managers at the local level. The simple corporate infrastructure encourages responsibility on the front line of projects, while providing the vital link between its thousand business units. ABB's flexibility allows it to move quickly to take advantage of shifts in the global economy. ABB constantly relocates its operations to benefit from local competitive advantages and to serve developing countries. With it slogan "We are global worldwide" and its multidomestic concept, ABB faces fewer obstacles in dealing with the internal politics of the countries that are its customers. Its Place is defined as the globe.

Along with the unprecedented changes in technology discussed in the first chapter, we also have seen many new forms of organizing economic activity emerge such as networks and alliances. We are just beginning to see these changes being manifested in the way we build and occupy our Places. How will we think about the Places our organizations occupy in the future?

RECONCEPTUALIZING PLACE

Let's consider how that icon of the organization, the office, will evolve in the future. Virtual technology and new ways of organizing mean that the workplace will look very different than the box full of boxes we used to think of as an office building. There are changes ahead in where we locate, how we develop and build the outside, and how we plan and use the inside of our workplaces.

OPTIMAL LOCATIONS
FOR INFORMATION-AGE COMPANIES

This section discusses trends in location preferences for information-age companies identified through one of my research projects. The experience of these companies, which all made major location decisions during the 1990's, offers insight into Place decisions knowledge-based businesses will make in the future.[3] We looked at forty companies with attractive high-paying jobs in businesses where knowledge was the key product. For the most part, these companies were deciding where to locate offices, not manufacturing, distribution, or retail sites.

As companies globalize their product distribution, the range of locational options is increasing. With communications technology and distribution logistics improving, the only link in the production process which cannot be fully automated, people, will grow in relative importance when selecting a business location. Throughout this book we have argued that with ubiquitous electronic communication, face-to-face communication will play a more important role in the ability to differentiate. It will be managed as a distinct and precious resource. More than ever before, corporations must integrate their real estate and facility management decisions with their human resource and information technology goals and policies in order to envision their future. The optimal location for the information-age company supports both people and technology. This has important implications for community economic development.

Access to Labor

The choice of new business locations in the information age is based more upon attracting and supporting a quality workforce than on old assumptions about proximity to customers and suppliers. Instead, relationships with customers and suppliers are more likely to be carried out using virtual technology, either through shared information, or by locating employees at the customer's or supplier's site and connecting them back to the "mother ship" using technology. For example, Procter & Gamble, which still retains a massive presence in the Cincinnati area, set up a facility adjacent to Wal-Mart's Bentonville, Arkansas, headquarters to better coordinate logistics with this essential retailer.

Geographic clusters of industries—the tendency of companies in similar or related businesses to locate near each other—are becoming more distinct.[4] This clustering will be increasingly influenced by the presence of labor pools with specific industry expertise rather than by access to suppliers or customers. In an era of downsizing and rapid change, skilled employees may prefer to stay located in an area with multiple employment opportunities, encouraging even more clustering of information-age industries in the future.

Quality of Place Considerations

Companies today must locate where knowledge workers want to live. The most attention is paid to community attributes which directly impact their employees' daily lives—their *ease of living* in terms of both costs and conveniences. Quality housing is viewed as essential for supporting the information-age workforce. A range of housing options for income levels varying from clerical to executive that is within an easy commuting distance is necessary. Educational institutions, both those that train potential employees and those that serve the needs of current employees' families, are the most critical public policy factors. Recreational amenities for families also are considered essential. Access to other major public institutions (such as libraries, parks, sports venues) are less influential as key decision variables.

Community Services Information-Age Companies Require

Information-age companies are seeking areas with strengths consistent with their goals:

* *High-quality educational institutions:* Along with high-quality primary and secondary schools, information-age companies rely on a variety of advanced educational programs. While big research institutions may provide some glamour, the vocational and community college resources which train the rank-and-file workforce are even more important. Although education and economic development usually are managed under different jurisdictions in cities and states, the educational infrastructure which both prepares potential employees and serves current

employees' families is far more crucial in attracting businesses than any sort of direct economic development incentive programs. While the emphasis on educational resources is not an original observation, it cannot be emphasized too much.

- *Advanced telecommunications infrastructure:* High-speed data transmission, redundancy, and access to lower-cost alternative providers are now "table stakes" that companies expect to be provided. Developers and local communities need to have strong partnerships with local telecommunications companies in order to provide state-of-the-art access. Advanced telecommunications infrastructure must be integral to any economic development strategy.[5]
- *Economic development incentives:* The presence of a local workforce with the appropriate industry-related skills and the local resources to train potential employees in those skills are more important in the final location decision than are financially based economic development incentives.[6] Companies also emphasize the need for speed and responsiveness to their specific concerns when negotiating with municipalities and economic development agencies; they considered these more important than financial economic development incentives.

Developers will need to offer more of a total package than just the land or a building. Companies will look for the ability to occupy a facility quickly, with attractive support facilities and amenities already in place. Shortening the time from decision to occupancy will become an even more important goal as rates of competitive change increase. The appeal of successful business locations such as Research Triangle Park (North Carolina) or Legacy (Plano, Texas) is that much of the front-end work has already been done and there is a solid assurance that the surrounding development will remain at a high level of quality. Shared facilities also will become more attractive as companies try to focus on their core business functions and leave the conference, fitness, and food operations to others. This may help make urban locations more competitive in the future.

A Growing Preference Toward Colocation

While technology today allows companies to link functions electronically rather than physically, there appears to still be a bias toward colocation of company facilities whenever possible. The geographic separation of major facilities from the founding site occurs under two scenarios: either the company reaches a size where it must geographically diversify its work-force to obtain sufficient talent or it must act to lower its cost position if its home location imposes a cost disadvantage in comparison to the company's competitors.

Many of the large companies we studied seem to prefer occupying clusters of low-rise buildings, which resemble a college campus, rather than high-rise office towers. The corporate campus offers many attractions—the ability to bring together a large number of employees who can be reorganized and reassigned more easily, control over employee activities (harder for them to have lunch with your competitors), and control over who neighbors the site. However, a large tract of land is needed to build a campus of any significant scale, and these usually are found only far from urban, or even established suburban areas, which fuels sprawl. This preference for isolated campuses offers a real challenge to central cities, which must compete even more now as attractive places to live and work.

The consolidation trend implies that communities should pay more attention to their local branch locations of major corporations. Those locations in which the company already has some facilities beachheads are almost always put on the short list of locations to be examined in further detail when companies consolidate. Cities in which the company had positive experiences in the past (i.e., cooperative local governmental agencies, a good workforce, and reasonable costs) were favored in the search process, although many of the companies strive to be as objective as possible.

Along with more employee-driven location decisions, corporations are now, more than ever before, building Places with the expressed goal of meeting employee needs. As we have seen throughout this book, some companies are seizing the opportunity to build Places which truly fit their culture and strategic needs. What trends can we observe and what questions might we ask about further innovation in the planning, construction, and occupancy of our Places in the future?

NEW APPROACHES TO BUILDINGS

Say farewell to the corporate Taj Mahal built in honor of the chairman's ego. The public capital markets have lost respect for companies with grand building schemes at a time when so much corporate infrastructure needs replacing instead. Now more attention is paid to what the building does for the occupants, rather than how it appears to the outside world. The key word here is *amenity*—features offering comfort to the occupant—as well as providing the best technological infrastructure with maximum flexibility. Rosabeth Moss Kanter claims that to succeed in the future, companies need to possess the three Fs; they need to be fast, flexible, and friendly.[7] We also can apply that criteria to our buildings. Some of these ideas are within our ability today, others pose a challenge to the planning, design, and real estate development professions.

Fast: We need ways to speed the planning, permitting, and construction of office facilities. In most municipalities it takes way too long to plan and build. The ability to build and occupy space rapidly is now a critical factor in selecting a site. Some companies try to solve the time problem by building very generic, low-risk offices that do little to enable or inspire. Can we find ways to quickly develop buildings that can still reflect the personality and special needs of their users? Can these facilities then be converted to other uses when needs change?

Flexible: We can't predict what we need from a particular place very far into the future. Can we find ways to quickly change our use of interior space, even the purpose of the building, and not lose the value of this expensive asset? Companies should be able to easily and affordably change a building's use and the kinds of activities it houses. Rather than assume we have found a perfect design solution, the basic premise should be that whatever can change will change, from technology to organizational structure, to the type of workers we hire and the work that they will do in the space. Further, the structure's use should easily convert to other uses, such as a school or housing, or myriad other options. Interestingly, it is the older, industrial pre-World War II buildings that are often the easiest to convert, while the stand-alone steel and glass towers of the 60's, 70's, and 80's are the least recyclable.

Friendly: Friendly buildings provide comfort for the whole body and inspiration for the soul while making a minimal impact on the natural environment. We have developed a great deal of knowledge over the years about how space affects behavior. Let's make use of it. We also have realized that the seemingly simple physical tasks technology requires, such as hours in front of a screen or on a keyboard, are actually pretty tough on our bodies and demand the correct surroundings. Technological advances in lowering energy consumption and greater use of recycled materials can help minimize the building's impact on the natural environment. Investment in these building systems must be judged against not only their initial cost and utility savings payback, but also take into account the health of the building's occupants and the cost of environmental damage from excessive energy consumption. Ultimately, the building must prove its worth in facilitating the flow of quality information throughout the organization by contributing to the creation of knowledge.

The need for buildings that are faster to build, more flexible, and friendlier is a great challenge for the real estate, design, and construction professions. Real estate developers must fill the need for fast occupancy with shorter commitment horizons, and a greater number of on-site amenities. They should view their properties more like hotels than annuities with 20-year tenant commitments. Designers have a tremendous opportunity to broaden the services they provide and reclaim their profession's role as the central coordinator of the planning-to-occupancy process. Many of the greatest challenges organizations will face in the virtual world will be spatial. Designers can offer both process facilitation as well as physical design solutions. Such services require a different concept of what a designer is—and it is not a sole genius foisting a grand design scheme upon a passive client. This attitude challenges how we currently educate and train architects. Builders also can make a contribution by streamlining their activities for greater efficiencies and by greater partnering with both client and designer.

Most notably, buildings are changing on the inside. New concepts of office design are now commonly advanced but still too rarely used. We need a new metaphor for a person's place in the organization.

CHANGING PLACE FROM THE INSIDE OUT

The office of the future, indeed of the here and now, requires us to think in terms of space and time, rather than about desks and chairs. This new concept of the office is not based upon the old person-place metaphor; instead it provides different spaces for different types of work.[8] Rather than allocating space based upon a person's position in the organizational hierarchy, spaces are set aside for different kinds of behavior. This activity-settings approach recognizes that a person may do several different types of tasks over the course of a workday or workweek. Some time is spent on solitary tasks, computing, reading, or writing. Other time is spent with co-workers. There are many different approaches, and as many different names, for alternative office designs. All these approaches vary along two dimensions: space and time. Space refers to the use of the space for either an individual working alone or people working in groups. Time is representative of whether the space is permanently assigned to an individual or group or whether it is assigned on an as-needed basis. Figure 12–1 illustrates these dimensions and the various design alternatives they generate.

As we discussed in earlier chapters, some companies have completely eliminated any assigned space for individual workers. People may share a workspace with someone who is there at a different time (hot desking), they may be assigned a workspace only for those times they are actually in the office (hotelling), or they may just move from space to space equipped with a portable computer and wireless telephone (free address). However, these are still the exceptional designs. Today, most companies still provide some individually assigned space for quiet work and two-person meetings, sometimes in closed offices but more often in partitioned cubicles. The

Figure 12–1
Place Varies Along the Dimensions of Space and Time

SPACE

		Individual Space	Group Space
TIME	**Pre-assigned**	• Cave • Personal harbor • Home base • Sequential shared offices, hot-desking	• Commons • Group address • Open areas and flexibly furnished conference rooms/libraries
	Assigned as needed	• Hotelling • Just-in-time offices • Telecenters/satellite offices	• Same design options as above • Contingent spaces

greater emphasis must now be on encouraging social connections in space and time. We are still in search of creative ways to balance between personal and organizational needs within the context of place.

As the primary purpose of the office shifts from providing access to equipment to providing places for personal interaction, people will come to the office more to be with their colleagues than to work alone. Offices must be designed accordingly. The allocation and use of space must support interpersonal and social contact. Along with more meeting rooms, bump spaces with couches and tables can be scattered about to encourage impromptu discussions. I call these spaces corporate living rooms. Some corporate offices now resemble Italian piazzas. Aisles widen into streets with places to stop and talk. Rather than being relegated to a hidden corner or closet, the water cooler and coffee machine now are celebrated in centrally located cafes where people are encouraged to meet each other. Quiet spaces also are deliberately provided in the form of small assigned spaces or shared spaces in libraries or quiet rooms.

Many barriers still exist to the widespread adoption of these office design concepts. The greatest of these is our own mental image of a position in the organization being equated with an individual physical place in the organization. Providing sufficient conference and group space to support new ways of working is often the biggest practical stumbling block. Unfortunately these spaces are lost through conversion to individual offices when the head count grows and additional space capacity is not added.

If Place is merely seen as a source of cost, rather than as an opportunity to encourage communication and innovation, organizations will not have the courage to try new ways of working. Clearly, reconceptualizing Place is not a task for corporate real estate and facility managers alone; it requires close partnering with your business and the view that place is an opportunity to build competitive advantage. This in turn requires corporate real estate and facility managers skilled in developing and managing relationships as well as projects.

RAISING CORPORATE AWARENESS OF STRATEGY AND PLACE

How do you promote the strategic perspective on Place in your own organization? Part of the answer depends on your role. Both line management and the corporate real estate support staff can embrace the opportunities to enable competitive advantage through Place.

Line managers can begin by better acquainting themselves with the broad range of choices to be made about Place—this book will have given you a good start. Encouraging communication with your corporate real estate and facility managers is key. Do you view them as vital business partners or as a necessary evil in the bureaucratic maze of getting your job done? Do they have a clear understanding of your organization's needs? If so, are you including them in strategic-level discussions so they can help you anticipate future changes to Place? If they don't seem to have a good understanding of your part of the business, find out why not. Demand more from your real estate and facility management organization but make sure they have the tools and the access to your organization which will help them fulfill those demands.

The essential starting point for corporate real estate and facility managers is the strategic perspective described in Chapter Three. However, the strategic perspective requires a wide range of managerial tools, well beyond the functional skills of real estate development and building management. The new breed of corporate real estate professional must be a jack of all trades and master of many. Not only must you understand a wide range of design, construction, and technology concerns, you must be able to translate these concerns into the language of the business. You can't fall back on using real estate or building jargon to communicate. To promote Place as a strategic tool for enabling competitive advantage, you must help to integrate across the businesses to identify synergism of scale and scope. The focus must be on building relationships with the various parts of your company over time, not just serving the needs of specific projects. There is no substitute for face-to-face relationship building and that takes time. It also takes repeated positive interactions for the senior managers in the businesses to trust their corporate real estate representative with highly confidential information.

At many of the companies I have studied and worked with, the organizational emphasis of corporate real estate is shifting from a functional, project management approach based upon how buildings are delivered to one which aligns with the structure of the company and the way work is conducted. This shift is necessitated not only by the strategic perspective but also by the increased use of service providers outside of the company that assume many of the routine functions of real estate and facility management.

FROM PROJECT MANAGEMENT
TO RELATIONSHIP MANAGEMENT

At its simplest, the relationship management model assigns a single point of contact between corporate real estate and a part of the business, such as a business unit or division. Responsibilities are assigned by line of business, rather than by property or project type. Relationship managers are empowered at many levels but at minimum must be able to exert influence in both directions. It takes time and an investment of management energy to develop this level of knowledge and rapport with the business.

In spirit, a relationship management model focuses on serving the needs of the business, not on the management and control of the real estate. There are many benefits to this approach. By building a relationship over time and through influence skills rather than positional power, trust is built. It is then more likely that corporate real estate will get vital information earlier and be able to help managers identify and act upon the real estate and workplace implications of foreseen changes. Since time is an increasingly important competitive weapon, a relationship management focus must emphasize taking time out of the problem identification, decision making, and physical implementation process. Effective relationship management should be able to provide one-stop shopping for the business, saving them both time and effort which then can be focused more appropriately on the business. Relationship management goes far beyond filling orders, however. The manager must proactively educate the business about the wider range of workplace design options available today. Understanding the business helps the development of relevant metrics to translate costs into benefits. Over time, a relationship manager becomes a partner in developing and implementing competitive strategy. This becomes the most effective way to position corporate real estate as the organization's integrator of strategy, people, and technology. Especially in turbulent periods, solid relationship management keeps corporate real estate responsive to change. Robert Patterson, now Senior Vice President of Corporate Real Estate at Bank of America, credits the relationship management structure he put in place at NationsBank with greatly facilitating the integration of the portfolio when the two banking titans, NationsBank and Bank of America, merged in 1998.[9]

The demand for a broad range of analytic, technical, and strategic skills is demonstrated in the Sun Microsystems job description for workplace manager, their job title for a relationship manager. A workplace manager at Sun is responsible for directly coordinating the delivery of real estate and facility management services to a single line of business. When I first read this job description, I wondered why they did not add "walks on water" and "leaps tall buildings" to the long list of desired skills. Yet Sun is able to find and develop such talented individuals who are viewed by the businesses they serve as highly effective and valued business partners.

Sidebar 12–1
SUN MICROSYSTEMS
WORKPLACE MANAGER JOB DESCRIPTION

Nature and Scope: The Workplace Manager is responsible for assuring that the business's organization, work practices, and processes are accurately assessed for their workplace implications, and that workplaces are designed and delivered to meet these requirements. The goal is to positively impact sales growth, employee recruitment, and productivity. Therefore, the nature and scope of the Workplace Manager's position is: Know the assigned business(es). The Manager will need to develop an intimate, intuitive knowledge of the business, including its markets and competitors, at multiple levels. Therefore, the incumbent will need to have strong business acumen, be familiar with the language of the business, have a strong grasp of business, planning and financial concepts, and be well skilled in building relationships. Understand the work practices of the business's employees, both as they exist and as they need to evolve. Therefore, the incumbent will need to be curious about and sensitive to how employees, as individuals and as a team, achieve high levels of productivity in their work. Based on knowledge of the business and understanding of work practices, assess how business and organizational needs align with the business's real estate portfolio, workplace strategies, and services required. The incumbent will then need to act on his/her assessments; therefore, the incumbent will need to conceptualize and then specifically scope, budget, and schedule projects and services to support the business and its work practices. Drive the processes for designing and delivering workplaces and services. To carry out these implementations, the incumbent will call upon outside service provider alliances and the function's Shared Services unit as the primary service delivery system.

Key Results and Accountability: Reports to the Director of Real Estate and the Workplace. Aligns design and workplace strategies and services with OpCo, cross-OpCo and SMI business objectives. Provides a comprehensive description of client's business environment and its impact on the way in which the client must organize and work to compete, and assure that the workplace supports these business objectives. Specifically defines scope of services and project requirements including locational choices, lease terms and conditions, adjacencies, block plans, square footage, design criteria, budgets, schedules, and performance measures. Manages move process. Defines on-going support service needs such as janitorial, mail, reprographics, transportation, food service, move management. Fully integrates functional objectives of IR, HR, and Finance. Participates in the selection of outside service providers. Measures the performance of all service against client requirements and provide feedback to the Shared Services Unit. Skills Required: *Interpersonal Excellent Communication skills, particularly listening skills. Both a conceptual thinker and a project manager, able to assess client work process needs and to deliver workplaces that support them. Comfortable with change and ambiguity in a rapidly changing work environment and functional business model. Takes initiative, can perform with little supervision. Is politically astute and sensitive in a complex Sun culture. Has strong interest in the way people need to work and the way workplaces can be used to support them. Is appropriately tough-minded; able to coach and council in a direction which may conflict with OpCo or business unit, which may not achieve business results. Appreciates that the primary role of our function is to help Sun achieve its financial goals. *Technical Familiarity with general business and financial concepts. Space planning experience in a high technology or other high performance and rapid changing environment. Experience on work process and organizational design and development. Exposure to project management in space acquisitions, interior design and tenant improvement projects and move management. Knows how to effectively utilize service providers. Excellent planning and organizational skills. Excellent written and verbal skills. Able to make effective presentations and to prepare work materials in a manner similar to the best approaches available in the service industry.

Education and Experience: 7–10 years in a workplace planning and project design with recent experience utilizing emerging workplace concepts. Could have worked in HR with a focus on work process and organizational design. May have come from a production environment focusing on industrial engineering and work processes. Has significant experience delivering space planning, project management, and real estate transaction with or without the efforts of others. BA in Architecture, Design or Human Resources Management. MBA or other graduate work in Human Resources helpful.

DEVELOPING CRE PROFESSIONALS TO MEET THE CHALLENGE OF CHANGE

People come to corporate real estate from a broad range of professional backgrounds: engineering, accounting, law, architecture, and general management. As of 1999, no formal graduate degree program existed in the United States for corporate real estate, and only a couple address facility management. Indeed there are only a few graduate, or even undergraduate courses offered in corporate real estate related topics.[10] Learning the profession happens on the job over time.

Companies are finding that they must invest in growing their own corporate real estate talent, through a combination of on-the-job experience, participation in industry seminars and activities, and company-sponsored management development programs. Functional skills, which are obtained through technological training, are the easiest to find and can often be obtained by hiring outside service providers when their specific skills are needed. Rather than relying on narrow technical specialization, today's corporate real estate professionals must have a little knowledge about lots of things so that they can effectively identify when to bring in outside expertise to help supply the right analysis. Knowledge bases include but are not limited to building operations and technologies, capabilities and demands of computing and communications technologies, project management, financial analysis and performance measurement, negotiation, human resources, and alternative workplace design.

Strategic skills that link real estate to the needs of the business are the most difficult to develop. They require a general management perspective and an intimate understanding of both the external and internal demands on the company. The bad news for companies today is that people with the full range of these strategic and functional skills are difficult to find. The good news for those already in this profession is that there is a great opportunity for professional advancement if the strategic perspective is embraced.

THE CHALLENGE AHEAD

Sir Winston Churchill once proclaimed, "We shape our buildings, thereafter they shape us."[11] Although you may be familiar with this quote, you may not be aware of the context in which it was proclaimed. Churchill was remarking upon how the design of the space in the House of Commons, which had just been destroyed by Nazi bombs, profoundly influenced the behavior of its members. Advocating that it be rebuilt in its original layout, he claimed that the rectangular shape of the room helped Britain sustain its two-party system, and its crowding (a result of not providing an assigned seat for every member) encouraged the lively debate that nurtured the country's democracy.

We are now at a point in our development as a society where we need to change our very concept of what role Place has in organizations, where it is located, how it is used, and even what it looks like. Technology is allowing us a whole new set of space and time dimensions to build up our ideas. As the shapes of our organizations change, Place must change in response. Virtual space lets our organizations function in three dimensions; we no longer can represent them in merely two-dimensional structures made of steel.

Buildings have always reflected the aspirations, as well as the practicalities of their eras. In light of more rapidly changing competitive conditions, the real challenge we face is making Place an opportunity for greater competitiveness, rather than an obstacle and an expense. We have many choices, different and exciting choices, about how we will live and work into the twenty-first century. It is not the time to avoid the corporate real estate dilemma—long-term commitments to Place in a short-term world—it is the time for bold vision. Let our corporate buildings reflect our highest aspirations and enable our greatest advantages.

ENDNOTES

INTRODUCTION

1. By *virtual* I mean any substitution for face-to-face transactions which utilizes electronic media, as the term is popularly applied. Immediacy is often an attribute of virtual interaction. Technologies which make the virtual world possible include computers which are part of a network, including those linked to the Internet, and telecommunications, including those enhancing voice contact, such as videoconferencing.

2. *Build* refers to any acquisition of facilities, whether owned or leased.

3. Alfred Dupont Chandler, Jr. *Strategy and Structure: Chapters in the History of the Industrial Enterprise* (Cambridge: MIT Press, 1962).

CHAPTER ONE: THE ROLE OF PLACE IN A VIRTUAL WORLD

1. Economic organizations are changing their structures, and these structural changes in turn are impacting office design. When Chandler wrote *Strategy and Structure: Chapters in the History of the Industrial Enterprise* (Cambridge: MIT Press, 1962), the dominant organizational form was the pyramid—a functional hierarchy with a clear chain of command. It was ideal for coordinated large enterprises which produced simple products. This formal hierarchy was represented in the design of office space; the higher an employee ranked, the more space and privacy he was allocated. By the 1970's, the matrix form of organization emerged to help solve more complex production problems and people reported to both a functional supervisor and to a project manager. Stanley M. Davis and Paul R. Lawrence, *Matrix* (Reading, MA: Addison-Wesley, 1977). Today, the network is more often a structure, with parallel production processes to speed time to market and unleash innovation. Membership on project teams is often fluid, requiring a great deal of internal movement in the work environment.

2. The length of leases has not significantly changed in recent years, typically from a minimum of five to a maximum of twenty years, but the number and complexity of options allowing for early exit or for additional space, have increased in importance. Kenneth A. Posner, "The Value of Options in Real Estate Leases," *Journal of Property Management*, May 1994.

3. The argument that traditional offices, even cities, will obsolesce in the virtual world has been put forth by Nicholas Negroponte of MIT (*Being Digital*. New York: Vintage Books), Roger Naisbitt (*The Global Paradox*, New York, Avon Books, 1995), and William Knoke (*Brave New World: The Essential Road Map to the Twenty-First Century.* New York: Kodansha, 1996).

4. The realization that the physical setting influences not only behavior but also the actual structure of the informal organization goes back to the seminal work of Elton Mayo, *The Human Problems of an Industrial Civilization* (Cambridge MA: Harvard University Press, 1946); George Homans, *The Human Group* (New York: Harcourt, Brace, Jovanovich, 1950); and Fritz Reothlisberger and William Dickson, *Management and the Worker* (Cambridge: Harvard University Press, 1947).

5. Peter L. Berger and Thomas Luckman. *The Social Construction of Reality* (New York: Doubleday, 1966).

6. A study conducted by the Institute for the Future and the Gallup Organization of 972 workers at large companies found an average of 31.8 phone calls, 13.6 E-mails, 11.2 voice mails, 8.8 faxes, and 11.1 written notes were received each day. Neither postal mail nor cellular telephone calls were even counted in this total. Alex Markeles, "Memo 4/8/97, FYI: Messages Inundate Offices," *The Wall Street Journal*, April 8, 1997.

7. According to the U.S. Department of Labor's Occupational Safety and Health Administration (OSHA), repetitive strain injuries are now the most common, and most costly, occupational health problem in the nation. Workers with carpal tunnel syndrome typically missed 30 days of work in 1995, the longest period of time of any major job-related injury reported by the Bureau of Labor Statistics Survey of Occupational Injuries and Illnesses. (BLS Web site: http://stats.bls.gov).

8. A U.S. Commerce Department study in a report released in the fall of 1997 forecast that between 1998 and 2005 an average of 95,000 new computer scientists, systems analysts, and programmers will be needed every year. However, only about 25,000 U.S. students earned bachelor degrees in those fields in 1994. *America's New Deficit: The Shortage of Information Technology Workers,* September 29, 1997.

9. The telework center is a type of office environment that supports work outside the central office and the home by providing facilities for occasional use by clients for a fee. Clients are motivated to use a telework center by preference for a near-the-home alternative to working at home, need for an easy commute, and office equipment that's available on a time-sharing basis. Sharon Tepper, "Telework Centers: An Analysis of the Physical and Economic Factors Which Contribute to Their Success." 1997 International Development Research Council Research Assistantship. Published by the IDRC.

10. The seminal discussion is found in Philip Stone and Robert Luchetti. "Your Office Is Where You Are," *Harvard Business Review* 63, no. 2 (1985). Stone and Luchetti went on to consult on the design of office furnishings and workplaces at Herman Miller and Steelcase.

11. Johnson Controls USA Office Costs Index documented the overall facility costs per occupant in the fourth quarter of 1998 to be $2,690 per person. This does not include the capital costs of the real estate asset, which Johnson Controls estimates to be an average of $7,481 per occupant for a total average occupancy cost of over $10,000 per employee per year. Correspondence with Barry Varcoe of Johnson Controls, Alpharetta, Georgia, March 10, 1999.

Expenditures on travel and entertainment have increased steadily. Expenditures of $156 billion in 1996 represent a 25% increase by U.S. companies since 1991 according to the National Business Travel Association. There is some speculation however, that companies are becoming more price sensitive to high airfares. From *The Wall Street Journal.* "As Air Fares Take Off, Business Travelers Stay Home," *Chicago Tribune,* March 1, 1998. American Express saw a 7% to 8% increase in spending from 1996 to 1998. Jane L. Leverre, "American Express Expects Travel Costs to Continue Rising Next Year but at Less Torrid Pace," *The New York Times,* September 17, 1997. In Canada, business travel costs doubled in the ten-year period from 1988 to 1998. David Israelson, "Business Travel Is Booming," *Toronto Star,* February 17, 1998.

12. Lorel McMillan, "Ernst & Young Calculates a High Return from Hotelling and High-Tech," *Facilities Design and Management,* 12, no. 14 (April 1993): 32–37. Dun & Bradstreet described in "This Old Office," *Journal of Business Strategy,* (September 1994). Andersen Consulting discussed in "Space/Time Office," *Facilities* (July 1993) and in "No Such Thing as a Corner Office," *Workscapes* 1, no. 1 (1997).

13. John Byres of IBM quoted in the *National Real Estate Investor* (May 1996).

14. Dana Dubbs, "Have Office Will Travel," *Facilities Design and Management,* 14, no. 12 (December 1995), 44–47.

15. In 1997, it was estimated that from 9 to 14 million American workers are telecommuters, "defined as those who work from their homes on a regular basis (at least two days a week) for an outside company." Further, from 10 to 12 million people run home-based independent businesses and another 12 to 16 million are independent contractors working from multiple companies. *The New York Times,* September 17, 1997, Section F. The Gartner Group Inc. estimates that some 55 million individuals worldwide will be telecommuting on a regular basis by 2000. "Speeding up the Telecommute," *Computer Reseller News* 734, 130 (1997).

16. See Arlie Russell Hochschild, *The Time Bind: When Work Becomes Home and Home Becomes Work* (New York: Henry Holt and Company, 1997) for an in-depth examination of how workers at one company managed the work-family balance.

17. A 1995 survey of 33 member companies belonging to the International Society of Facilities Executives, in cooperation with Knoll (an office furniture manufacturer), found that most of the ISFE companies were using some forms of alternative officing. However, even in the next five years, these companies did not foresee more than 10% of their workforce using home office or shared workspace approaches. On the other hand, most companies planned to use forms of a universal office (providing similar-size space to all employees) or team space, for many job functions. These changes in traditional office design were projected to yield space reductions per employee of about 4% for clerical employees, and up to 12% for professional employees. This survey, which comprised a larger proportion of professional service companies, could be considered optimistic since service companies have been the forerunners of alternative office use. See Christine Barber, "Alternative Officing: Where Are We Headed?" *Facilities Design and Management*, 15, no. 12 (December 1996): 38–41.

CHAPTER TWO: FORCES DRIVING CHANGE IN THE MANAGEMENT OF CORPORATE REAL ESTATE AND FACILITIES

1. McKinley Conway, *Development Highlights of the Twentieth Century* (Norcross, GA: Conway Data: 1997).

2. By 1998, IDRC had 2,500 members, NACORE 3,600, and IFMA boasted 15,000.

3. IFMA fact sheet prepared for the 1997 Annual National Summit on Building Performance, October 30, 1997, Washington, D.C.

4. Association of Foreign Investors in Real Estate. 1997 AFIRE Annual Meeting Proceedings, October 5–7, 1997. AFIRE 700 Thirteenth Street, Washington, DC 20005.

5. "Solving the Fulfillment Issue: Focus: Internet Retailing," *Chain Store Executive with Shopping Center Age* 74, no. 5 (May 1998).

6. By 1994 more than 8 percent of the U.S. population was foreign born, with the rate of immigration at its highest point since the 1911–1920 period. Maryann J. Gray et al., "Immigration and Higher Education: Institutional Responses to Changing Demographics," Washington, D.C., *RAND*, 1996.

7. Tom Peters, "The Brand Is You," *Fast Company*, August–September 1997.

8. According to economist Juliet Schor the average worker has added an extra 163 hours to his work year over the past two decades. Juliet Schor, *The Overworked American*, (New York: Basic Books, 1991).

9. "Sought After Workers now Have the Clout to Demand Flexibility," *The Wall Street Journal*, September 1, 1997.

10. See C. K. Prahalad and Gary Hamel. "Core Competence of the Corporation," *Harvard Business Review* (May 1, 1990) for one of the seminal discussions of this principle.

11. "Emerging Trends in Real Estate 1998," ERE Yarmouth and the Real Estate Research Corporation, October 1997, Chicago, Il.

12. Formed under the name Hines Corporate Properties, LLC. Raised a pool of $500 million to purchase sites and work with corporate tenants to develop the property. "Hines Announces Formation of 'Hines Corporate Properties.'" Hines Corporation press release, February 1998. www.hines.com.

13. One example is AMC Entertainment's sale/leaseback of 12 megaplex movie theaters to Entertainment Properties Trust (EPT) in 1997. While legally not a spin-off from AMC, EPT went public with nothing more than an option to purchase the twelve theaters, and then used the money from the initial public offering to actually pay for the transaction. Further, the bulk of EPT's management team came from AMC. However, EPT is a completely independent company from AMC, and it pursues sale/leasebacks with direct competitors of AMC. Example courtesy of Kevin E. Deeble of TriNet Corporate Realty Trust, San Francisco, California, December 1998.

14. Charles Handy, *The Age of Unreason* (Boston: Harvard Business School Press, 1990), chapter one.

15. Testifying before the Federal Trade Commission, Hewlett-Packard Company's chief executive officer remarked that the typical product life-cycle is six to twelve months today. Five years ago the typical cycle was three to five years. 3M Corporation expects to have 10% of its annual sales come from new products introduced in that year. "Anticipating the 21st Century: Competition and Consumer Protection in the New High-Tech, Global Marketplace, Volume One: Competition Policy in the New High-Tech, Global Marketplace," June 3, 1996. Copies of both volumes of the report are available from the FTC's Public Reference Branch, Room 130, 6th Street and Pennsylvania Avenue, N.W., Washington, D.C. 20580. June 3, 1996.

16. George Stalk Jr. and Thomas M. Hout, *Competing Through Time: How Time-Based Competition Is Reshaping Global Markets* (New York: The Free Press, 1990).

CHAPTER THREE: CHAMPIONING THE STRATEGIC PERSPECTIVE

1. For a discussion of how cognitive biases influence decision-making, see Max H. Bazerman, *Judgment in Managerial Decision Making*, (New York: John Wiley & Sons), 1997.

2. See Michael Joroff, et al. *Strategic Management of the Fifth Resource: Corporate Real Estate.* Published by the Industrial Development Research Foundation, May 1993.

3. The late 1970's were characterized by high inflation and low vacancies. The 1981 tax act made it easier for investors in real estate to write off losses against ordinary income. The deregulation of the savings and loan industry, starting in 1982, unleashed a large supply of capital seeking higher returns. These factors combined to produce rampant overbuilding of commercial space and projects lacking economic justification. In 1986 the ability to write off real estate losses was severely curtailed limiting the attraction of many real estate investments. Source: David Shulman, "A Graphic History of U.S. Office Space Supply and Demand, 1972–1990," *Solomon Brothers Real Estate Research Bulletin,* February 6, 1991. See also Anthony Downs, "What Have We Learned from the 1980's Experience?" *Solomon Brothers Real Estate Research Bulletin,* July 1991.

4. Source: CB Richard Ellis/Torto Wheaton Research, 200 High St., Boston, MA 02110.

5. Since the fieldwork was done, both of these local telecommunications providers have been acquired by other regional companies. Pacific Bell and Nevada Bell merged into Pacific Telesis after the 1984 telecom industry deregulation. Pacific Telesis merged with Southwestern Bell in 1996 and is now part of Southwest Bell Communications, although it uses the name Pacific Bell in its local service area. New England Telephone merged with NYNEX in 1989 and NYNEX was then acquired by Bell Atlantic in 1997. In July 1998 Bell Atlantic announced its merger with GTE. Throughout the book, these companies will be referred to by the name they operated under at the time the event under discussion occurred.

6. Measures such as economic value added (EVA) take into account a manager's use of capital when evaluating performance. Since real estate and facilities are capital intensive, a business unit of the company with a lot of corporate property on its books adversely affects its EVA performance. "Valuing Companies: A Star to Sail by?" *The Economist* (August 2, 1997).

7. These ideas were first put forth by C. K. Prahalad and Gary Hamel in their article, "Core Competence of the Corporation," *Harvard Business Review* (May 10, 1970) and subsequently expanded upon in their book, *Competing for the Future* (Boston: Harvard Business School Press, 1994).

INTRODUCTION TO PART TWO

1. Among the companies studied, other attributes such as size, age, or location did not correspond with the dominant approach to real estate decision making as well as strategic uncertainty did.

2. The initial research questions were stated broadly: "How do organizations make corporate real estate decisions and which sort of organizational theo-

ries best describe the process?" The research effort posited that both rational-instrumental and valuational-symbolic processes play important roles in real estate decisions, but at different times and in different ways. I sought to understand when and why these differences occur. To investigate my questions, a thorough understanding of how physical structuring decisions are made by organizations was required. Eight companies were selected to represent a variety of sizes and ages. Companies with high-technology products were chosen because typically they must cope with factors that challenge the design and management of facilities: rapid rates of technological and competitive change, a highly professional workforce, and extensive use of office automation. The companies and projects are listed in Exhibit N-1.

Research Design: The research design was based upon a sociological method referred to as grounded theory (first presented by B. Glaser and A. Strauss in *The Discovery of Grounded Theory: Strategies of Qualitative Research*, London: Wiedenfeld and Nicholson, 1967) that emphasizes the use of inductive reasoning grounded in the constant comparison of empirical observations. The goal is to generate new theories, not test existing hypotheses, therefore the researcher attempts to keep an open mind about what is observed. To use the grounded approach, the outcome of the decision being investigated must be clearly identified so it is less likely that the decision criteria will be reinterpreted later. In this research, the outcome was either the resulting physical setting such as the site location, the appearance and use of the building, the design of the interior space, or a specific policy outcome such as the structure of a project management team. Care was taken in this research to accurately reconstruct or to observe in real time the activities leading up to a facility decision, the decision-making process, and the implementation of the decision.

Some advocates of the grounded theory approach encourage the use of theoretical constructs during data gathering and analysis. I followed the recommendations of Kathleen Eisenhart as presented in "Building Theories from Case Research," *The Academy of Management Review* 19 (1989). Drawing upon the organizational behavior literature, I developed theoretical constructs to compare and categorize observations from the fieldwork.

Data Collection and Analysis: Information on real estate decisions was collected using interviews, observations, and reviews of company documents. Among the eight sites, 96 one-to-two hour interviews were conducted using snowball sampling, starting with the head of real estate or facilities and including the executive to whom these functions reported as well as the occupants of the space under discussion. Where appropriate, service providers also were interviewed. During the fieldwork, both the process by which decisions were made as well as the specific design outcomes of these decisions were examined. Physical outcomes—what facilities looked like, how they functioned, and the policies in place for their use—were evidence of the intentions and the priorities of the planners. Simply put, it did not matter what color the

Exhibit N-1
Companies and Projects in the Original Study

Company	Location	'90 sales (000)	'95 sales	Age in '95	# interviews	# mtg. observ.	Projects	Year project complete	Year of follow-up
Digital (DEC)	Maynard MA	12,942	13,813	33	19	5	New England site reorganization NE facility management reorganization	84 89	90–96
G-Tech	Warwick RI	150	147	14	7	1	New HQ Warwick mfg. Facility	91 85	94
Millipore (M'pore)	Bedford MA	717	594	28	8	2	Third site study Expansion of Milford facility	89 87	92
Molecular Devices (MD)	Palo Alto CA	10	na	6	8	4	First headquarters	90	91–94
New England Telephone (NET)	Boston MA	3,602	acquired	100+	11	3	New headquarters	88	92
Pacific Bell (PB)	San Ramon CA	8,651	9,040	84	11	3	Move Info Services organization New headquarters	89 83	93
Pacific Bell Directory (PBD)	San Francisco CA	810	na	75+	13	1	New headquarters	88	92
Sun Microsystems (Sun)	Mountain View CA	2,466	5,902	8	19	5	New headquarters Training center Milpitas manufacturing	90 87 85	91–98

wall was painted; I questioned who made the decision and what reasons they gave for the color selection. Decisions were judged neither bad nor good, popular nor despised, although attention was paid to how people in the organization reacted to these decisions.

Interviews were conducted using an outline of open-ended questions about real estate and facility management practices and policies. Over time, distinct facility projects, either ongoing or completed within the past four years, were identified and examined in further detail. Facility planning meetings were attended at each company (24 meetings) to see whether those discussions used the same criteria claimed to be true in the individual interviews. Organization charts, written policies, department and project memorandums, and secondary-source publications provided supplemental background on the projects. Most sites were visited a minimum of four times each over a period of three months. Photographs were taken to help remember the sites and to illustrate the companies during oral presentations of the research. The primary fieldwork was completed over the course of one year and some of the companies have been followed over the past decade.

To help condense and report the extensive field research material collected in a way that also enhanced the reliability and replicability of the study, a variation of the *case cluster method* was used. As advocated by Charles McClintock (et al.) in "Applying the Logic of Sample Surveys to Qualitative Case Studies: The Case Cluster Method" published in *Administrative Science Quarterly* 24 (1989), this method applies the underlying principles of sample survey design to qualitative data analysis by identifying units of analysis and forming categories for their comparison. Among the eight companies, fourteen distinct projects became the units of analysis, which then made it possible to compare decisions within the same organization at different times and for different types of projects. Physical structuring decisions were broken down into four categories: site selection and property acquisition, exterior design, interior design, and workstation design. The field notes from each organization and project were also written up as separate cases that followed a consistent outline and format.

Theoretical scenarios were developed for each type of structuring decision which predicted what the decision criteria should be if it followed either the rational-instrumental or the valuational-symbolic perspective. These theoretical scenarios are summarized in Exhibit N–2. Reasons given for decisions leading to the development of each of the fourteen real estate projects were then compared with these scenarios and categorized as either rational-instrumental or valuational-symbolic, based upon the researcher's judgment. The resulting ratings are shown in Exhibit N–3. Some companies used mainly rational-instrumental reasons for their decisions, others were far more valuational-symbolic. And the same company might use one or the other more at different times. To explain the different approaches, I compared the organizations I studied along a variety of dimensions: size, age,

Exhibit N–2
Theoretical Scenarios

REAL ESTATE ACQUISITION AND SITE SELECTION
(includes leasing, selecting new property, disposal)

Rational-Instrumental:

Closely aligned with production requirements and access to resources. Quantified cost-benefit analysis. Decisions primarily made by specialists in real estate site selection.

Valuational-Symbolic:

Heavily based upon preferences of local manager. Input from marketing, human resources, and public relations as well as facilities.

EXTERIOR BUILDING ARCHITECTURE AND SITE PLAN

Rational-Instrumental:

Either highly specified by standards which are functionally based or subject to what is available in the market when the need for space arises. Concern is primarily with functional use of building and cost management. Design aesthetic judgments are not made by the organization other than what is previously specified as a corporate standard.

Valuational-Symbolic:

Building is individually programmed and designed. High level of involvement by senior management. Concerned with image, aesthetics, and amenities.

INTERIOR ARCHITECTURE

Rational-Instrumental:

Highly specified by standards based on functional requirements. Expenditures monitored for functional impact. Colors, finishes, and other design features selected for ease of maintenance, durability, low cost.

Valuational-Symbolic:

Individualized design for each product with autonomy by the occupants for many design decisions. User involvement in programming beyond the technical requirements of the space. Concerned with image, aesthetics, and amenities. Aesthetic as well as functional concern with finishes.

WORKSTATION DESIGN

Rational-Instrumental:

Standard design based upon functional programming. Same standards applied for all projects. Colors, finishes, and other design features selected for ease of maintenance, durability, and low cost.

Exhibit N–2
Theoretical Scenarios

WORKSTATION DESIGN (continued)

Valuational-Symbolic:

Individualized design for each product with autonomy by the occupants for many design decisions. User involvement in design beyond the technical requirements. Concerned with image, aesthetics, and amenities. Aesthetic as well as functional concern with finishes. Individuals can adjust their work area to serve individual preferences.

Exhibit N–3
Ratings of Fit with Theoretical Scenarios

PREDOMINATE MODES OF STRUCTURING DECISION MAKING

Highly rational-instrumental: (4–0)

Sun Milpitas, NET new HQ, Pacific Bell ISG move

Moderately rational-instrumental: (3–1)

Molecular Devices first HQ, Digital organization of NE, Digital FR reorg.

Attributes of both rationales: (2–2)

Sun training center, Sun new HQ, Millipore Milford expansion

Moderately valuational-symbolic: (1–3)

Pacific Bell Directory HQ, Pacific Bell HQ

Highly valuational-symbolic: (4–0, 3–0)

Millipore new site, G-Tech new HQ

structure, location, and competitive environment but none explained the differences in behavior I observed. The managers I interviewed for the study frequently mentioned uncertainty in their organization's competitive environment as a factor which influenced their real estate decision making and inhibited their efforts to make long-term plans. This led me to develop a way of comparing, identifying, and measuring strategic uncertainty at these companies.

3. The valued use of symbolic design in corporate buildings is discussed in Peter Olof Berg and Kristian Kreiner, "Corporate Architecture: Turning Physical Settings into Symbolic Resources," in *Symbols and Artifacts: Views of*

the Corporate Landscape by Pasquale Gagliardi. (New York: W. de Gruyter, 1990). In general, European scholars have paid a great deal more attention to the symbolic role of facilities than American researchers have.

4. This work drew upon the work of organizational theorists Jeffrey Pfeffer *(Organizations and Organization Theory,* Marshfield MA: Pittman. 1982), Graham Astley and Andrew Van de Ven ("Central Perspectives and Debates in Organizational Theory," *Administrative Science Quarterly* 28, 1983, pp. 245–273), and Charles Perrow (*Complex Organizations: A Critical Essay,* New York: Random House, 1986).

5. Rational-instrumental functions of the physical setting are discussed in a variety of sources including: Everett Rogers and Lawrence Kincaid, *Communication Networks: Toward a New Paradigm for Research* (New York: The Free Press, 1981); Richard Edwards, *Contested Terrain* (New York: Basic Books, 1979); Jefferey Pfeffer, *Organizations and Organization Theory* (Marshfield MA: Pitman, 1982); Paul Lawrence and Jay Lorsch's seminal work *Organizations and Environments* (Cambridge: Harvard University Press, 1967); and James Thompson in *Organizations in Action* (New York: McGraw Hill, 1967).

6. Peter Berger and Charles Luckman put forth these concepts in *The Social Construction of Reality* (New York: Doubleday, 1966).

7. The book edited by Peter Frost, *Organizational Culture* (Beverly Hills: Sage, 1985) contains articles by John Van Maanen and Stephen Barley, "Cultural Organization: Fragments of a Theory" and by Meryl Reis Louis, "A Investigator's Guide to Workplace Culture" highlighting the role of the workplace in reinforcing organizational culture.

8. See Igor Ansoff: *Implanting Strategic Management* (Engelwood Cliffs, NJ: Prentice Hall, 1984).

9. Of the long line of articles defining various sources of environmental uncertainty, an early work by Robert Duncan, "Characteristics of Organizational Environments and Perceived Uncertainty," *Administrative Science Quarterly* 17, no. 3 (September 1972): 313–327, remains among the most useful.

10. To objectively measure strategic uncertainty, I developed rating scales indicating the typical conditions under which either high or low levels of strategic uncertainty would describe a firm's competitive environment. Using sources which included articles gathered through the ABI/Inform system, investor reports, annual reports, company financial statements, and company-published documents such as project descriptions, newsletters, and internal memorandums, I ranked each company's level of strategic uncertainty for the calendar or fiscal year of each project under investigation. A version of the ratings instrument is presented in Chapter 7.

CHAPTER FOUR: INCREMENTALISM

1. Scott McNealy quoted in "Silicon Valley's Rising Sun," *Newsweek* (March 21, 1988).

2. Scott McNealy quoted in "Sun's Sizzling Race to the Top," *Fortune,* (August 17, 1987).

3. "Sun Microsystems Turns on the Afterburners," *Business Week* (July 18, 1988).

4. Source: *1997 Millipore Annual Report* and www.millipore.com.

5. This discussion of Millipore is based upon fieldwork completed for my dissertation.

6. The following discussion is based upon interviews with corporate real estate executives and managers at Fidelity Corporate Real Estate and from publicly available information about Fidelity Investments.

7. James Brian Quinn, *Strategies for Change: Logical Incrementalism* (Homewood IL: Richard D. Irwin, 1980).

8. Interview with Jean Kovacs, cofounder of the Qualix Group. Hillsborough, California, April 5, 1996.

9. Michael Lewis, "The Little Creepy Crawlers Who Will Eat You in the Night," *New York Times Magazine* (March 1, 1998).

10. Interview with Donna Horton Novtisky of Clarify. Woodside, California, October 25, 1997.

CHAPTER FIVE: STANDARDIZATION

1. Enabling technologies are defined and discussed in further detail in Chapter Eight.

2. The evolution of the bureaucratic form was explicated by Max Weber, *The Theory of Social and Economic Organization,* translated by A. M. Henderson and T. Parsons. (New York: The Free Press, 1947). The original German version was published in 1924.

3. Frederick Taylor in *Scientific Management* (New York: Harper & Row, 1947).

4. Based upon field interviews at Pacific Telesis, spring 1989.

5. Institutional isomorphism and other topics examining the institutionalization process are found in the excellent compilation: *Institutional Patterns and Organizations: Culture and Environment,* edited by Lynne G. Zucker (Cambridge, MA: Ballinger Publishing Company, 1988).

6. As quoted in the *National Real Estate Investor,* special supplement, Fall 1991.

7. Karl E. Weick, *The Social Psychology of Organizing, 2nd. ed.* (New York: Random House, 1979).

8. Telephone interview with Bethany Davis of Andersen Worldwide, June 6, 1998.

9. "Hotelling" refers to the use of unassigned offices reserved in advance by employees who need a place to work for a particular period of time. The Andersen Consulting offices in Wellesley, Massachusetts, were profiled by Laura Pappano of the *Boston Globe,* "Freedom from Chores," July 22, 1997.

CHAPTER SIX: VALUE-BASED STRATEGY

1. O'Mara interview.

2. O'Mara interview.

3. O'Mara interview.

4. Scott Kirsner, "Every Day It's a New Place," *Fast Company* (April–May 1998): p. 131.

5. Semiotics, the study of human behavior as a formal system of signs, has its base in linguistics but has a rich tradition of examining the symbolic meaning of cultural artifacts, particularly art and architecture.

6. In a study of new-tech firms, Price Waterhouse found that distinct corporate life cycles drove the corporate real estate life cycle. At each of the four stages—start-up, expansion, maturity, and diversification, the lease terms, typical lease rates, mix of leased/owned, tenant improvements, and amenities varied. They also found a strong correlation between revenue growth and employment growth two years prior to the decision to build a facility. Price Waterhouse Working Paper, "High Technology Firms: Corporate Real Estate Life Cycle Modeling," June 1998. Available from elliott.farber@notes.pw.com.

7. We will look at only office buildings in this discussion, not retailing.

8. Occupancy of highly customized facilities tends to be locked in for a long time horizon, although some companies choose financial arrangements other than ownership for balance sheet considerations.

9. Thomas Walton explored how companies used their building's architecture to promote their marketing image in *Architecture and the Corporation: The Creative Intersection* (New York, Macmillan, 1988).

10. Paul Goldberger, "A New Disney Building Mixes Art with Whimsy," *New York Times,* May 12, 1991, section 2, p. 38.

11. Thomas W. Haines, "Intel: A Chip Above," *Seattle Times,* June 30, 1996.

12. For more on corporate art collections, please see Chapter Eleven.

13. The *Reinventing the Workplace* Series of publications by the International Development Research Council (IDRC) summarize a variety of programming methods. Also see *Workplace by Design* by Franklin Becker and Fritz Steele (San Francisco: Jossey Bass, 1995); and *Excellence by Design—Transforming Work-*

place and Work Practice by Turid Horgen (Editor), Donald A. Schon, William L. Porter, and Michael L. Joroff (New York; John Wiley & Sons, 1998).

14. "Case Study: Nortel Builds a New HQ—and a 'New City.'" *Site Selection* October/November 1997. (No author given.) "Nortel Opens New Global Headquarters," Nortel company press release, May 1, 1997.

15. In different ways, the following authors identify the need for premise controls—those things which influence employees to behave consistently in novel situations. Other sources of premise controls include: use of mission statements, selecting and training of employees, various organizational development activities, and compensation systems. See Richard Edwards, *Contested Terrain* (New York: Basic Books, 1979); and Rosabeth Moss Kanter, *The Change Masters* (New York: Simon & Schuster, 1983).

16. The design of the workplace to serve as a source of unobtrusive control is discussed by Charles Perrow in *Complex Organizatoins: A Critical Essay* (New York: Random House, 1986), p. 129.

17. Sharon Machlis, "For Many, Digital Died a Long Time Ago," *Computerworld* (February 9, 1998).

18. Paul Lawrence and Davis Dyer, *Renewing American Industry* (New York: The Free Press, 1983).

19. Mark Golen, interview by author, Mountain View, California, April 12, 1997.

CHAPTER SEVEN: REAL ESTATE STRATEGIES ARE DYNAMIC

1. Source: Case, Shiller, Weiss Research, 1698 Massachusetts Avenue, Cambridge, MA 02138; web address is www.cswcase.com.

2. O'Mara interview. Quote attributed to Scott McNealy by William Agnello, June 30, 1994.

3. Bob Graystone interview by Hillary Lewis, June 14, 1994.

4. Paul Donnelley quoted in the *National Real Estate Investor,* Special Supplement, December 1994.

5. Source: Merrill Lynch company documents, interview with Alan White, July 1996.

6. Quoted in "Fast Growth at Cisco Systems, Inc." by Martha O'Mara. Case study published by the Harvard University Graduate School of Design, June 1998, for the IDRC symposium "Infrastructure Challenges for Fast-Growth Companies."

7. Brent Schlender, "Computing's Next Superpower," *Fortune* 135, no. 9 (May 12, 1997).

8. A synthetic lease is considered a purchase according to a company's federal tax return, so the firm can expense its depreciation like an asset. At the same time, the lease is accounted for as an operating lease, and the lease cost is

deducted as an operating expense yearly. The asset and corresponding liability do not appear on the balance sheet although the obligation is footnoted in the financial statements. Because they are considered low risk, synthetic leases are charged at the corporate borrowing rate, which is typically lower than the rate real estate developers can obtain in conventional real estate financing. See James Blythe Hodge, Esq., "The Synthetic Lease: Off-balance Sheet Financing of the Acquisition of Real Property," *Real Estate Finance Journal,* Fall 1998.

CHAPTER EIGHT: UNDERSTANDING YOUR STRATEGIC ENVIRONMENT

1. A notable effort to link corporate strategy with corporate real estate decisions, particularly those involving the negotiation of real estate transactions in the external markets was set forth by Stephen E. Roulac, "Strategic Decision Models: Multiple Perceptions, Unifying Structure," *The Journal of Real Estate Research* 10, no. 5 (1995). An earlier incorporation of Porter's models is found in H. O. Nourse and S. E. Roulac, "Linking Real Estate Decisions to Corporate Strategy," *The Journal of Real Estate Research* 8, no. 4 (1993). See also Mahlon Apgar IV, "Managing Real Estate to Build Value," *Harvard Business Review,* November 1995.

2. Michael E. Porter, *Competitive Strategy: Techniques for Analyzing Industries and Competitors* (New York: The Free Press, 1980) and *Competitive Advantage: Creating and Sustaining Superior Performance* (New York: The Free Press, 1985). For an update on Professor Porter's work, see *On Competition* (Boston: Harvard Business Review Publishing, 1998).

3. I am grateful to Richard Audie, of the Center for Executive Development in Cambridge, Massachusetts, for this set of examples.

4. Robert R. Faulker, *Music on Demand: Composers and Careers in the Hollywood Film Industry* (New Brunswick: Transaction Books, 1983).

5. Martha O'Mara, "Strategic Drivers of Location Decisions for Information-Age Companies," *The Journal of Real Estate Research* 17, no. 1/2 (April 1999).

6. Marshall L. Fisher, "What Is the Right Supply Chain for Your Product?" *Harvard Business Review* (March–April 1997).

7. "Will GM's Long Shot Pay Off?" *Ward's Auto World* (June 1996); "GM Leadership Team Establishes Residency at New Global Headquarters," PR Newswire (November 11, 1997).

CHAPTER NINE: NAVIGATING ENVIRONMENTAL CONSTRAINTS AND OPPORTUNITIES

1. Microsoft Bookshelf reference.

2. Gensler and Associates, "An Agile Approach to Facility Design," (Internal publication, 1996).

3. Thomas J. Allen, *Managing the Flow of Technology: Technology Transfer and the Dissemination of Technological Information Within the R&D Organization* (Cambridge: Massachusetts Institute of Technology, 1977).

4. Jill Smolowe, "Noble Aims, Mixed Results," *Time* 146, no. 5 (July 31, 1995).

5. Scenario planning techniques for modeling major change in your industry structure are explained in Peter Schwartz, *The Art of the Long View: Planning for the Future in an Uncertain World* (New York: Doubleday, 1991).

6. *Operating* refers to the direct costs of producing your product or service which are claimed as expenses against income each year. *Capital* refers to those purchases which have a longer life, are carried as assets on the balance sheet, and are partially expensed every year as depreciation. Rates of depreciation are based upon Internal Revenue Service regulations, not necessarily the true life of the asset. See Robert K. Brown, Alvin A. Arnold et al., *Managing Corporate Real Estate* (New York: John Wiley and Sons, 1993).

7. This discussion benefited from the NACORE Masters in Corporate Real Estate thesis of Genevieve Krumm, "Leasing Versus Purchasing," *Corporate Real Estate Core Readings,* vol. 1 (West Palm Beach, FL: NACORE International, 1996).

8. To be considered a capital lease, a lease agreement must meet one of four criteria: "(1) The lease transfers ownership of the property. (2) The lease contains a bargain purchase option. (3) The lease term (the 'fixed noncancelable term of the lease') is equal to 75 percent or more of the estimated economic life of the property. (4) The present value of the minimum lease payments (the *noncancelable* rental payments that a company is required to make) is equal to 90 percent or more of the fair value of the leased property, less any related investment credit retained by the lender." Brown, Ibid.

9. Synthetic leases are discussed in Chapter Seven, endnote 8.

10. Reduced corporate ownership of real estate assets is strongly urged by Peter Linneman in "The Coming Disposal of Corporate Real Estate," *Wharton Real Estate Review,* Fall 1998.

11. See K. L. Alli, G. G. Ramirez and K. Yung, "Corporate Headquarters Relocation: Evidence from the Capital Markets," *AREUEA Journal,* 19, no. 4 (1991), 583–99; S. H. Chan, G. W. Gau and K. Wang, "Stock Market Reaction to Capital Investment Decisions: Evidence from Business Relocations," *Journal of Financial and Quantitative Analysis,* 30, 1995, 81–100; and C. Ghosh, M. Rodriguez and C. F. Sirmans, "Gains from Corporate Headquarters Relocations: Evidence from the Stock Market, *Journal of Urban Economics,*" 38, 1995, 291–311.

CHAPTER TEN: DIAGNOSING STRUCTURAL DEMANDS WITHIN THE ORGANIZATION

1. Steelcase Inc., "The Emerging Integration," (videotape).

2. Information about the Serviceability Tools and Methods (ST&M) process can be obtained from the International Centre for Facilities, 440 Laurier

Avenue West, Suite 200, Ontario, Canada K1R 7X6, or on the Internet at http://www.icf-cebe.com.

3. For a simple discussion of these methods see Toni Hupp, et al. *Designing Work Groups, Jobs, and Work Flow* (San Francisco: Jossey-Bass, 1995).

4. The concept of the *value chain* and its applications for strategic analysis are fully presented in Michael E. Porter's *Competitive Advantage: Creating and Sustaining Superior Performance* (New York: The Free Press, 1985).

5. Thomas J. Allen, *Managing the Flow of Technology: Technology Transfer and the Dissemination of Technological Information Within the R & D Organization* (Cambridge: MIT Press, 1984).

6. Debra Cash, "Office Space and Cyberspace—Striking a Balance: Two American Companies Face the Options." 1995 International Research Development Foundation Research Assistantship paper. Supervised by Martha A. O'Mara.

7. Although reengineering and downsizing are used synonymously, they are two different phenomena. Reengineering is the fundamental examination and redesign of work systems to take optimal advantage of new technology and operating methods. Reengineering may result in downsizing if the process identifies ways to accomplish tasks with fewer people.

8. "Team Funds Hold Less Cash and Generate Less Turnover," *Bloomberg Personal* (November–December 1996,) p. 86. Also in 1998, Fidelity Investments Fixed Income division migrated to a team-based organizational structure.

9. The Buffalo Organization for Social and Technological Innovation (BOSTI) report for Teknion, (a furniture manufacturer) 1993. Also see Michael Brill, *Using Office Design to Increase Productivity,* published in association with the Westinghouse Corporation, vol. 1, 1984; vol. 2, by Workplace Design & Productivity, Buffalo, NY, 1985.

10. Mark Alpert, "Office Buildings for the 1990's," *Fortune,* November 18, 1991.

11. Quoted in *The Wall Street Journal,* June 29, 1994.

12. *Facilities Design and Management* (March 1994).

13. Glenn Rifkin, "The Future of the Document," *Forbes* (September 9, 1995).

14. "New Technology News in Brief," *Management Services* (June 1996).

15. Mark Leibovich, "Sleepless in Silicon Valley," *San Jose Mercury News,* June 21, 1996.

16. Susan Farmer, "Corporate Ladders, Jungle Gyms," *The Columbian,* April 21, 1996.

17. Kirsten D. Grimsley, "On-site Child Care Takes Care of Parent's Business," *Washington Post* (March 12, 1996).

18. Susan Canfield, "On-site Child Care Is No Small Matter," *The Seattle Times,* (May 13, 1996).

CHAPTER ELEVEN: DIAGNOSING CULTURAL DEMANDS WITHIN THE ORGANIZATION

1. "IBM Finds It Can Go Home Again," *The Wall Street Journal,* (May 13, 1998).

2. Interview with Guy Snowden, March 1989, in Providence, Rhode Island.

3. Henry Mintzberg, *The Nature of Managerial Work* (New York: Harper & Row, 1973).

4. "Informix Drops Project Despite OK by City," *San Jose Mercury News,* November 6, 1997, p. 1B.

CHAPTER TWELVE: THE FUTURE OF PLACE FOR ORGANIZATIONS

1. From *International Directory of Company Histories,* Volume 6. Edited by Thomas Derdak (Chicago: St. James Press, 1988), pp. 257–260.

2. Interview with Walter J. Stuecklin, Senior Vice President, Corporate Real Estate, ABB Asea Brown Boveri Ltd. The interview took place on March 11, 1998, in Cannes, France.

3. Martha A. O'Mara, "Strategic Drivers of Location Decisions for Information-Age Companies," *The Journal of Real Estate Research* 17, no. 1/2 (April 1999). Companies covered in the 1996 study include Adobe Systems, AMOCO, Apple Computer, Applied Materials, Avis, Bank of America, Bausch and Lomb, Bayer, Charles Schwab, Chrysler, Ciba-Geigy, Citicorp, Corning Bio, Dayton Hudson, Duracel, EDS, Executone, Fidelity Investments, Ford Credit, Ford Fairlane, Ford Primus, General Motors, Hertz, Heulbein, IBM, IP ResourceNet International, JC Penney, Eastman Kodak, Mobil, National Semiconductor, Nortel, Octel, Packard-Bell, Reichhold Chemicals, Phone-Poulenc Rorer, St. Paul Companies, Southwestern Bell, Sylvan Learning Systems, United Parcel Service, U.S. West.

   A typology of location decisions was developed based upon the magnitude of the relocation and the impact on the workforce:

   MOVES TO A NEW GEOGRAPHIC AREA

   Pick Up and Go: An entire function of the company is moved from one part of the country to another along with a significant amount of the existing workforce.

   New Horizons: A company selects a location to start-up or grow a new business, or to reposition an existing business and hires most of the employees from the new location.

   Consolidation to Beachhead: Geographically dispersed operations are consolidated to a location where the company already has some presence. Some senior employees may be relocated, but the bulk are hired from the expanded location.

MOVES WITHIN THE SAME GENERAL AREA/MUCH OF THE WORKFORCE IS RETAINED:

Green Acres: Both moves from an urban location to a suburban location and moves from one suburban location to another in the same general area but to a different municipality.

New Urbanites: Moves from a suburban location to an urban one.

Recommitment: This represents the company that conducts a serious relocation analysis but in the end decides to stay either at the same location or to locate nearby in improved facilities. The category is further divided into *Urban Recommitment* and *Suburban Recommitment.*

The strategic business drivers for these location decisions are identified as follows:

Exhibit N–4

Location Decision	Primary Strategic Driver
Pick Up and Go	Major strategic repositioning of the company
New Horizons	Achieve cost advantages for new or existing businesses
Consolidation to Beachhead	Increase scale economies, flexibility, and control over geographically dispersed operations
Green Acres	Greater control over surrounding site—ability to easily expand operations on-site
New Urbanites	Increase cosmopolitan exposure of its workforce
Recommitment	Historical affinity to a community which has retained its quality of workforce and living standards

Future trends and their implications for corporate real estate strategy and economic development priorities also are suggested in the paper.

4. Michael E. Porter, "Clusters and the New Economics of Competition," *Harvard Business Review* (November–December 1998). Also see the work of Michael Enright, "The Geographic Scope of Competetive Advantage," in Elke Dirven et al., Editor; *Stuck in the Region: Changing Scales for the Regional Identity,* Utrecht: VUGS, 1993. Also, "Regional Clusters and Economic Development: A Research Agenda," Harvard Business School Working Paper, 1995.

5. T. Venable, "Telecommunications: Paving the National Information Highway," *Site Selection* 1994, 39, no. 2 (1994): 214–216.

6. A study by the Corporation for Enterprise Development (Schweke, Rist, and Dabson, 1994) concluded that most financial incentive packages did not

return their value to the community over time and that the moneys might be better spent on long-range investments which increase the quality of the workforce and improve the community.

7. The attributes "fast, flexible and friendly" are introduced by Rosabeth Moss Kanter in *When Giants Learn to Dance: Mastering the Challenge of Strategy, Management, and Careers in the 1990's* (New York: Simon and Schuster, 1989).

8. This idea was first advocated nearly fifteen years ago but is just gaining acceptance today. See the seminal work by Philip Stone and Robert Luchetti, "Your Office Is Where You Are," *Harvard Business Review* 63, no. 2 (1985). Their work subsequently influenced office furniture manufacturers such as Herman Miller and Steelcase to offer products for use in alternative office settings. In 1986, the Urban Land Institute also began to explore these ideas in an edited volume by Thomas Black et al. *The Changing Office Workplace* (Washington, D.C.: The Urban Land Institute and the Building Owners and Managers Association). The Corporate Real Estate 2000 effort by the International Development Research Council also publicized and urged adoption of these ideas.

9. Interview with Robert Patterson of Bank of America, Palm Springs, California, January 28, 1999.

10. Cornell University offers both undergraduate and graduate degrees in Facility Planning and Management, Human Factors and Ergonomics, Interior Design, and Human Environment Relations under their College of Human Ecology. Other schools such as the University of Southern California, Massachussetts Institute of Technology, New York University, Wharton, Michigan State and Harvard Graduate School of Design offer graduate study in real estate. Of the professional associations, the International Association of Corporate Real Estate Executives (NACORE) has the most complete education program, offering a highly regarded Masters in Corporate Real Estate certification program. NACORE courses are offered several times a year at various locations. The International Development Research Council (IDRC) initiated its own certification program in 1998. Self-study courses are offered by both associations. The International Association of Facility Management (IFMA) also offers a certification program.

11. From his speech to the House of Commons, October 28, 1943. Sir Winston Churchill, *Churchill Speaks: Winston S. Churchill in Peace and War: Collected Speeches, 1897–1963*. Robert Rhodes James, Editor. (New York: Chelsea House, 1980), p. 820.

INDEX

ABOUT THE AUTHOR

Martha A. O'Mara is an independent real estate strategy and executive development consultant in Cambridge, Massachusetts, and serves on the core faculty of the Institute for Corporate Real Estate, sponsored by NACORE.

She has designed and conducted corporate real estate strategy seminars for Merrill Lynch, Fidelity Corporate Real Estate, IDRC, IFMA, NACORE, Sprint, the General Services Administration, and NationsBank, and as a Faculty Partner in the internationally renowned executive education firm Center for Executive Development, she has conducted management seminars for AT&T, IBM, British Telecom, Johnson & Johnson, RR Donnelley, and GTE.

Having worked in the fields of management consulting and workplace design since the late 1970's, she was Assistant Professor of Real Estate Development in the fields of Management and Organizational Behavior at Harvard University's Graduate School of Design from 1989 to 1998. Her articles have appeared in *The Journal of Applied Real Property Analysis*, *The Journal of Real Estate Research*, and *The Journal of Corporate Real Estate*, and she has presented talks and papers on corporate real estate strategy at international meetings of the Academy of Management, the Strategic Management Society, the American Sociological Association, the Environmental Design Research Association, the International Research Development Council (IDRC), the International Facility Management Association (IFMA), the American Real Estate Society (ARES), the Association of Foreign Investors in U.S. Real Estate (AFIRE), and the International Association of Corporate Real Estate Executives (NACORE).

Dr. O'Mara holds a Ph.D. in Organizational Behavior, jointly awarded by the Harvard Business School and Harvard's Graduate School of Arts and Sciences, an M.A. in Sociology from Harvard, and an M.B.A. from the Harvard Business School. She received her B.A., in Social Ecology, from the University of California, Irvine.